JOHN BAYLEY

SHAKESPEARE AND TRAGEDY

ROUTLEDGE & KEGAN PAUL
LONDON, BOSTON, MELBOURNE AND HENLEY

First published in 1981
by Routledge & Kegan Paul Ltd.
39 Store Street, London WC1E 7DD,
9 Park Street, Boston, Mass. 02108, USA
296 Beaconsfield Parade, Middle Park,
Melbourne, 3206, Australia and
Broadway House, Newtown Road,
Henley-on-Thames, Oxon RG9 1EN.

Set in Garamond
and printed in Great Britain by
Ebenezer Baylis and Son Ltd,
The Trinity Press,
Worcester, and London.

Reprinted in 1982

British Library Cataloguing in Publication Data

Bayley, John
Shakespeare and tragedy.
1. Shakespeare, William – Tragedies
I. Title
822.3'3   PR2983   80–42076

ISBN 0-7100-0632-2
ISBN 0-7100-0607-1 Pbk

CONTENTS

INTRODUCTORY

❧

Modern techniques of criticism should find a good field for exploitation in Shakespeare's plays: it is surprising that they have not so far been much used. Treating a text as a purely verbal experience, they read it as a multiple code to be deciphered by a number of signifying keys. They remove the author, and so should find it convenient that few attempts are now made to discover Shakespeare the man in his work. The author is his language and its functions, extending into all our own further acts of imagination about his text. And oddly enough something very like these conscious tenets of structuralism and semiotics have long been unconscious assumptions where Shakespearean criticism is concerned: Shakespeare critics have talked about him in this way without knowing it. Working inside a code of significance, they have understood and interpreted him according to their own lights and their own ideas of enjoyment.

These up-to-date critical methods have tended none the less to prefer more modern texts. Balzac, Flaubert, Goethe, George Eliot, Henry James – they can not only be shown to mean a very great deal but something in their language codes already meets the critic half-way and acquiesces in the infinite extensibility of their meanings, They have no objection to the critic excluding them from a text which has become themselves. To remove the author in these cases is paradoxically to take for granted that he is and cannot be other than wholly identified with his work. As V. S. Naipaul has commented: 'Fiction never lies; it reveals the writer totally.' This makes for an intimacy between critic and author which the transformation of the latter into a linguistic code does nothing to compromise.

Intimacy with Shakespeare is of a different kind: not with the text as author but with the text as world. About the world there is nothing to say, though there is everything to say about our relations with it. But intimacy is not based on an invisible mutual understanding, as between author–text and client–decoder, about the text's significance and seriousness. And though Shakespeare's world is inside the words, these have a special and open relation with gesture, intonation, and sound. The ghost of Hamlet's father cries

> But, soft! methinks I scent the morning air:
> Brief let me be.

Our pleasure in the text as speech here is quite complex. The pause, the appeal to a pre-verbal sense instinct, enclose a wariness, something almost furtive, as if ignominious death had turned a king among men back into something from Circe's animal kingdom. This both reverses and enhances the marvellous wordiness of the ghost, his verbalisation of his predicament. His words move Hamlet intensely, and impress the audience, but the contrast between the ghost as speaker, and as a subtly and disquietingly physical being, has its own sort of comedy: not the author getting at the ghost, or giving any hint to the audience to do so, but as if both parties were separately savouring, and intently examining, the problematic nature of its existence.

When Ophelia says to Hamlet 'You are keen, my Lord, you are keen', the words reveal her instantly and as if inadvertently; they do not seem to be a part of the code of *Hamlet*. Because Flaubert is decipherable at constant speed in his own code, *Madame Bovary* is gradually built up and identified wholly in terms of it and its creator. Ophelia's words give us a more authoritative glimpse of a girl's predicament than does the whole of Flaubert's novel. They do so because of the suddenness and unexpectedness with which an impression is first received, and then derecorded, vanishing in an absence of uniformity and of tone.

All authors, including Shakespeare, make appeals to a 'metanarrative' which purports to come from outside the coding of the text. 'How many times shall Caesar bleed in sport?' The author gives a meaning glance at the audience over the heads of his characters. A complete story by Somerset Maugham begins like this. 'One of the inconveniences of life is that it seldom gives you a complete story. . . . Generally nothing happens. The inevitable catastrophe you foresaw wasn't inevitable at all, and high tragedy, without any regard for artistic decency, dwindles into drawing-room comedy.' This is a way of introducing the reader to the conventional use here of the tragic and the comic, and of confirming the author's authority on both. Shakespeare's presentation of the murder of Caesar is confirmed as literature by its reference to the original event, Maugham's story from the life as coincident with the text it has become. Like the various modes of 'naturalism' in any fiction, such effects serve to propel us more surely into the world of the work of art.

But Shakespeare's plays are not 'theatre' in the sense in which the ordinary play is expected to be, and usually confirms itself as. Brecht's plays are plays in this sense, and so are Marlowe's or Ibsen's, Shaw's, Pinero's, or Chekhov's; they are designed to render specific effects which actors in the theatre can give, and to transmit certain ideas to the audience (ideas which in Brecht's case have usually been taken in by the audience well before the end of the performance). But impressions from Shakespeare are not like those from plays, or from any other genre of art. Maurice Morgann anticipated the methods of Roland Barthes when he 'cracked the code' of Shakespeare's Henry IV plays, in his essay of 1777, 'On the Dramatic Character of Sir John Falstaff', and announced that Falstaff is not a coward and buffoon but a man with the kinds of courage that go naturally with a strong character. What the play requires Falstaff to be is not what its language actually reveals him as.

Morgann's key word, 'impression', corresponds in some degree with the modern conception of 'code', and the suggestions based on it can be as enlightening in the case of the eighteenth-century critic as of the modern one. Both reveal the extent to which the pleasure of a certain kind of text goes with our readiness to exploit its unexpectedness, and believe in what it seems to suggest. Like everything else in art this unexpectedness of impression, these sensations unconfined to and undifferentiated by form and genre, are of course themselves produced by art; and yet they do not seem to lead us back to the author as text, as they would in the case of Balzac or Henry James or Flaubert, but to a new aspect of the text as a world.

Morgann was the first critic of Shakespeare to imply that such investigations had an authority of their own; and that an impression received from Shakespeare, however apparently subjective, also had a certain right to self-confidence. In general the impression we may receive from the tragedies written by Shakespeare is that the tragic form exists for him as a means of giving its freedom to every *other* aspect of life and art. Such an impression would suggest the only real distinction – a formal one – between the tragedies and the histories, comedies, and the last plays. In them he seems to define the form and achievement of each play, as Henry James said of *The Tempest*, 'by his expression of it exactly as the expression stands'. His tragedies, showing that they are tragedies, seem also to avoid being themselves. In a sense that would also be true of *Henry IV*, which the presence of Falstaff turns into something different from a history play, but there an inspired addition suffuses the historical narrative. The tragedies add nothing to a traditional tragic formula but produce a different result. The tragic characters avoid their roles by performing them in their own way.

Such an avoidance creates its own freedom, as in the case of *Hamlet*. Hamlet needs tragedy in order not to be exactly expressed, as comedy would have expressed him. This is not a question of different kinds or versions of Hamlet, but of the general freedom with which the tragic process surrounds him. By its action Shakespearean tragedy vividly suggests other worlds in which its operation is irrelevant, has no place. The code's indications lead us outward. Hamlet is a man dispossessed of himself, or rather one who has no chance to become himself. Even more indeterminate, less dramatically enticing, is another world in *King Lear*, in which the ego lives by language and the family by silence. The hidden worlds implicit in Shakespearean tragedy, but not revealed by its formal specification, can also seem to encapsulate, in unnervingly realistic terms, a different sort and centre of artifice. Farce enters the marriage bed of the lovers in *Othello*. As if in a comedy, where beds are for everything but love, they are interrupted by a disturbance and appear to spend the rest of the night discussing it.

But no suggestion of incongruity threatens the coexistence of these worlds, or flattens them into diagram. Tragedy as a catalyst reveals both different modes of being and separate kinds of art. It is this relation between the form and idea of tragedy, and the modes of Shakespearean creation in relation to it, that I shall be trying to analyse and explore.

Shakespeare is not one of the English tragedians in the sense that Lydgate had been, or as some of his own contemporaries were, like Ben Jonson and Webster and Massinger: or as Dryden and Addison were to be, and then Tennyson and Sir Henry Taylor in the nineteenth century and T. S. Eliot in the twentieth. These authors variously had ideas of adding to the art and form of tragedy, defining it in relation to English drama and the English poetic tradition, in concert with other schools and theories of the genre. Shakespeare's tragedies depend on the form in a different sense. They need it for diversionary, often almost parodic, excursion. With no apparent intention of doing so they evade its most characteristic commitments, fulfil them too literally, transform them.

Nor are they in any way a uniform body. There is a greater resemblance among the Greek tragedies, those in the classic French or Spanish genre, or in the German Romantic tradition, or among the tragedies of Shakespeare's own contemporaries, than there is between *Macbeth* and *Timon of Athens*, *Troilus and Cressida*, *King Lear* or *Coriolanus*. The stories in each of these seem to have engendered in Shakespeare's imagination a different way of looking at the world, and a new way of creating it in art. No doubt a measure of chance was involved. Sometimes the idea and the intellectual challenge of the form may have operated, at least initially, as it did upon other tragedians of the time. Then there was the success of the history plays as *exempla* of historic misfortune and political lesson, the rise and fall of princes and dynasties; and Shakespeare's supreme gift for turning chronicle and received tradition into popular drama. A readiness to imitate others goes with this, and a lack of assertive impulse. Ben Jonson's scholarship about the ancient world as source of tragedy, or Massinger's interest in social, legal and moral problems, are aspects of those writers' individuality, a source of ambition, of status and pride. But in relation both to the past and to the tragic form Shakespearean intelligence does not work like that.

This unusual relation with the materials of tragedy was held a fault and often censured in the century and a half following Shakespeare. It was seen in a different light from Morgann's time onwards, when Shakespeare's example seemed godlike and his influence was at its height. I suspect it was something about the atmosphere of that influence which made Schiller say, of his own tragic trilogy on the history of Wallenstein, that he took it on because it was a subject that did not interest him particularly. Perhaps he felt that this avowed lack of reflective interest might confer on him something of the detachment, the primal strength in creation, which he and other writers had begun to revere in Shakespeare. What is natural in Shakespeare begins, in the focus of Schiller's attitude, to seem portentous. It seems clear that Shakespeare was not in this self-conscious sense detached from his material, but in the bustle of his demanding profession there was no doubt an element of luck in how subjects for plays turned out.

Tragedies exemplary of the genre depend either on action or idea. The uncompromising finality of action in Greek tragedy is as remote from Shakespeare as is that exposition and catastrophe in terms of an evolving idea which distinguishes Romantic tragedy in the nineteenth century, or the stately resolution of dilemmas which is the engine of the neo-classic. The satires and *autos* of the Spanish school are no nearer to Shakespeare, except in point of time, than are Hebbel's and Grillparzer's Hegelian-style conflicts between history and the individual, or the confrontations arranged in modern poetic tragedy between individual and myth.

But with Shakespeare the mere fact and story of consciousness replaces both action and idea. It is the imminence of action which brings that consciousness into prominence, but it remains independent of action. The tragedy itself may be bounded in a nutshell, but the minds of Hamlet, of Macbeth and Othello, make them kings of infinite space. F. R. Leavis writes that the world of action is where Othello has his 'true part'. But there is no such thing as a true part for any hero of Shakespearean tragedy, and certainly not in action. It is his consciousness that fills the play. In Othello's case the action is supplied by Iago, who has no proper existence outside it. As he exclaims, after a successful bout of it, 'Pleasure and action make the hours seem short'. As short as those of an enacted play, which the hero's consciousness transcends. The usurpation by the mind of both practical action and purposeful idea in tragedy – the mind of a murderer, a revenger, a man and a woman in love – this is far from being the sum of Shakespearean tragedy; but it is the most important feature of Shakespeare's relations with the tragic form.

CHAPTER 1

THE KING'S SHIP

On Dover cliff

In the fourth act of *King Lear* the blinded Gloucester comes to the edge of Dover cliff, led by his son Edgar in the disguise of a Tom of Bedlam. Or rather he does not quite come to the edge; how near it he gets is not clear.

> GLOU. When shall I come to the top of that same hill?
> EDG. You do climb up it now; look how we labour.
> GLOU. Methinks the ground is even.
> EDG.   Horrible steep.
>   Hark! do you hear the sea?
> GLOU.   No, truly.
> EDG. Why, then your other senses grow imperfect
>   By your eyes' anguish.
>   IV. vi. 1–6

Keats was haunted by 'Hark, do you hear the sea?' It is a sea heard in the mind only, for Edgar will soon revise his deceit and say that he cannot hear it either. Their little exchange has a kind of intimacy deep inside it, as if the pair had grown accustomed to one another in the course of their long walk. But however far the pair may be from the cliff's edge, Edgar's next words bring us all to it.

> Here's the place, Stand still. How fearful
> And dizzy 'tis to cast one's eyes so low!

The crows and choughs that wing the mid-way air
Show scarce so gross as beetles. Half-way down
Hangs one that gathers samphire, dreadful trade.
Methinks he seems no bigger than his head.
The fishermen that walk upon the beach
Appear like mice, and yond tall anchoring bark
Diminish'd to her cock, her cock a buoy
Almost too small for sight. The murmuring surge
That on the unnumber'd idle pebbles chafes
Cannot be heard so high.

IV. vi. 11–22

In the company of Garrick and some others Dr Johnson observed of this that 'the crows impede your fall.' If you expect to be in fear of falling Johnson is probably right. But in fact, as the speech takes you, you are doing something more like soaring. The workaday intimacy in that little exchange between the pair now bursts exuberantly out. In his mindless emphases ('horrible.... fearful.... dreadful trade....) Edgar apes a cheerful working-man's relish in the way things are. In the midst of tragedy we briefly glimpse the daily round of hazard and accident – fires, floods, falling off ladders – and with Edgar we rise to the pointless occasion of them. However unexpected, there is here a proper moment for Dickensian enjoyment. And we have got there at last, to the cliff's edge, for whatever purpose.

But there is no purpose, only the sudden sense of freedom and exhilaration. The crows and choughs, the mice-like fishermen, the samphire gatherer, are beheld by the spectators as if they had abruptly floated off into a world outside the play. Johnson's logic makes us realise this. If the play had a mental world it must needs engross us in, and the characters along with us, then we should need to feel in that precipice the terror of what Gloucester thinks he is about to do. Then indeed, as Johnson says, we should need to feel the description to be 'all precipice, all vacuum'. The crows then might certainly impede us from the play's cliff of fall – 'frightful, sheer, no-man-fathomed'. But we are outside the drama: the drama is nowhere; we have no need to pay attention to it but only to the goings-on at the foot of Dover cliff.

Those are not part of the play, but they do not disassociate themselves from it either. If they were either in it, or self-consciously out of it, the play would not be a Shakespearean tragedy, or rather not this tragedy by Shakespeare. All, but in various ways, disclose kinds of existence outside the preoccupations of their tragic matter. Sailors, fishermen and samphire gatherers, going about their occupation, are seen with the eye of joy, the joy of seeing the gift of 'the clearest gods'. The events of tragedy are going on in what is according to its lights an equally workaday world, in which the audience are doing their bit. Here they look up and look out of it. In Shakespeare's tragedies the transcendental takes many forms. But its effect is to make our consciousness feel homeless. There is in a way no tragedy other than the awareness of this. There are worlds which we can imagine and dream of in our philosophy but which we cannot live in – this is true even of the world we now see lived in by ships and waves, pebbles and people. The requirements of life make our sense imperfect through a necessary numbness; but the world Gloucester cannot see, and which only the play can show us, is also one which we recognise and delight in.

There is no question of any such worlds being 'true' ones, or truer than others. Shakespeare's idealism is only accidentally Platonic: it does not suggest that reality is elsewhere and that we are living in a world of shadows. Shadows and reflections are what we live in and by; enriched and presented by art they become the life and soul of consciousness. In giving us the pulse of life Edgar's description is none the less totally literature. Playing with shadows as it does – and 'the best in this kind are but shadows', as Theseus observes in *A Midsummer Night's Dream* – the play makes a vision of workaday life seen from the cliff's height seem inhabited by different beings, a tragic glass without the bitter liquid in it. The trick of Shakespearean art makes the illusion at a distance different from that closer to hand. 'Life's a dream', not in the sense in which Calderon's play asserts the idea, but because the mirage of art itself gives the different appearances of life that constitute a dream. There is no waking, though the art of this tragedy suggests that we endure in order to awake.

Literary consciousness has come to reject tragedy as something that feigns by contriving the worst; and thus cheering us up, paradoxically, by an obvious misrepresentation of the way things really and unremittingly are. Shakespeare's feigning is of a uniquely comprehensive kind which creates the appearance of tragic reality not by reduction but by multiplication. In his essay 'Tragedy and the Whole Truth', Aldous Huxley draws attention to the difference between the way in which tragic grief is represented and the ways in which it actually has to fit in to the priorities of existing. The overwhelming desire for a drink or

g to eat never anticipates the proper expression of grief at the
tragedy. But Homer records in the *Odyssey* that after Scylla
ybdis had seized and devoured some of their party, Ulysses
survivors managed to land, and after recruiting themselves with
the best supper they could make, began to lament and shed tears for
their absent comrades. This account of Homer, says Huxley, is the
whole truth as human beings have to experience it.

A valid point, for tragedians do not look at things but at the human
version of them: they are concerned with what people create about
themselves inside their minds, and what images and defensive
overlookings they foster there. As a form, tragedy flourishes at times
when language has the confidence of a specially rich and active function
in relation to human fates – an elaborately protective function. The
language of tragedy has words for any situation. Shakespeare represents
grief, and the self-protector's need to express it, in rhetorical modes of
range and subtlety, from the noisy outburst of the nurse and the
Capulet parents over the seemingly dead Juliet, to the response of the
Scottish lords to Duncan's murder, and the symphonic ritual of the
survivors at the end of *King Lear*:

KENT.   Is this the promis'd end?
EDG. Or image of that horror?
ALB.   Fall and cease!
                    V. iii. 263–4

The language of tragedy does not describe events but takes them over,
and in Shakespeare it does more. Words can redeem both protagonists
and audience from those events by darting off outside them, under the
impetus of their own self-generative ardour, 'in the quick forge and
working-house of thought'. A Greek chorus does this with more
energy and obviousness, bringing a unity to the response of spectators
and actors that does not exist in Shakespeare.

Coriolanus is too exhausted from the reaction after his bout of
fighting in Corioli to remember the name of his former benefactor in
the city whom he wished to be spared. He gives up the attempt and
thinks only of a draught of wine. There is a small parallel there with
Huxley's point about Homer, the kind of resemblance that is sure to
turn up somewhere in the tragedies. But the Dover cliff scene is itself,
and amongst other things, an indicator of what Huxley was getting at.
It releases us from the point of view, the preoccupation that, in

rhetorical form, dominates tragedy. Romeo is dominated by it when he
recalls the Mantuan apothecary who might sell him poison, but the
poetry also shows us the apothecary as Edgar's account showed us
Dover cliff:

> Let's see for means: O mischief, thou art swift
> To enter in the thoughts of desperate men.
> I do remember an apothecary,
> And hereabouts he dwells, which late I noted
> In tattered weeds, with overwhelming brows,
> Culling of simples; meagre were his looks,
> Sharp misery had worn him to the bones:
> And in his needy shop a tortoise hung,
> An alligator stuff'd, and other skins
> Of ill-shap'd fishes: and about his shelves
> A beggarly account of empty boxes,
> Green earthen pots, bladders, and musty seeds,
> Remnants of packthread, and old cakes of roses,
> Were thinly scattered to make up a show.
>
> V. i. 35–48

By contrast Macbeth's rhetoric is wholly illustrative of himself:

> Howe'er you come to know it, answer me.
> Though you untie the winds and let them fight
> Against the churches: though the yeasty waves
> Confound and swallow navigation up;
> Though bladed corn be lodged and trees blown down;
> Though castles topple on their warders' heads;
> Though palaces and pyramids do slope
> Their heads to their foundations; though the treasure
> Of nature's germens tumble all together
> Even till destruction sicken; answer me
> To what I ask you.
>
> IV. i. 51–61

That war of shadows is working for Macbeth, not carrying on a life of
its own. And yet there seems a real froth of surf: a real cornfield
flattened by wind and rain. Our glimpse of them is as brief as possible
but it exists: the shadows are defined as sharply as possible.
Performance is eked out with the mind in the fullest sense, and in the
mind's capacity for multiple response, each separated from the other.

The language of Shakespearean tragedy exactly comprehends and endorses the simplest religious premise: that we live in no abiding city but in a world of shadows out of which thought aspires to regions that seem to it everlasting. Religion needs a transcendental truth; Shakespeare's transcendentalism is equally ideal but implies nothing but differentiation. It is brief, with a brevity that intensifies the relation between language and the mind, and often draws its own kind of attention to the process. Marvell, the most Shakespearean of poets, has the same sense of the possible relation in art of mind and language.

> The mind that ocean, where each kind
> Does streight its own resemblance find;
> But it creates, transcending these,
> Far other worlds and other seas. . . .

We seem to feel the process going on all round us on the cliff-top. The sense of exhilarating space is in one area: the knowledge of Gloucester and his ruined sense, in another. The freedom of mind and sense, in this poetry, is often exulted in by the poetry itself; the power of its charge to leap from point to point with telegraphic economy is a feature that grows more marked in Shakespeare's style as the plays go on.

> I boarded the King's ship; now on the beak
> Now in the waist, the deck, in every cabin,
> I flam'd amazement: sometimes I'd divide
> And burn in many places; on the topmast,
> The yards and bowsprit, would I flame distinctly,
> Then meet and join.
>
> I. ii. 196–201

Ariel's description of his magic is also a description of the height of Shakespeare's tragic style. Parodied and exuberant, it reveals itself in his words and actions: on Dover cliff it gives itself to us without consciousness, through the sole medium of what is created. It is a typical paradox that Shakespearean tragedy should consist so much of angelic moments – another is Banquo's reference to 'the temple-haunting martlet' that makes its nest on the wall of Macbeth's castle – which bring home the nature of the tragic, as his poetry gives it to us, more unmistakably than all its rhetoric of loss and darkness, misfortune and disaster.

The tragic relates here to the ideal, and how momentary it is;

consciousness apprehends it as it declares itself, with the rapidity of magic. We think of Shakespeare as down-to-earth, and as a universal model sensibility, adjustable to any age. As regards his finest sense of the tragic neither of these assumptions is true. The distance, in Shakespearean tragedy, of 'living' from 'writing' is what gives him his complete anonymity, but it also reveals such writing to be an angelical activity. A coincidence with Renaissance idealism is conferred upon us, more or less, by our boarding the king's ship, not to do as Ariel does, but to share in the rareness of his magic. Shakespearean tragedy depends upon the fact that angelic perceptions are too good for this life, but they are none the less what creatures who have to live this life, and live it with an unsuitably godlike apprehension, depend on.

We are accustomed today to think of the writer's sensibility as what he lives in all the time and shares with us; must do so, totally, in order to be himself as a writer for us.

> What I want to do now is to saturate every atom. I mean to eliminate all waste, deadness, superfluity: to give the moment whole: whatever it includes. Say that the moment is a combination of thought; sensation; the voice of the sea. Waste, deadness, come from the inclusion of things that don't belong to the moment; this appalling narrative business of the realist. . . . Why admit anything to literature that is not poetry – by which I mean saturated?

That is Virginia Woolf in *A Writer's Diary*, talking about her novel *The Waves*, and how to read it. Her idea of the 'saturation' of consciousness is as different as possible from that elevation of consciousness which we have in Shakespeare. The logic of Virginia Woolf's method is already present in Sterne, naturalised by Hegel and the German philosophers, explored by Wordsworth and Coleridge. Today it is taken for granted – 'One life, one writing' as the poet Robert Lowell puts it. Whitman would have understood that, and so would every American writer today. What is comprised is not so much the autobiographical, though that comes into it, as the homogeneity of consciousness manipulated by art – 'the voice of the sea' becomes a part of thought and sensation. In Shakespearean tragedy the voice of the sea, which Keats heard, comes from another world which our consciousness visits, aware that it cannot live there, or even remain there for more than a moment.

Shakespearean fish swam the sea, far away from land.
Romantic fish swam in nets, coming to the hand.
What are all those fish that lie gasping on the strand?

Yeats put it succinctly. But to gasp upon the strand, the strand of our consciousness, is just what the modern writer wants to do. Keats himself is the remarkable case of instinctive understanding of the Shakespearean tragic principle. In one sense he is the most confiding of poets, but his notion of the heroic subject is a wholly Shakespearean one. Heat, cold, grief and joy, sensation itself, become for him in art tragic intuitions which can be visited only in a distant and formal medium corresponding to tragedy, the medium of 'The Eve of St Agnes' and 'La Belle Dame Sans Merci'.

And they are gone. Aye, ages long ago
Those lovers fled away into the storm.

A modern Keats, even a Wordsworthian Keats, would write something more like a history of his life and sensations, the realities of the medical school, the realities of his brother Tom's death from tuberculosis. But Keats had to find a tragic reality, as far away as possible from such events, and yet intimately in contact with them.

Shakespeare is so accustomed to going out of himself in order to write in the tragic manner that his attitude towards it is ultimately insouciant. His obligations to the form mean a lack of obligation to what he himself makes of it. All is avowedly pretence, all is unconcerned. And this, more than anything. divides his genius from the modern era. The modern spirit is, as Hegel said, 'shameless', and this shamelessness is a symptom of its sincerity. It is so seriously itself, and can be no other; its single-mindedness can be hypocritical but not deceitful, for it has ceased to understand instinctively the deceitfulness once practised by great art. Shakespearean tragedy never begins at home, as the modern spirit of sincerity feels it must do. Ariel never lights his flames in his own backyard, but in the King's ship or the cliff-top, the heath where earth has bubbles, the stormy shore of Cyprus. Ariel is never personally responsible for what he does; his magic is not his own but a gift to be exercised at remote control.

It is difficult to exaggerate the importance of this secret freedom, even though the freedom of creation and perception has no warrant in the thing perceived. Creator and client possess above all the freedom which is denied to the tragic protagonists. We are not held in their situation, as Virginia Woolf for instance wants to hold us in the satura-

tion of her artist's consciousness, as most post-Hegelian writing wants
to engulf us wholly in its own totality of being. The art of Shakespeare
draws our attention to how free we are from its own material and
manipulation. Dover cliff gives us a special awareness of such freedom;
and it seems the same kind of awareness that tantalises the consciousness of Lear and Macbeth, Hamlet and Othello. To be aware of it, and
yet to be deprived of it, is for them the most absolute part of tragedy.

Our apprehension of space and joy on the cliff, bestowed on us by
Shakespeare's sudden exuberance of fancy, also shows us what it means
to be excluded – the most absolute of exclusions being that of the eyeless Gloucester. Shakespeare's tragic characters are close to us
principally because of the kind of loss they undergo, a loss whose
nature we know of because of our own exemption from it. The play
that frees our spirits has cabined and confined theirs, enclosed them
within the walls of predicament.

> For who would lose
> Though full of pain, this intellectual being,
> These thoughts that wander through eternity,
> To perish rather, swallowed up and lost
> In the wide womb of uncreated night,
> Devoid of sense and motion?

Milton in *Paradise Lost* almost certainly had a recollection of Claudio
in *Measure for Measure*. The freedoms of the play make us aware of
what constitutes their loss to the participants. Macbeth knows he has
given his 'eternal jewel' to 'the common enemy of man': he knows too
that he has lost his soul's receptive, nimble, and 'delighted' powers, to
the living death which Duncan's murder has brought him.

Claudius is aware of the same thing, and we with him. Unlike
Macbeth, 'All may be well' is his sanguine hope, attending his relation
with the queen and his satisfaction as king: we share in his hopes and
fears. And in his happiness in the queen's affections. She pronounces a
threnody on Ophelia.

> There is a willow grows aslant a brook
> That shows his hoar leaves in the glassy stream;
> There with fantastic garlands did she come,
> Of crow-flowers, nettles, daisies, and long purples
> That liberal shepherds give a grosser name,
> But our cold maids do dead men's fingers call them.
>
> IV. vii. 167

And it is also a farewell to her own pulses of life, the happiness of being herself, and loving others. Othello's loss is on an appropriately grand scale, the loss of a state of mind out of which love was first born, and for which he had sacrificed the 'unhous'd free condition' of military life.

Travelling as he does in tragic creation into what seems a distant country, Shakespeare makes us feel for that reason that his plays too are full of events elsewhere. All the tragedies seem to know of worlds in which 'the mystery of your loneliness' might, it seems, be appeased. Yet this too is part of insouciance. We may have the feeling that something beyond the play beckons to us, but this is not because truth is concealed behind falsehood. In this art lying is as irrelevant as sincerity, for the art exists to breed the possibilities that make up the specification. There is no central core of truth in a Shakespearean tragedy. The artist is away from home, in a place where he can do what he wants.

Compare him here with another traveller, who found himself investigating the dark heart of a tragedy. In Conrad's *Heart of Darkness* the narrator, Marlowe, tells us 'I hate and detest and cannot bear a lie, not because I am straighter than the rest of us but simply because it appals me. There is a taint of death, a flavour of mortality in lies'. Any serious writer of the modern age would see the point of that. Art, the art of the novel, has become directly and supremely a truth-telling mechanism; and the narrator here is its instrument. Lies smell of mortality because society and its arrangements are the biggest one of all. Kurtz, the tragic figure examined in the novel, comes to see that his sense of himself and his vocation is a lie; exposed to the darkness of the Congo he finds the same negative anarchy in himself. Kurtz has found the truth, but Marlowe, the man who hates lies, has to tell them in order to conceal the truth of what has happened, from Kurtz's fiancée and from decent people.

Such a work as *Heart of Darkness* makes one see how little responsibility weighs upon Shakespearean tragedy and its author. He has travelled for the practice of his art to a land where everything is made up anyway, and where 'the truest poetry is the most feigning.' Enjoying the status of triviality the plays make use of it as no other works of art have ever done. They have no points to make about the idea of darkness, though they are full of it. Nor, where the heart of man is concerned, do they distinguish between illusions and realities. As for Kurtz's discovery of himself, the tragedies – like the essays of

Montaigne – are quite at home with the idea of self-knowledge, and yet do not take it very seriously. The self is too fleeting and ambiguous an entity, existing in relation to queries and possibilities. In fact, for a Shakespearean tragic hero, queries and possibilities form the concept of a personal being. Knowing yourself is something that other people, with a vested interest in the predictability of the individual, would like you to do more of. Keeping sturdily to their single appetitive course, Goneril and Regan are critical of their father's vanities and divagations. 'He hath ever but slenderly known himself.' True, as regards the knowledge that they and their world expect of him. Not so very differently from the sisters do authors and critics demonstrate self-discovery, or self-deception, in the characters they invent, like Conrad's Kurtz, or analyse, as with Shakespeare's Othello. When Shakespeare's heroes refer to self-knowledge what they disclose is an awareness of the possibilities among which they live, and the drama of choice or necessity among them. They are not concerned with the truth about themselves but with what might be lost and gained in those worlds of the flesh and the spirit that they intimate and crave. 'To know the deed 'twere best not know myself', says Macbeth. He knows that the deed was planned and would be carried out in a different world from others which his senses had warmed to, which his consciousness had been touched by and moved towards. If he is to be the deed's creature and live with it, those other intimations of what he might be will have to go. But they will not; and he remains trapped in different versions of himself.

Most persons will recognise the situation, though the artist employs on it no investigative rigour. There is a clear connection between the fact that Macbeth's process is not one of self-discovery, and the fact that Shakespeare is not mounting in the play an inquiry into the heart of Scotland's darkness. The main reason for this is his pleasure in the limitations of his art. It never aspires to the condition of life, as Conrad's novel has to do, or – in the modern theatre – a play by Beckett or Pinter. There is no purposive movement in a Shakespeare play except in the logic of its artifice, expanded in the outcome of the plot.

> the fire i' the flint
> Shows not till it be struck; our gentle flame
> Provokes itself, and like the current flies
> Each bound it chafes.
>
> I. i. 24–7

The words of the Poet in *Timon of Athens* correspond to the strange saying in *King Lear*, 'Ripeness is all.' Our process, whether life or art, is carried by its own vitality as far as it will go. The mysteriousness in Edgar's three words is also the mysteriousness of a Shakespearean tragedy.

Mystery in this context is a feeble word but one none the less full of meaning. In Shakespearean tragedy, as for Wittgenstein, 'the riddle does not exist . . . the solution to the problem of life is seen in the disappearance of the problem'. But for Wittgenstein, as for a modern artist like Beckett, the point in art would be precisely to make that point. Shakespeare's art does not realise its existence: nothing in *King Lear* suggests to us – 'What I am trying to get at in this play is that ripeness is all.' The mystery is in the art's unawareness of any such implication. The art of Marvell again suggests a close parallel, in its combination of exuberant artifice and mannerism with a strangeness that touches us by its irreducible simplicity. Marvell's spirit has also boarded the king's ship, darting with agility and levity all over the robust appearance of things. His poem 'On Appleton House' is a masque that shows scenes more fantastic than those at top or bottom of Dover cliff.

> And now the salmon-fishers moist
> Their leathern boats begin to hoist:
> And, like Antipodes in shoes,
> Have shod their heads in their canoes.
> How tortoise-like, but not so slow,
> These rational amphibii go!
> Let's in; for the dark hemisphere
> Does now like one of them appear.

Those fishermen, not mice-like figures on a beach, are employing an ingenuity in transporting their craft which Marvell's metaphysical wit is well able to take advantage of. The scene, though, makes the same kind of simple exuberant statement. The dark hemisphere becomes one with the actors and the scene is closed. An angel looking from Dover cliff, or from where Marvell is standing, might in his nature see things as this poetry describes them for us; but only such art gives us the momentary trick of angelic apprehension. From it we turn back into nature, to live and die.

The inappropriate world

Gloucester cannot see what Edgar's words put before us. The tragedy itself needs to go no further than that. We have always felt a kind of intimacy with him, like that we may feel for Stiva Oblonsky in *Anna Karenina*. One difference between Tolstoy's novel and Shakespeare's play is that we know Stiva could not suddenly be made blind, and we know Tolstoy knows it too, and resents intensely Shakespeare's irresponsibility in doing things another way. Tolstoy has to allot 'fates' to people, and it is Stiva's allotted fate to be a happy survivor of any débâcle, just as it is Sonya's, in *War and Peace*, to be adoringly and helpingly outside the family circle, never at one with it. This allotment of roles gives their solid authority to Tolstoy's novels, and Shakespearean tragedy is neither solid nor authoritative.

And yet Gloucester is done with as instant an accuracy as anything in Tolstoy. He is as proud of his bastard son, Edmund, as Justice Shallow of his youthful exploits at Clement's Inn. It is no shame to acknowledge his misdemeanours; they are of the kind any age tolerates easily and perhaps – as the transgressor well knows – with a certain envy as well. But we are to be surprised by Gloucester. As the family crisis deepens he becomes increasingly distracted, and the final explosion of Lear against his daughters distresses him deeply. When he has to be involuntary host to Cornwall and Regan. who arrive on his doorstep unexpectedly, he can open to them his woe at Edgar's supposed treachery ('O madam, my old heart is crack'd, is crack'd'), and get some comfort from the matter-of-fact way they ask about the gossip of it. It feeds Regan's malice.

> What, did my father's godson seek your life?
> He whom my father nam'd? Your Edgar?

He is touchingly pleased again ('For him I thank your grace') when Edmund is noted by Cornwall as a likely man to be used in the impending emergency. This part of the play is distinguished by a horrible domesticity ('Your Edgar', 'My Regan counsels well') and this cosiness on the side of the evil party takes no account of poor Gloucester's assiduous helplessness. We have the impression that the shock to Gloucester, brought about by Edmund's deception, has left him as Cordelia's ingratitude left Lear: determined to adjust to the new family situation and yet inwardly still committed to the old.

Between Lear and the odious Cornwall he is, perhaps for the first time, in a position where his offices of good nature can do no good at all. Surely his role is to be merely ineffectual? But no, he sees what he must do, and he says as much to Edmund, the only comfortable person, as he now feels, in whom he can confide. 'If I die for it, as no less is threatened me, the king, my old master, must be relieved.' Under interrogation and torture the point that sticks with this natural host is that it is being done to him in his own house. His effective act was to have the king carried to Dover, and it seems natural after this that Dover should become his home, and the place to die at. Dover in *King Lear* has something of the same odd dream-like insistence, as goal and geographical symbol, that Milford Haven has in *Cymbeline*. Gloucester's tormentors seem aware of this power when they thrust him out to smell his way to Dover.

At this point that Gloucester we know surprises us again, but for a reason the play can hardly be expected to reveal to us. Shakespeare has so far been supplying the role of Gloucester himself; now he becomes the character on whom he is based, the Paphlagonian king from Sidney's romance of Arcadia, the king deposed and blinded by his bastard son, who had contrived to turn his father against the legitimate prince. As so often happens in *King Lear*, a different mode of displaying or discoursing tragedy appears and makes its own way along, producing its own species of effect. The account in the *Arcadia* is moving; doubtless Shakespeare found it so. In the undefined area in which the play wanders, the Paphlagonian king and Gloucester are quite assimilable to one another, but Sidney's sweet and confiding narrative decorum deals with two aspects of the sad story. One is the rise and fall of the great, to power and thence to impotence, and from grandeur to wretchedness – the threnody being 'pittie for so great a fall'. The other is a survival of courtly debate. 'Within that rude carapace of a hollow rock', lashed by hail and 'the pride of the wind', the king and his son are heard engaged in 'a strange and pitiful disputation'. We hear that the good son Leonatus, the equivalent of Edgar, has given up the promise of a great career in a foreign country to come and attend on his father; and that the blind king's constant task – since his son will not lead him to a place where he may throw himself down and die – is to persuade the young man to return abroad and flourish.

Endless and high-minded discussion, in incongruous circumstances, is typical of the *Arcadia*'s world, as in that of *The Faerie Queene*, and all 'cabinet' tragedy and romance of the Renaissance, up to Dryden and Racine. In this context high-minded stoicism and bodily affliction appear in dignified contrast to each other, increasing both the uplift and the pathos. There is nothing in the least stuffy or formalised about Sidney's narrative, which for all its convolutions is confiding and sweetly direct in feeling. But it has the convention of dividing the physical world from that of thought and discourse, whereas in *Lear* the two are brought closely together – the physical overpowers. Gloucester is 'poorly led'; Edgar filthy and half-naked; the fugitives and victims are in 'loop'd and window'd raggedness'; and this in fact may be a recollection of the pair in the *Arcadia* – 'poorly arrayed, extreamly weather-beaten . . . and yet through all those miseries, in both there seemed to appeare a kind of noblenesse, not suited to that affliction.'

The relation of Gloucester and Edgar is far more primitive. Everything has gone down before the fact of Gloucester's blindness. He does not know the creature who leads him, the instrument to help him to get to Dover cliff and fall. The jelly of the eye and the bleeding face, the flax and whites of egg that may still be sticking there, are constantly before us, as the fact of darkness is before Gloucester. A blind man by himself might well fall over a drop and be killed by accident, but a more awful sense of the condition is brought about by an opposite event. Convinced that he is on the verge of destruction Gloucester falls on to the safe and familiar lap of the grass.

Shakespeare goes to the heart of the *Arcadia* situation by speeding up, as he also does in *Othello* and *Timon*, a situation static in the source, and suitable for that reason to an atmosphere of moral discussion. The speeding up of drama is also a way of removing the human tendency to make literature into cool debate. But the change from the *Arcadia* does not only make the situation more physical but also in a way more empirical. The doleful and dignified debate becomes a crude experiment. The audience enters into this, and its risks. Edgar displays them.

> Why I do trifle thus with his despair
> Is done to cure it . . .
> And yet I know not how conceit may rob
> The treasury of life, when life itself
> Yields to the theft. Had he been where he thought,
> By this had thought been past.
>
> IV. vi. 33–4, 42–5

The final ignominy of this so real and positive blindness is that it can persuade him he has really fallen.

GLOU. But have I fall'n, or no?
EDG. From the dread summit of this chalky bourn!
  Look up aheight: the shrill-gorged lark so far
  Cannot be seen or heard. Do but look up.
GLOU. Alack I have no eyes.

IV. vi. 56–60

Edgar, as the stranger on the beach, tells him he has fallen perpendicularly the height of ten masts. The fact would be as striking to the audience, who would respond to the idea of amazing escapes as they would to that of risky trades and experiments in shock therapy. The fall of the great from prosperity to wretchedness seems literally enacted in the imagined height of those masts, and Edgar feigns wonder at 'so great a fall', here transposed from the courtly atmosphere of the *Arcadia* into the workaday actuality of Dover cliff.

The change from the *Arcadia* could not be greater, though it is one of atmosphere and, as it were, of *class* – Gloucester and his son are wholly declassed, the one by the outrage inflicted on him, the other by his becoming a fugitive and beggar. We may remember again Cornwall's servants at the castle, their participation in and revulsion at the act their master commits, and their pity for the blinded earl, pity that does not lament his fallen state but goes to get flax and white of eggs for his bleeding face. Most writers would have deliberately drawn to our attention the 'democratic' aspect of the business, the uniting of all persons in suffering and the utter loss of dignity sustained by Gloucester. In the cliff-top world it is taken all for granted. The homeliness and literalness of the whole scene greatly exercised the eighteenth-century editors, always a sign that expectation has been confounded. No wonder, for even Dickens is a great stickler for the retention of class conditioning and refinement under all tribulations. The reason for the scene being at once extraordinary and to be taken for granted may lie – as so often happens in *King Lear* – in the presentation of two modes together without any recognition of each other: in this case the 'gentility' of Edgar, and Gloucester's awareness of his 'better phrase and manner', together with their appearance as very 'ordinary people'.

Through the prism of Shakespearean effects Gloucester appears as he is to himself – a man afflicted past bearing, like Job.

> This world I do renounce, and in your sights
> Shake patiently my great affliction off . . .

The idea of doing oneself in 'patiently' is a remarkable paradox, of the sort that Gloucester and those in his position might well commend to themselves. But he is also a man subdued to suffering and seen as a victim of its incongruous pathos: any further tricks played on such reduced persons, would seem wanton even if unintended, for Gloucester is also the anonymous, helpless old party found in difficulties by kindly bluff strangers – in this case Edgar, simulating the bystander at the foot of the cliff. The most important thing about tragedy in Shakespeare is how it conceals itself. Or alternatively we could say that, like Chesterton's postman, it makes itself too obvious to be taken in, elucidated, emphasised. And it lays false trails, that look, and indeed are, very authentic. This is especially true of *King Lear* because in it the main characters are claiming tragedy in their own right, and on their own behalf. No one could deny their right to it, but this makes it all the more elusive. Neither Lear nor Gloucester contrives to coincide with it, though they go through all the motions of doing so.

Thus the play slips out of every area for which there is something appropriate and intelligible to be said. Everybody knows that when Gloucester exclaims

> As flies to wanton boys are we to the Gods
> They kill us for their sport

he is saying something obviously appropriate to his experience, his own reaction to that experience. He is not touching a central core of tragedy, voicing a discovery the play wants to 'leave' with us, or anything of that sort. But it might seem a different matter when he exclaims 'I stumbled when I saw', or 'I see it feelingly', when Lear says 'You see how this world goes'. And yet in *King Lear* these comments seem almost equally inappropriate, equally on a wrong note. The wrongness of the note seems equable, even inevitable, more totally because more subtly wrong than anything Gloucester says about flies and gods and wanton boys, or his 'Paphlagonian' utterances about shaking patiently his great affliction off.

Something in the play knows about this comprehensive wrongness and accepts it as quite natural. It is part of the dolour of human fate to be wrong in that way, part of its necessity. That necessary human falsity occurs again and again in *King Lear*, as if the self-preoccupation of human beings in pain was bound to produce it. But of course, and as with all such things in Shakespeare, what we receive is an impression and not the sense of contrived effect. No deliberation seems involved. By contrast, there *is* deliberation, and of the most effective kind, in the ways Shakespeare secures tragic appropriateness in its proper place and context, for example at the end of *Julius Caesar*. The last hours and death of Brutus are admirably arranged for maximum tragic effect – 'tragic' itself being the formally appropriate word here for the limitations involved, and accepted, as it were, both by audience and playwright. When Brutus says 'Thou seest the world, Volumnius, how it goes,' the sentiment, unlike Lear's, is wholly satisfying in terms of his and our participation in what is being enacted and shown.

> Farewell to you; and you; and you, Volumnius.
> Strato, thou hast been all this while asleep.
> Farewell to thee, too, Strato. Countrymen,
> My heart doth joy that yet in all my life
> I found no man but he was true to me.
> I shall have glory by this losing day.
> More than Octavius and Mark Antony
> By this vile conquest shall attain unto.
> So, fare you well at once: for Brutus' tongue
> Hath almost ended his life's history.
> Night hangs upon mine eyes; my bones would rest
> That have but laboured to attain this hour.
>   V. v. 31–42

Appropriateness is all the more effective because of the relaxed touch ('Strato, thou hast been all this while asleep') suited to the great man's last meticulous courtesies to friends and attendants.

Brutus shows how appropriate man can be to his idea of tragedy; Lear and Gloucester show how unsuitable he can be for it. For Brutus everything works out like an audit: life has been a preparation for this, and this is the proper ending and meaning of life. It is the point so compactly made by Oreste at the end of Racine's tragedy *Andromaque*: 'Hé bien! Je meurs content, et mon sort est rempli.' True, that is not the end for Oreste. He goes mad. Racine's finale has his hero announcing the proper end for himself in a tragedy of this sort, and then succumbing to another kind of fate, though one equally suited to the conventions of tragedy. Racine shows his highly individual kind of mastery in the quiet way he combines the two.

Gloucester and Lear attempt both, in their various ways, but succeed in neither. A Racine tragedy is perfectly successful in the way it matches what happens with the right way of describing and reacting to what happens. Such an exact beauty of fitting and responding not only does not exist in *King Lear*, but the fact that it does not exist is itself the most incalculable and mysterious part of the play's art. That is what gives its quality to the cliff-top scene, a scene so joyous in its art and yet so indifferent, as it seems, to any Shakespearean mastery of appropriateness. Consciousness looks on while action expends itself, as it does in Greek drama. In the *Philoctetes* of Sophocles, the betrayed hero attempts to throw himself off the cliffs of his island, and is restrained by Odysseus and his men who have come to carry him off to Troy. This attempt and its frustration is enacted as self-sufficiently as a tableau. In the similar kind of pattern in *King Lear*, such action becomes a vigorous but shadowy parody of itself, attempted by a blind man who declares by his unawareness of what is really happening the fact that he has passed beyond its sphere. But in parodying action the scene none the less remains meticulously literal, more emphatic in its literalness than any scene of conspiracy, confrontation or battle.

Indeed the literalness of the scene greatly exercised the eighteenth-century editors. As Edgar tells his father that he is now within a foot of the verge, he says; 'For all beneath the moon/ Would I not leap upright.' Warburton objected that an upright leap would bring one safely back in the same place, and wanted to change the Folio reading to 'outright'. Mason remarked on the fact that the phrase gives better idea of the imminence of space than if Edgar had said he wouldn't for all the world go another step forward; and Malone commented that if Warburton 'had tried such a leap *within a foot* of the edge of a precipice, before he undertook the revision of these plays, the world would, I fear, have been deprived of his labours.' In such a context old scores tell us something: the editors were very much aware of the physical situation involved. The impression they had (Warburton excluded) and that we still have, if we think about it, is of the odd pair *crouching*, as if on the verge: a position instinctively taken up so near the edge of the cliff, so one could crawl away from it (Lear's expressed desire in the first scene to 'unburdened crawl towards death'). Gloucester is kneeling to say his last words, and his fall is the merest subsidence, a blind man diving like a baby into a cot.

This kind of literalness means there can be nothing 'right' about the scene, the rightness that is appropriate to tragedy. In the scene there is helplessness and blindness, and there is also the joy made visible in Edgar's words, the joy of human life and natural beauty. These have nothing to do with each other, and nothing to do with the attempts of the characters to make sense of what is happening to them, the sort of sense that Oreste made so economically in that line from the end of Racine's play.

Such a lack of appropriateness, unemphatic as it is, is the deepest singularity in *King Lear*. It extends to almost all personal observations, claims, discoveries and pronouncements. And one important consequence is the position of the author himself. It is a commonplace to say that Shakespeare the man is not 'present' in his work, but as an artist he frequently is ; at the end of *Julius Caesar*, for instance, he can be seen getting the proper effects in a manner that is all the more straightforwardly personal, where the artist is concerned, for being so masterful and brilliant. This would be more obviously true of much in the history plays, and, in a different way, of *Coriolanus*, or of that piece in the scenario of *Sir Thomas More* which is generally thought to be by Shakespeare. Such a discernibility of the artist in his successful effect is evident in the whole ghost scene in the first act of *Hamlet*, and in the first scenes of *Othello* – perhaps indeed throughout that play.

But in *King Lear* the sense of mastery is obscured by something clumsy and basic in the feel of things, and that does not seem obviously attributable to design on the part of the writer. Indeed it could be said that the writer is showing himself in his usual way in Edgar's speech on the cliff, but in a way that is not related to what is in hand, except in some obscure and wonderful sense quite unconnected with his being present to us in his superb fulfilment of a tragic specification. Critics have in fact been quick to discover an appropriate area of specification in *Lear*, and to invent ways in which Shakespeare can be seen filling it in.

> A central paradox in Lear is epitomised by the blind Gloucester's realisation, 'I stumbled when I saw'. Sight blinded him, while blindness heightens feeling and insight, just as Lear's temporal destitution brings spiritual richness . . . .

That kind of judgment is sympathetic: the only trouble is that it is no more true than the reflections of Lear and Gloucester themselves. It gets things into the kind of order they also come to depend on, but which their experiences as we see them do not bear out. This is a more complex matter than saying that Lear and Gloucester are unreliable, as all dramatic characters may be more or less, and that anything they say is far from defining the shape and meaning of the play or the attitudes of its author. It is more a question of anything that is said about life in the play seeming wrong and off-key. Edgar is not exempt when he says that ripeness is all, that men must endure their going hence even as their coming hither, and when he tells his father to 'bear free and patient thoughts'; Cordelia herself is not exempt.

One might say too, neither is the playwright. He has got hold of something that undermines the kind of expression that a play relies on. That is why there is such a burst of joy when language can soar away, Ariel-like, in the vision of Dover cliff, free for once from human speciousness, even though that language is itself performing its own shiningly dishonest act of making us and Gloucester see something where there is nothing. But here, unlike all the human sentiments in the plays, nothing is off-key. The Fool in this sense is also 'human'. His position is certainly different, though not fundamentally so. Compare him with Lucky, in Beckett's play *Waiting for Godot*, and it can be seen at once how deeply compromised Beckett is with the success of his character as an instrument of truthtelling rhetoric. The Fool is not like that. He shares in what I have called the comprehensive human wrongness which the play accepts as quite natural.

The Fool, though, is in the family. And the family is in its nature inimical to all kinds of sentiment and self-expression. Lear goes against this when he demands expressions of love, and Goneril and Regan give him what he deserves, But Cordelia cannot herself escape a comparable falsity, which is produced by the inherent falsity of Lear's demands. In a family context all that produces a kind of intolerableness. The off-key note of everything human in *Lear* comes from the primal violation of family silence. Tolstoy, whom I shall have to refer to again, understood this very well. His hatred of the play is a hatred of the language and atmosphere produced by this violation of family decencies and silences, a violation which he – not unnaturally for the kind of writer he himself was – laid at the door of the playwright. (Tolstoy's attitude may well be elaborated from the famous comment in a poem by Tyutchev that a thought expressed is always a lie.) What it feels, a family does not express.

As a stage play *King Lear* is not 'conscious' of the ways in which something in its subject makes for its impossibility as normal theatre. Charles Lamb, and those who followed him in saying it should not be acted, did so on the grounds that it was too sublime. The reality is rather different. It defeats the quality of acting – the quality that makes an actor superb in that last scene of Brutus in *Julius Caesar*. If the characters themselves sound off-key, how much more so will the players? Actors can hardly, in all their circumstances, reproduce the subtlety of the off-key note, especially when so much in the play itself is barely aware of it. It goes with that sense in the play of a family forced into the open, the good members compelled into unnaturalness by the unnatural evil of the others. And this does not form part of the acting potential of the play, as for instance does the sugared pretence and· animal practicality of the two sisters, or the gusto of Edmund. Such an acting potential can be very artfully comprehensive in Shakespeare: a case would be acting inside the acting, with the player in *Hamlet* weeping over the Hecuba speech, observed by the player Hamlet, who can use the contrast with it to act his own sources of grief. But there are so many moments in *King Lear* when the characters themselves are off-key, producing kinds of false note which cannot be acted, kinds of naked exclamation which cannot bear acting.

The two modes contrast maybe, but in no happy or definable sense, the sense which the critic constructs when he talks about the 'central paradox' of *King Lear*. This is also the objection against interpreting the play as a 'tragedy of the grotesque', as Wilson Knight did so memorably in an essay in *The Wheel of Fire*. Once accepted, such a word is voracious, eating up everything in the play. *Wozzeck*, the powerful piece written in 1836 by the young German dramatist Büchner, who had been much influenced by Shakespeare and *King Lear*, really is a tragedy of the grotesque in this purposive sense. Like those phrases about 'a central paradox', the idea of the grotesque puts a constructive purposefulness on the action, indicating what Wilson Knight calls 'the appropriate forms which the Lear vision as a whole expresses.' Such an 'appropriateness', and the idea of 'vision' too, seem as off-key as the many generalising and meaning-giving phrases that are used by the characters inside the play.

Emphasised in this way the idea of the grotesque becomes purposeful, as if the cliff-top scene, for instance, had been designed to get both a shudder and a laugh. We are conditioned now to the ways in which dramatist and producer manipulate anti-climax and incongruity to the point where they become a theatrical formula conditioning us in their turn to look for the the same things in Shakespeare. The danger here is that the pursuit of, and response to, humour and the grotesque becomes standardised in the expectation of the audience, as in the author's method. Once its overriding authenticity has been established, the idea of humour and the grotesque as the proper response in art to life is apt to drive out anything else. The balance, the distinction, and the compartmentalisation that great art requires disappear.

They are obviously required in Dickens, where farce is never far off, and yet the genius of the author, in collaboration with his audience, is able to sense the natural gap between the closeness of laughter and tears, the comic and the sentimental. The gap shows how close, how very nearly interchangeable, the two are: the art itself asserts its own kind of barrier between them. Much Victorian art domesticated and gave its characteristic and sometimes gruesome respectability to the sentimental formula of *Tristram Shandy*, even to Byronic gaiety and freedom. To many Continental writers of the first part of the nineteenth century, including Pushkin, this mixed-up creation of the funny and the sad, the conventional and the incongruous, was the essential spirit of Romanticism, and Shakespeare was for them the greatest of Romantic writers. It is probably significant that Pushkin created, in the old Countess of his story 'The Queen of Spades', a female version of King Lear with much of the simplicity and poignancy of the original. Like Shakespeare he enters both fully and simply into the state of being old.

But the once-inspiring techniques of incongruity and the grotesque were soon vulgarised, until in our time they have come to be practised mechanically by every uninspired novelist (the standard blurb always claims that its novel is 'profound and yet outrageously funny', 'obscene but tender', 'heart-breaking but hilarious' etc.) and they have also come to be the effects sought for in every theatrical production. The 'roaring farce' which Hardy felt was Modern Tragedy is now the standard article. In fact the post-Romantic age only recognises the idea of the tragic if it is presented in comic–grotesque form, a form which usually excludes the possibility of real humour. It is against this background of convention that Wilson Knight's conception of *King Lear* has become the one we take for granted. What he called 'the absurdity of the Lear situation', and 'the demonic laughter that echoes in the Lear universe', have come to seem the natural thing to us.

As well they might. Like previous critics Wilson Knight was expressing the spirit of his age, a vision of the play in keeping with the modern theatre, where enactments of the comic–grotesque are the norm, and can readily be found in Gloucester's delusion that he has fallen over the cliff, in Kent's being put in the stocks, in a captain who appreciates that a regular job and prospects depend on his readiness to act as hangman of Cordelia. And to audiences at a modern production these things may well seem as pointed, as much part of an overall design, as they would in a play by Beckett or Pinter. But though we may see them as parts of a grotesque pattern if we wish to, in the world of *King Lear* there cannot really be any such pointers. For one thing there is too much in it of the natural world. There is the storm and the sound of the sea, the larks singing, men busy on the beach, weed-flowers among the corn in the fields near Dover. Having invisibly arrived, all these have become more important than the playwright's treatment of the *Lear* material.

And there is certainly nothing grotesque about them. *Lear* is in many ways Shakespeare's most realistically rural and domestic play, with a wide suggestion not only of lives being lived in their usual variety, but of physical continuity too, of getting from A to B and back again. The sequence of Gloucester's castle, the open country, the hovel and the farm, is done with an almost pedestrian accuracy, akin to the background of temperate but penetrating observation of families and quarrels, men of business, retainers, servants, and beggars. The perfunctory battle at Dover helps to emphasise by contrast how well done and visualised is the home front in *King Lear*. The play's atmosphere is unremittingly domestic, full of home's dull cruelties and brisk virtues. Home life in *Romeo and Juliet*, in *Coriolanus* and *Antony and Cleopatra*, is by contrast done with a total stylisation, with infinitely greater verve and vivacity, economy and wit. And there are no 'characters' in *Lear* such as we meet in these plays; no one is presented as being the perfection of his own particular type. Edmund is an atypical villain; the two women he makes up to do not seem monsters – in terms of their speech and consciousness they seem more repulsive than that, and also more trivial – and their rivalry over Edmund seems less the result of honest passion than of a venomous whim. Like everyone else in the play they seem *not up to it* – up to it in the sense which a Lady Macbeth so dramatically is.

One way to say this would be that the creative power which makes a Falstaff or Henry V, a Shallow, Helena, Beatrice, Polonius, Macbeth, seems to be going elsewhere in the play, running in some other way, difficult to describe or analyse. The idea of Lear as himself a titanic figure is contradicted here, though not with any emphasis. Where, we might wonder, does an overall impression of the sublime, and of Lear's stature, come from? Or is that idea only suggested by what we have read about the play?

The grotesque, well contrived, has its own form of total effectiveness, and one that never appears in *Lear*. The storm, and Lear's reaction to it, make a scene which might be grotesque and terrible but in fact is not: it seems full of a subdued understanding of the ways in which the persons in it are not up to its occasion. No 'demonic laughter' here-abouts, only the sense of an understanding of human weakness, working its way through the properties needed by the play; and seldom coinciding with the kinds of creative pressure those properties require. There is so much calm in the play, and a sort of reasonableness in episodes like the successful treatment of the two old men: Gloucester ministered to by Edgar at the cliff, Lear by the Doctor and Cordelia, as he lies witless and exhausted at the French camp. The humanity here bypasses any formula of tragedy, as well as what Wilson Knight calls 'the purposeful working-out' of the theme of the grotesque.

This goes together with the absence of fantasy in the creation of the characters of *King Lear*. Fantasy has no place even in the joyous account of Dover cliff, and it does not touch the dramatis personae and what happens to them. Polonius with Hamlet, the drunkenness of Cassio, Anne Boleyn and the old lady in *Henry VIII*, Falstaff and Shallow and the impressment scene – these demonstrate not only the scope and ease of a creating genius but a use of humour and incongruity (as with the manly heart and sentiments of the woman's tailor, Feeble) which is obviously purposive, and which moreover puts such scenes securely in the realm of high art, way above the debatable area of what can actually happen. We no more believe in the practical reality of Falstaff than we could experience a Feeble presented as the masterful scene presents him; but both are wholly 'right' in terms of Shakespeare's powers of drawing nature, and bestowing on it his own total appropriateness of temper and tone.

The kind of truths about ageing and the family in *King Lear* are not such as can be put into the realm of high art by temper and tone. The play accepts inadequacy and exhaustion, as well as a pedestrian sequence of labour, of coming hence and going hither. Any element of *tour de force* is absent, and a formula based on the idea of the grotesque must always appear a *tour de force*. Achievement, in the obvious sense, seems written neither into the events of the play nor its method. In *Macbeth* or *Othello* or *Hamlet* such achievement seems paramount in both. The achievement that some writers on *Lear* have seen is a kind of redemption, but what really happens to the two old persons – and it is surely much more affecting – is a sort of temporary physical alleviation, a homely cure, brought about by simple empirical means. The play can make nothing big out of either case: the patients are wholly passive, like persons in a casualty ward. Their needs are physical; the tone of the Doctor, and of Edgar and Cordelia too, is one found in circles where good doctors meet relatives, one of sympathetic and unsurprised humanity.

Unsurprised, in particular, by anything that Lear says. Going on about old army experiences ('Yon fellow handles his bow like a crow-keeper') is as commonplace in geriatric wards as senile obscenity ('Behold yon simpering dame') railing on women and sex, seeing through the shams of society and the way the world goes. Actors cannot face its simplicity, but we can take our cue from the bystanders on the stage itself, who hear Lear out without embarrassment, but with the normal indifference of solicitude. Pitifulness, when handled by art, has to be careful not to embrace us altogether into any mode of the histrionic. To avoid such a togetherness, in terms of the play, is the most difficult and unrewarding thing possible. It is easier to play up the scene, as the old *Leir* play did, into a facile mutuality of sentiment; or, as a modern production of Shakespeare does, into a *tour de force* of the touching and the grotesque. But all such effect is off-key, 'unnecessary' as age itself is. His lack of identification with what is going on could be said to produce in the onlooker a curious state, soothed, receptive, even a bit phlegmatic, as he listens to these unnecessary utterances. Tragedy has become a matter of deference to an unhinged old person, such as most or many of us shall become; and this old person is a king.

No wonder that critics have been anxious to establish a Job-like sequence of suffering, and a purgatorial way to redemption by love. But this falsifies what the play mysteriously suggests is true of both old men – the blankness of their experience. Lear and Gloucester continue to live, and those of good will help them to do so. That is the situation made out of the necessary dramatic sequence in which Lear will recognise Cordelia, and Gloucester die knowing that he has been attended by his son Edgar. The impersonal tenderness of the experiment Lear will accept in simple relief, as if it had stopped a raging toothache.

Acting and being

The mild pathos has nothing to do with drama and performance, just as Lear's situation itself has not. Gloucester's bewildered query: 'But have I fallen or no,' has something of the same simple vulnerability.

The story that Edgar then concocts is claimed by Wilson Knight as typical of the way in which the grotesque and absurd are at work in the play. But surely the impression most of us receive is rather different? As with Lear, the purpose is humanity, the humouring of the old in a tentative, rational way that is the irreducible part of the profession of human kindness. Edgar's devil – 'Methought he had a thousand noses, Horns whelked and waved as the enridged sea' – seems more like something out of the familiar childishness of fairy-tale than 'a fantastic picture of a ridiculously grotesque devil'. What Lady Macbeth calls, 'the eye of childhood' is a restorative and reassuring thing, to be invoked by those who have to 'trifle with despair', as Edgar says he must do. 'Trifling with despair' is routine practice to anyone trying to look after the old. More important, there is an affinity, 'above all strangeness', between Edgar's account of the sea-cliff, and of the creature that stood with Gloucester on its summit. Imagination depends on the sight, and the delight of Edgar's descriptions brings us back to Gloucester's eyeless state, knowing neither the cliff nor the thing that led him there.

In the old play of *Leir*, as in the *Arcadia*, the appeal to our pity came directly from the author and his text. Here there is no such appeal: feeling has to be supplied by ourselves and in our own way. Another instance of the overtly grotesque, and its effect upon the inward eye, is Theobald's anticipation of Wilson Knight's emphasis on the theme. Theobald thought it appropriate that Lear should enter 'fantastically dressed with wild flowers.' His direction, still lodged in the text, does its best to distort the way in which plain literalness, not fantasy, pity or terror, is put before us in the world of *Lear*.

CORD.   Why, he was met even now
   As mad as the vex'd sea; singing aloud;
   Crown'd with rank fumiter and furrow-weeds,
   With burdocks, hemlock, nettles, cuckoo-flowers,
   Darnel, and all the idle weeds that grow
   In our sustaining corn, – A century send forth
   Search every acre in the high-grown field
   And bring him to our eye. – What can man's wisdom
   In the restoring his bereaved sense?
   He that helps him take all my outward worth.
DOCT. There is means, madam;
   Our foster nurse of nature is repose,

The which he lacks; that to provoke in him
Are many simples operative, whose power
Will close the eye of anguish.
CORD.   All blest secrets,
All you unpublish'd virtues of the earth,
Spring with my tears.

IV. iv. 1–17

This is the reverse of fantasy; nor is there anything absurd in it. It becomes clear that Lear has not, like Ophelia, made something, something touching in his predicament, out of flowers; in his anguish he has plucked and torn at his surroundings and is bespattered with vegetable debris. And Cordelia's tone is quite unlike Queen Gertrude's. Gertrude is pronouncing a dirge, a sweet and touching lament over a young girl, the scene of whose end and her 'fantastic garlands' belong to the fantasies of girlhood. The fields over which Lear roved in his distractions are like the scene brought before us by Edgar at Dover cliff: Edgar and Cordelia lead us from the play's action out into the world, and its daily beauty and activity. Their words understand its relation to Lear and Gloucester, whom they try to bring back to everyday life by everyday remedies.

But all this is impossible for the theatre, which must take refuge in the grotesque, and above all in the *idea* of the grotesque. Lear, fantastically dressed in wild flowers by Theobald, is probably an accurate up-dating of the Lear who would actually have appeared upon the Elizabethan stage, just as Wilson Knight's vision of a comedy of the absurd would always have been implicit in the acting of the play.

The tragic in *King Lear* is sober, gentle, and enduring; at times joyful and spontaneous; nothing that can be effectively mimed, represented or repeated in the sense that acting must repeat each evening the big moment. There is something secretive in the play, which in a manner much more positive than with any other Shakespearean tragedy resists the notion of being played *in a certain spirit*. *Hamlet* has nothing like this, for whatever else may elude in that play, we can be sure that all kinds of stylishness, appropriate to the individual, the court, the old politician, the young girl crazed by grief, will give a firmness and confidence to the acting that avails itself of them. But the spirit of humour, of the grotesque, of what Wilson Knight calls 'cosmic mockery', seem alike ineffective in a rendering of *King Lear*. Nothing avails against the indeterminate nature of these experiences here undergone. Wilson Knight maintains that if we hold on to the idea of the comic grotesque it will 'cut out for analysis the very heart of the play, the thing that man dares scarcely face' – which is lunacy. But this of course is a way to face it, and the play shows no signs of facing it. We are told in this context that we must beware above all things of sentimentality, but sentimentality in such a context is a highly ambiguous concept. We can back straight into it while facing fearlessly in the opposite direction, rather like Bertrand Russell confronting the meaningless abyss of things in 'A Free Man's Worship'. Sentimentality in art today is usually a matter of a work of art, or its interpreter, having decided on the correct attitude to strike, having come to an understanding of the way things really are.

As we have seen, attempts to do this provide the off-key notes inside *King Lear*. But there is nothing beyond them. Here we are again at the source of Tolstoy's hatred of the play. Tolstoy of course grasped man's need to take the correct attitude and find the way things really are, however positive or negative the formulation of them may be. He himself was obsessed with a positive formulation. But Pierre, in *War and Peace*, makes a great discovery during the suffering and horror of the retreat from Moscow, in which he is involved as a prisoner. Pierre discovers that after all there is nothing 'terrible' – *strashno* – in human experience, and this gives him throughout all his hardships a sense of release and relief. This is a kind of parody of what tragedy normally tells us, but it is also very close to it. The desire to make sense of what is happening to one is very strong, and this is one way of doing it. But Pierre is answered (as something in Tolstoy may very well have perceived) by Edgar's comment in *King Lear*; 'The worst is not, while we yet live to say ''This is the the worst''.' Pierre's discovery is like all kinds of tragic discovery; and so would Edgar's comment itself be if it was advanced in the same spirit, instead of indicating nothing more than negation – a kind of blur. In the play every kind of metaphysical summation goes absent, like ghosts from the enchanter fleeing, but this is not seen to be done, only apprehended as we find the play more and more compelling in its simplest, least organised kinds of mastery. The most accurate parallels to *King Lear* tend to be pictorial ones: for example the great canvas of Velasquez known as *The Lances*. In that marvellously superficial picture the concentration on very ordinary delights of portraiture and perspective has come to produce the same sort of mysterious because open and unidentifiable effects of the non-terrible and terrible coinciding, in a vision that is neither one nor the other, neither tranquil nor appalling, neither pastoral nor tragic.

We escape into the metaphysical in order to deal with *King Lear*, where the eighteenth century took a simpler, more robust, way out. The Romantics, Keats and Lamb for instance, have accustomed us to the idea of 'burning through' the play, and Hazlitt to the idea, which even Wilson Knight would be a little shy of countenancing too openly, that it is the play in which Shakespeare 'was most in earnest.' Lamb's query – 'What gesture shall we appropriate to this?' – hits one nail on the head, but then opts for the metaphysical category of the sublime – the sublimest tragedy. Dr Johnson and his contemporaries took a different view. In spite of its formidable effectiveness as a tragic tale, the play had been made deliberately harrowing by Shakespeare: like *Titus Andronicus* only more so.

They were right. It is remarkable that though the play is without a spirit, without a style, it is none the less based on a version of the story which has clearly been used because it is the most painful conceivable. This might mean that the style itself becomes graphically agonising: *Titus Andronicus* is designed to enact stoicism and suffering as *Hamlet* is designed to enact a style and a despair in its own right. But in selecting the most painful way the story of *King Lear* could go, Shakespeare dispenses with any style that becomes the painfulness, and rises to it appropriately. Our general sense of this issue is in fact very much to the contrary of what the Gentleman says about Cordelia's grief for the sufferings of her father:

> In brief,
> Sorrow would be a rarity most belov'd
> If all could so become it.

The Gentleman adds his name to the many others in the play who try to respond appropriately to its pitiableness and outrage. This is his way of saying: 'This is the worst.' Cordelia, he thinks, is exactly *right* as the grieving daughter. But what is to come will deprive her of any such status, and what is to come is already implicit in the blur that surrounds her, the fact that no one looks the right way, if indeed there is a right way to look.

Tate solved the problem with a typical sort of eighteenth-century common sense. If the plot is to be changed, made both more melodramatic and happier, then she must be quite a different sort of person. The most important thing about his version is not so much the happy end as the thoroughgoing 'humanisation' of Cordelia. She is apparently the same girl, but it would be impossible to have hanged in the prison so engagingly commonplace a heroine as Tate provides – a Cordelia who has picked out Edgar to be her man, and behaves towards him with all the coquettish possessiveness that the new part demands. To kill such a girl in the way Shakespeare did would be worse than a crime, it would be a blunder. The ingenuity of the Tate version consists in making Shakespeare's look wrong. Shakespeare (they felt) made the error of creating a real and delightful and sympathetic girl, and then wantonly turning the screw of horror in order to create as succulently awful a finale as possible. And in a sense Tate and his contemporaries were quite right: Shakespeare does go too far in *King Lear*. But, having done so, he also produces no stylistic justification for doing so. That, to us, is the final effectiveness of his art here, but to the eighteenth century it must have seemed quite singularly uncalled for.

Even Dr Johnson thought so, and preferred Tate. But one wonders whether he was not accepting Tate's Cordelia as much the same sort of person as Shakespeare's. His praise of the play that 'hurries you irresistibly along', suggests that speed and excitement struck him as its leading characteristics, and these would be enhanced by the change and given the added justification of melodrama. Once Cordelia has become Edgar's sweetheart his cliffhanger rescue of her and her father is wholly proper to the form, as is Tate's Cordelia herself. Her chief preoccupation at the love-test ceremony, and it gives her just the kind of added personal motive such a heroine should have, is to avoid betrothal to her father's nominee, Burgundy.

One interest of Tate's Cordelia is that she is as 'right' in his version as all the pre-Shakespearean Cordelias were in theirs. Spenser's few stanzas in *The Faerie Queene* are concerned with a warlike and determined lady who gains a victory over her sisters and their husbands, restores her father, and is then deposed and imprisoned after his death by her nephews, – 'Till wearie of that wretched life herself she hong.' Heroic suicide is just the thing for this Cordelia, who is also suited to its leisurely dynastic anecdotes and tales of things 'done long ago and ill-done'. Cordella too, in the old *Leir*, is just right for the sentiment of that play, and in her romance relation with 'the Gallian king' seemed to Furness, the Variorum editor, 'more lovely and loveable' than the Cordelia of *King Lear*.

All these Cordelias are *right* for their situations: only Shakespeare's is not, in the sense that she is not the kind of character who can make

plain that   a situation is going on, and of what kind. On the part of
critics and directors the sure way to a vulgarising of the play is to
interpret her as fitting a situation, as her sisters do. This can be done in
the most popular version of the play current today, in which the
implications of the comic–grotesque are purposefully worked out. It
makes a situation and a play intended to be, to quote Wilson Knight
again, 'the most fearless artistic facing of the ultimate cruelty of things
in our literature'. And this suggests a play as clear-cut in what it
intends to be, and to do, as is the old sentimental *Leir* play, or Tate's
melodrama. In every case the appropriate Cordelia is fitted to her
situation, in the modern case in a play of grotesque incongruities,
which require her death as a part of them. Every age gets its *King Lear*
in the genre it requires.

And, more generally, its notions of the tragic. Every age has its own
way of imposing a stereotype on a Cordelia fitted neither to its notions
of tragedy, nor to its ideas – usually less variable – of how things should
be done on the stage. Cordelia is the embodiment of that aspect of *King
Lear* which tends to elude and disappear from itself, from its status and
form as tragedy. Not only is she not made for tragedy: she does not
seem to be made for art at all. Now this is obviously an inexact sort of
thing to say, because anyone in a play has been designed for and put
into it. Most modern drama in any case tries to give the impression
that the characters have wandered in from outside, that they are not in
any usual or conventional sense theatrical characters. But by not being
so, they become, of course, theatrical in a novel and opposing sense.
Cordelia is not like that; she does not seem an original or unusual
character to find in a play, but one who is not properly of it or in it.

The way this impression is created – and as always with Shakespeare
impression is everything – is initially quite simply done. Lear has cast
himself – quite deliberately as it appears – for a role in a play, a play in
which he as hero will be beloved father and wise ancient who
renounces his powers to the young and strong. And of course this goes
badly wrong, partly because Lear has cast himself for a role he does not
really believe in – does an old man really grasp that he is old? Lear's
big scene fails, and in failing produces the superbly effective drama of
his rage and his rejection of Cordelia. But in a less direct way the scene
goes wrong not because Cordelia insists on playing the wrong part, but
because she does not understand the business of playing a part at all.
Lear, one could say, would be less exasperated by a defiant daughter,
who opposed her own kind of part to his own, than by a daughter

whose non-playing threatens his whole dramatic conception of himself.

Lear is much more evidently concerned with a part than are Shake-speare's other tragic heroes, and this itself serves to increase the sense of Cordelia's non-participation. Tate, one feels, was determined to bring her back into the play, and make her as exuberantly a part of it as the Cordelia of the old *Leir*. Tate's Cordelia is as much concerned with the question of marriage as she is with gently opposing the part her father wants her to play, and substituting her own. To Shakespeare's Cordelia the question of marriage, as treated by her father and suitors, seems part of the whole unreality of the play situation. Lear himself draws attention to this: 'Sir, there she stands.' To stand there is indeed all that Cordelia can do. She does not even have to accept France formally, or to reply to his chivalrous speech. The 'hideous rashness' of her father reveals a theatre where the opposite number will not play at all. At this moment Lear is not just an old man. He has elected to over-come the disability by acting the part for all he is worth. As the play opens he chooses the play world, with all its passions and poses; the world in which Cordelia can only be uninvolved.

This brings up the question of what they have been doing until now, and how behaving? Here, as in so many other ways, the play is off-key, off-key to the usual Shakespearean harmony of character realisation. For, as Morgann observed, that realisation normally includes the previous, invisible, undisplayed experience of his characters, and makes it a part of themselves as we see them in the play. We have only to thnk of the unseen life of Gertrude and Claudius and Hamlet, or of Macbeth and Lady Macbeth. That life is so imaginable precisely because it seems part of the total life of the play. In the case of *King Lear* it does not seem so. Another factor operates. Something in the tragedy depends on the presences of matters not of the tragic world, not of the play world at all; and this effect goes with the other we have noted: the tendency of the characters to protect themselves from their experiences with utterances and sentiments suited to a play.

A play like *Hamlet* or *Macbeth* would reveal with instant and invisible mastery what Cordelia was *like*. It would reveal her past, and its relations with her present. In their elementary way the *Leir* play and the Tate version both do this. Their Cordelia is like any other character in art. The old *Leir* play indeed rushes in with relish here, informing us that Gonorill and Ragan couldn't abide their sister, because she was 'so nice and so demure/So sober, courteous, modest and precise'; and moreover that she had the exasperating habit of looking much more attractive in any new fashion of clothing they took up than they did themselves. Imogen, Portia, Helena, Desdemona – any other heroine of Shakespeare would thrive on this kind of disclosed domesticity. And in the Tate version there is the love relation with Edgar, which supplies instant intrigue, story and background.

In *King Lear* no background exists. Instead it is as if life and choice had been forced to begin together from scratch by the great ceremony of the opening. Everything till now has been in abeyance, in eclipse. Now Lear has resolved to be himself and act his part and require others to endorse it, most especially his favourite daughter. Cordelia cannot enter into existence on these terms. Her existence itself is absolute, it has no 'story' to it; and this is conveyed by the blankness of her acceptance of marriage with France, as by the blankness of her rejection of her father's need that she should play a part with him.

In the other tragedies characters not only have a past but have a future as well. Although they die they might have lived. They themselves, or their friends, can imagine what might have been the case if they had. Hamlet 'was likely, had he been put on,/ To have prov'd most royally.' Lady Macbeth 'should have died hereafter,' in the natural course of life's history: her story has a past and a possible future. Cordelia's life and death do not appear to come within the compass of this sort of fictional art, which Shakespeare is normally such an adept in supplying.

These aspects of Cordelia, suggested in the impression she makes in the great power of the piece, are none the less insubstantial enough – they do not have the air of an intention. The words she speaks are sufficiently like those of other people to excite no comment, as it were, in the context of a play in blank verse. And yet they *are* different, as everyone feels, and they produce subtle kinds of misunderstanding. Although Cordelia can heave her heart into her mouth perfectly well on occasion, as the overall convention of a play requires, she can also appear to discredit poetry, not intentionally, but by not embracing it, as the others do, as an extension of their wills and personalities. Lear, his other two daughters, Edmund and the rest, *use* poetry as they would use rhetoric. Shakespeare suggests – and it is an extraordinary feat of style to do so – that Cordelia cannot do this. She is as devoid of studied human eloquence as an angel might be. It is Romeo who says about Juliet

> O speak again bright angel, for thou art
> As glorious to this night, being o'er my head,

As is a winged messenger of heaven
Unto the white upturned wondering eyes
Of mortals that fall back to gaze on him
When he bestrides the lazy-pacing clouds
And sails upon the bosom of the air.

II. ii. 26–32

Poetry is being used, though for the most lyrical of reasons; the winged
messenger himself would have no need to command such eloquence.
The Gentleman speaks of Cordelia's tears in the same vein that Romeo
does of Juliet.

You have seen
Sunshine and rain at once? Her smiles and tears
Were like a better way. Those happy smilets
That played on her ripe lip seemed not to know
What guests were in her eyes, which parted thence
As pearls from diamonds dropped.

IV iii. 17–22

The fervour is undoubted, even though there is a comical incongruity
between the Gentleman's eloquence and our sense of its object. (His
phrase-finding has one point of real observation in it, none the less, and
that is how an impression of Cordelia is at a loss for ordinary studied
consistency: she baffles the summer-up by her unselfconsciousness,
even in the matter of her appearance in joy and grief.) But the use of
poetic eloquence contrasts with the odd plain word that comes from
Cordelia herself when she leaves with her new betrothed husband, the
King of France, and, as she says, 'with washed eyes'. When Lear sees
her again, on waking from distraction, her tears are the first thing he
sees. 'Be your tears wet?' This, the most moving moment of the play,
is so because it is the only time in it that the speech of father and
daughter coincides. Neither is using words for effect or purpose, but
like a kiss or touch. Lear has had no time to reassemble his sense of self
and the language that goes with it.

LEAR. I feel this pin prick. Would I were assured
    Of my condition.
CORD.   O look upon me Sir
    And hold your hands in benediction o'er me.
    No Sir, you must not kneel.
LEAR. Pray do not mock me.
    I am a very foolish fond old man,

Fourscore and upward, not an hour more or less,
And to deal plainly
I fear I am not in my perfect mind.
Methinks I should know you and know this man.
Yet I am doubtful: for I am mainly ignorant
What place this is, and all the skill I have
Remembers not these garments; nor I know not
Where I did lodge last night. Do not laugh at me.
For, as I am a man, I think this lady
To be my child Cordelia.
CORD.   And so I am, I am.
LEAR. Be your tears wet? Yes, faith. I pray,
     weep not.
If you have poison for me I will drink it.
I know you do not love me, for your sisters
Have, as I do remember, done me wrong.
You have some cause, they have not.
CORD.   No cause, no
                              cause . . .
LEAR.   You must bear with me.
Pray you now, forget and forgive. I am old and
     foolish.

IV. vi. 56–75, 84–5

His words – 'mainly', 'plainly', 'not an hour more or less' – have the
same ring as hers, and the most moving thing is not their 'togetherness' – so consciously emphasised in the old *Leir* play, but the seeming
incompatibility of both estrangement and taking each other thankfully
for granted. Since her sisters have done him wrong she can't love him
either; but he knows she does, and takes it now for granted as much as
he had once insisted on its expression.

Perhaps the most moving thing is the sense that, whatever happens,
it cannot last. Lear is not that kind of man, and taking things for
granted is not in his nature. There could be no greater contrast than
between this scene and the one after the battle, when Lear in the full
exaltation of assertive consciousness sees himself and Cordelia united
forever at last.

Upon such sacrifices, my Cordelia,
The gods themselves throw incense. Have I caught thee?

Tragedy for Lear is as much what would have happened as what actually does. In his relation with Cordelia, Lear enjoys at the close of his fortunes a transcendent and visionary moment of life. That the vision is impossible does not alter the truth and happiness of it in Lear's eyes:

> We two alone will sing like birds i'the cage.
> When thou dost ask me blessing, I'll kneel down
> And ask of thee forgiveness: so we'll live,
> And pray and sing and tell old tales and laugh
> At gilded butterflies, and hear poor rogues
> Talk of court news; and we'll talk with them too,
> Who loses and who wins: who's in, who's out,
> And take upon's the mystery of things
> As if we were God's spies.
>
> V. iii. 9–17

Mystery means mastery, in the sense that a craft or profession is mastered. Lear's vision is again one of power, of his kingship by other means, but that is not the most of it. Cordelia will now be entirely his, completing the fantasy of life that sprang into existence at the beginning of the play. And, in the face of this, Cordelia, like reality itself, again has nothing to say. Her last line has already been spoken, and in its intonation is one of her simplest and most characteristic and yet strangest in the play: 'Shall we not see these daughters and these sisters?' For her it is the matter in hand that counts and the relational aspect of her normal duty. Lear in any case has forgotten that she is a married woman, and that her husband the King of France has responded to her appeal to restore Lear to his kingdom.

Not surprisingly, for France is as shadowy a figure as the battle from which he is absent – rather necessarily absent – is perfunctory. But it is important that he exists, for he is part of the simple reality in which Cordelia lives. There are moments in the play, and this is one of them, when the impression with which it opens, of existence and choice beginning for two people, makes all the 'stories' in it seem not worth bothering about. In fact they are, as we shall see, and in a manner unique to this play; but the unstoried relation of Lear and Cordelia is none the less apart from them. The tragedy of the relation is that it cannot exist as Lear wishes it to, and she can do nothing to help the matter.

The play begins with a declaration of love. This means that, whatever the story tells us, nothing would satisfy Lear. He wants the impossible. Cordelia knows this and accepts it. It does not change her duty or her love, but the real significance of her reply is that she knows that what Lear wants is not hers to give. The mystery that surrounds her ordinariness is that of a plain and unacceptable truth. Goethe said that every old man is a king Lear, but it is also true that every man, old or not, tends to be one.

The play's universality is concerned with this. Browning must have intuited it when he took the line 'Child Roland to the Dark Tower came', and made it into a poem. Much has been written about the meaning of that poem, and its deliberate mysteriousness, but its allegory is clear enough. The Dark Tower is the end of strenuous illusion; it is the mere thing in itself. Browning wrote the poem in Paris, after the difficulties of his marriage had begun to reveal themselves. Now the reality had begun: the thing itself was there. At the beginning, Lear addresses himself to the achievement of his ideal, and to the part he will play to get it. The reality of Cordelia is itself the Dark Tower. But he neither knows it for what it is nor is he capable of accepting it.

A play in earnest

No wonder that Hazlitt said that this was the play in which Shakespeare was most in earnest. Everyone feels that, and the fact that he was not in earnest in the normal sense – the sense in which Dante and Milton were – does not alter the matter. The story let his genius work in the deepest understanding of things, and give the completest form and pressure to his sense of tragedy. It is concerned with discrepancy: the absolute difference between Lear and Cordelia, the absolute difference between life as a play to be arranged, and as the space between our coming hither and going hence. But out of this simplicity comes a very great deal of complication, complication that works on different levels and through different modes of discourse. In none of the plays are these more oddly related to one another, or more productive of further rewards and fascinations. In none does earnestness itself seem to become more earnest, however subtle and peculiar its relation is to what is off-key. In none do virtue and simplicity appear more evidently. In none does deliberation amount to so little.

'Oh the difference between man and man,' says Goneril. Such differences are especially marked not only between the persons in it, but between different aspects of the play. In *Shakespeare's Tragedies of Love* H. A. Mason took the bull by the horns when he called it not only the most irritating but even the most disappointing of Shakespeare's tragedies, because it is so good in some places and so extremely bad in others. Middleton Murry and critics before him made the same kind of point. That Shakespeare is sometimes 'bad' – mechanical or perfunctory or stereotyped – is of course a commonplace, but the objection here is that these things not only get in the way of the play's greatness but give it a quality of uncertainty, of the accidental.

Mason takes particular objection to Edgar's killing of Oswald, whom he thinks should merely have been frightened, and to the odious way in which he describes his disposal of the body ('Here in the sands/Thee I'll rake up, the post unsanctified/Of murderous lechers'). He cannot abide the contrivance by which Edgar and Edmund come to their armed confrontation, and particularly dislikes the complacency of the victorious Edgar's summing-up of the situation ('That dark and vicious place where thee he got/Cost him his eyes').

Such criticisms, exhibiting the pedantic or priggish views of a given age and society, have always been voiced. But their importance in relation to the world of *Lear*, and the particular vehemence with which Mason in particular has made them, do show something of importance. In fact such things are as essential to the world of *Lear* as anything else, for they help dispose of any conscious aura of its earnestness and sublimity. The story is part of the bewilderment of living and its minor incomprehensibilities. Meeting and divergence – as Lear's with Cordelia – go together with its humble necessities. In *Hamlet* plot contrivance is closely integrated with the intellectual atmosphere: the two are part of the same art. But in *King Lear* they are very different parts.

Lear and his daughter, like Gloucester and Edgar, are in one sense deeply attached, in another utterly apart and separated. That is in any case a normal family thing. But the unwinding of the plot emphasises it. The encounters of Edgar and Oswald, of Edmund and Edgar, are as hasty and provisional as the last we see of Lear and Cordelia in life together. In the context of action truth to life is a momentary truth, as we are hurried irresistibly along, and this is the most strangely and richly momentary of plays. There is no liaison between soliloquy and plot, as in *Hamlet* or *Macbeth*. Nothing profound, to be questioned or thought on or decided, interrupts the immediacy of experience. And yet of course the inquirer knows that in the midst of this medley is the most earnest, touching and profound of Shakespearean imaginations. No wonder he wants to separate one thing from another, the chaff from the wheat.

But it cannot and should not be done. Triviality will have its say:

again, not in the sense that *Hamlet* has the Osric scene, and the
Polonius and Reynaldo scene, to remind us of other aspects of life. All
aspects cohere here, and in cohering reveal the sort of sensationalism
on which living is based. The most startling example, which a modern
audience cannot respond to as the old one would have, but which is
none the less of great significance, is the loss of the battle by Lear's
party. This is signalised by Edgar rushing in to carry off his old father
from a spot now grown mortally dangerous.

EDG. Away old man! Give me thy hand. Away! . .
GLOU. No further sir – a man may rot even here.
EDG. What, in ill thoughts again? Men must endure
   Their going hence even as their coming hither.
   Ripeness is all. Come on.

                                  V. ii. 5, 8–11

Lear's eloquence in the next scene, his vision of a motionless Elysium
of loving and detached repose in the prison with Cordelia, is swept out
of the way by the next bit of action. The better informed among the old
audiences must here have been in a state of high curiosity and
expectation. In the old play, and in all versions they might have heard,
Cordelia and her father win the battle, though in a ballad (afterwards
collected by Percy) the victorious girl herself dies in action. What an
audience would not have expected to see is the triumph at this point of
the play of the forces of evil, even if they were British. Again, all is
uncertainty, and immediately the pair are led away *something* sinister –
but what? – passes between Edmund and one of his captains. From this,
and from Edmund's soliloquy before the battle, it is clear that he
intends to make away with the pair if he can – but will he succeed?

   This suspense overlays the ensuing action and separates itself from it.
In the same way action both overrides the family theme and is
irrelevant to it. The chivalry of the encounter between Edgar and
Edmund, and their 'exchange of charity' after it, is not eclipsed by
what may be going forward in the unseen prison, as a result of that
secret instruction. All aspects of the play are now proceeding
independently, each insuring that no general tone or atmosphere will
dominate it. These separate actions are each as valid in their way as the
sentiments uttered as a result of them: sentiments like Edgar's about
the 'dark and vicious place', like Albany's about the 'Justicers' above,
and the heavens sending down to 'tame these vilde offences'. Only
someone determined to make sense of the play, according to a pre-

conception, or desire to sort out the good and bad in it, is exasperated by the way in which such action and sentiment moves separately, and regards it as evidence of confusion or weakness.

All are in a way echoes of the fact that the gap, the distance between Lear and Cordelia, remains as constant as the love. One thing so unexpected and effective in their scene together after capture is how they have changed places, though the same gap remains. She is stoical, but her passionate desire is to confront 'these daughters and these sisters' and passionately to express her indignation and abhorrence, if it is the last thing she does. There is nothing in her 'personality' to explain this, but it is her simple desire to do it, as were her previous needs to speak the truth to her father, then to rescue and shelter him. By contrast there is a great deal in Lear's personality to explain his exaltation. He no longer has the slightest interest in catching and killing his daughters and sons-in-law, for he has 'caught' Cordelia herself.

> Have I caught thee?
> He that parts us shall bring a brand from heaven
> And fire us hence like foxes.

Have *I* caught *thee*? should be the intonation. Their capture has given him his chance to be her captor, a state of affairs still more satisfactory to his imagination than to be the tyrant of her 'most kind nursery'. And indeed no one can part them, for they have never been joined.

She is as distant from him as is Edmund from the two sisters to whom he makes love. The 'difference between man and man' is again well exemplified. Compared to Macbeth's actions, or those of Claudius or Richard III or Iago, Edmund's activities display only the contented self-absorption of most human business. His orders for the prisoners' death, like his plot against his father, and his sudden reversal of fortune, seem like an interlude in the foreground of the suffering and bereavement which they cause, but with which they do not appear connected. As so often in *King Lear* one is reminded of the technique of great narrative painting, with its apparently uncoordinated detail of separate event.

Edmund's 'repentance' has the same lack of co-ordination here as Cordelia's obstinate wish in defeat to confront her sisters. It used to be a critical question whether his repentance were genuine or not, one body of opinion inclining to the ingenious idea that he deliberately postponed repentance and reversal of orders until he knew it could do no good, thus achieving the maximum 'Oh if only we'd remembered a bit earlier' effect. But this sort of criticism is like Mason's and Middleton Murry's, seeking to excuse where they wanted to censure, but both trying to tidy things up and put them in order. Edmund is a wholly spontaneous figure, his part lying on that side of the canvas where impulse naturally joins hands with the hurry of action. The audience see the arrangement that leads them to look into every scene in it, however disjunct, as parts of a spacious whole. Having lost, why should Edmund not have the impulse to undo mischief, just as he did it? The appalling damage he does is not what he deliberately wants, but the result of his will to action, as if he had accidentally killed several people when deciding to drive very fast from A to B. This now is a last flourish of his will, for which he finds an appropriate formula: 'Some good I mean to do,/Despite of mine own nature.' In the same spirit he says of Goneril and Regan: 'I was contracted to them both: all three/Now marry in an instant.' It gives him joy that they loved him, and even that 'The wheel is come full circle: I am here.'

Edmund's last scene and lost death is typical of the *ease* of *King Lear*, the way in which corny historical-type drama becomes a part of it. Edmund is so well fitted for this part that the casualness with which he ruins those against whom he has no hate helps to spread the load of the play still wider, to reduce even more the sense in which it demonstrates itself as an earnest play on a sublime theme. The effectiveness of Edmund, in terms of his own self and of a simplistic convention, is the way in which he helps to show how little intensification the play needs, how much more moving it is without invoking it. His death 'is but a trifle here', as Albany says, but because it is a death of melodrama, or of tragedy, it shows the nature of such a death in contrast with death of another kind. The difference between one and another is no less, in this context, than that between man and man.

The natures of Cornwall, of Goneril and Regan, are as different from his as both are from those of Kent or Cordelia. They are bad and dreadful in the family sense, like the kind of children who torment animals and pull the wings off flies. They are dreadful but also sluggish, without the gaiety and will to achievement that is in Edmund, and to which they respond, the women idolatrously. Edmund, who does the most harm, is none the less outside that family area in which both the real harm and the real good are done. Gloucester's blinding, from which Edmund is excluded, is a family scene, its Cordelia being the servant who served Cornwall since he was a child and now bids him 'hold his hand' and refrain from the wanton wickedness of the action.

CHAPTER 2

THE NATURES OF DEATH

Enacting and dying

Critics who, like Mason, would like to separate the good from the bad in *King Lear* do not distinguish between the good and the bad, the sublime and the trivial, where dying is concerned. Perhaps they should, for the variation is certainly remarkable and tells us much about the place of death in Shakespearean tragedy, where we have, as it were, dying of all kinds. Death is sometimes the most cursory sort of dramatic convenience – the dialogue of Albany, Edgar and the wounded Edmund is a case. Death is a way of ending a necessary dramatic discourse that tidies up the plot, and in its artificiality makes the other story impending over us more disturbing, more evidently and terribly true. Edmund's 'getting ready for the end' line – 'But speak you on;/you look as you had something more to say' – would be comically flat in the most lowly history play: here it seems to make the right sort of contrast with what is to follow. Paradoxically it is more necessary to the story itself than to the acting of it. The state of the text – the Folio omits it altogether – seems to indicate that the actors abridged as far as they could Edgar's explanation of how his father died of joy at recognising him, and how he left Kent 'tranced' at this new metamorphosis when the trumpets sounded for the duel with Edmund.

The account of Gloucester taken by death unawares occurs inside the tableau in which Edmund enacts the waiting for it. But actors could hardly get that point across, and this is one of many occasions when Shakespeare seems more faithful to the story than to the play. That faithfulness has its own kind of chivalry, a moving one, and yet

Shakespeare can free himself momentarily from the tale too, as Dover cliff shows, soaring into a world outside both story and play. But most of the time he is as faithful to both forms as Ariel to Prospero; and the element of mummers' simplicity and banality in them seems a kind of reassurance for his art, and for ourselves with it. The business of deaths and recognitions here is in direct but uncomprehending relation with Lear and his loss.

Simple concentration on loss can produce superb tragedy, as Racine shows. But it is interesting that the attempt to combine naturalism with such concentration always leads to pretentiousness on the stage. Tragedies are no good if, like O'Neill's, and a hundred others of every date, they concentrate fiercely on showing how stark and awful life is. Able to concentrate on nothing but effective moments, the tragedian emancipated from any local necessities often impresses the groundlings but makes the judicious grieve. Tragic emotion of the Shakespearean sort requires – and never more so than in *King Lear* – placing among homely and traditional kinds of distraction, consolation and pretence, before it will appear both simple and unacted. It is because Edmund acts that Lear at the end seems not to, and it is because Edmund has a stage-tragedy death that Lear and his daughter seem not to.

A moment before Lear enters with his cry of total loss, Edmund gave a characteristically jaunty expression to his own. 'I was contracted to them both'. It is his version of 'Hé bien je meurs content.' As such it expresses the important convention in Shakespearean tragedy of death as a ritual, or as a piece of dramatic propriety and convenience. The most effective use of such formality in Shakespeare is Laertes's forewarning of Hamlet's death, and with it, the end of the tragedy:

> Hamlet, thou art slain;
> No medicine in the world can do thee good;
> In thee there is not half an hour's life.
>
> V. ii. 305–7

And neither is there in the play. In theatre terms it is the formal equivalent of Brutus' Roman sentiments: 'Night hangs upon my eyes; my bones would rest/That have but laboured to attain this hour.'

In *Macbeth* death's ritual appears in the guise of longing and weariness. Banquo bides safe in a ditch, 'with twenty trenched gashes on his head,/The least a death to nature.' But in Macbeth's imagination he is not dead, and hence his ghost is the most frightening in Elizabethan tragedy. Macbeth envies one of his victims, King Duncan, because he knows that Duncan is in his grave. To his imagination the murdered king sleeps well, but the murdered rival, whose offspring survives, lives on in the fever of his mind. Grave and ditch are two kinds of death as seen by the need and imagination of the living. The audience is taken more absolutely into Macbeth's imagination than that of any other character in Shakespeare, and there is no more vivid proof of this than the quiet desperate query he addresses to friends and attendants when he sees Banquo sitting at the table – 'Which of you have done this?' Macbeth knows, and we know, that there is nothing there, so he longs to think this a real body, or some dreadful practical joke played on him, as it is played on Antonio in *The Duchess of Malfi*.

Death is so much a fellow of Macbeth's imagination that his own has no significance: it has been conceived and acted out in that of his victims and his wife, in the theatre of his consciousness. He himself is persuaded that he cannot die, that no man of woman born can kill him, and that he has been condemned to live in the torture of the mind as he is to sleep no more. For Antony and Cleopatra death seems a way of extending their consciousness of each other; they ritualise their endings as they have done their loves; and though Antony's agony is prolonged by his own indecisiveness, it gives him more time to die into his queen and impress his death upon her. The rite of death is mixed with hard and homely fact, as their rites of love have been. Othello's death re-enacts a deed of suicidal daring, making amends to himself and the world for the murderous passions and jealousies that have been sated with an equal swiftness upon Desdemona.

All these show that for Shakespearean tragedy death is very much a part of life; and, in the sense of the play, to be lived through and endured as life itself is. Death is so common in, and so proper to, such tragedy, that the existence of the characters is confirmed by it and not extinguished. Within the form of the art death becomes the experience Wittgenstein said it could not be. ('Death is not an event in life: we do not live to experience death.') Elizabethan tragic decorum regarded death as a ceremony in which all the players participated and were united into a whole. Curiously enough it is irrelevant whether the Christian idea of survival is present or not. In the tragedies it is glanced at, as it is in *Othello*, or more deliberately excluded, but the effect is not dissimilar to that in the history plays, with their specifically Christian ethos and their pattern of descent and continuity. Vaughan, Rivers and Grey, about to be executed on the orders of Richard III, take solemn farewell of each other, 'Till we do meet in heaven.' Although for Hamlet the rest is silence, the communion is the same, and it both survives and perpetuates him. Tragedy re-enacts itself in its cycle of death and rebirth; the form of Hamlet remains, his function never dies.

This is what makes the enactment of death in *King Lear* such a remarkable exception. Though it is performed by players who will 'rise and fight again', our apprehension of it is clean contrary to what we feel in the other tragedies. It usurps life without rhyme or reason. Cordelia and her father, who are without a past and seemed to begin life by making their choice, end it, as it were, without a future. The death of Cordelia appears to overwhelm the other characters in the play, as well as her father, because of the irrelevance that brings home its finality. Persons in a tragedy are normally accustomed to view death in a different spirit.

Cordelia has not only failed to live through death, by the aid of the tragic convention. She also seems to show that she has not been aware of taking part in the formal world of tragedy: she has lived in it through no choice of her own. That suggests something of importance about the way the play works. For Cordelia does not appear to discredit, even by implication, the tragic conventions, with their appropriate discourses, that are going on around her. Her sudden removal strikes them dumb, but there is no suggestion that the author and the play have contrived that this should be so. Death takes its place beside death-in-tragedy unobtrusively and without drawing attention to itself, or proclaiming itself as a new and startling device of art, as does the death at the end of Pirandello's *Six Characters in Search of an Author*. There the specific point is made of death as reality, versus death as enactment. Death in *King Lear* leaves us to feel our own impression of it.

Cordelia's death is as unassuming as her whole being, her marriage to the King of France and her reappearance in England to help her father. And it is of course her unawareness of herself as a tragic or a pathetic character that makes her death so painful. Its painful unfairness is felt by everybody, by the critic in his study just as much as the mass audience.

Dr Johnson undoubtedly felt that *King Lear* had forfeited, in a formal sense, its right to be called a tragedy. No doubt, in other senses, other plays of Shakespeare could be said to do the same thing; and this would not have worried him, for he makes it plain that the 'rules' of tragedy, as formulated after Aristotle by various neo-classic critics, neither apply to Shakespeare's particular genius nor have much virtue in themselves.

But he implies that because of the treatment of Cordelia *King Lear* is a different case, and merited the treatment it received at Tate's hands.

Dr Johnson, after all, lived in the century in which *feeling* was coming to be valued as the dramatic quality *par excellence*, the great quality of literature in general. The Romantics only added an extra emphasis to this general view. Though it is classic in form Johnson's own tragedy, *Irene*, depends on feeling as much as Sheridan's *Pizarro* or the early plays of Kotzbue and Schiller, which made Hazlitt weep 'like a madman'. The nobility, the sentiment and the pathos that could be put into a part were all-important.

And pathos on the stage is a very soothing thing. The deaths of Paul Dombey, or of Little Nell, are in many ways the culmination of a couple of centuries of acted deaths – with them Dickens is very close to the traditions of the stage. There is nothing specious about the pathos; it is perfectly genuine, as real as the floods of tears which accompany it, and in the same way the audiences at a Greek tragedy probably groaned and rocked themselves from side to side like the mourners at a wake. Their response was not like the feeling induced by a good part and a good actor, but it had that much in common with it.

There is no pathos in this sense at the end of *Hamlet* or *Macbeth* or *Julius Caesar*: the rites and community of death are accomplished there by other means. But there is a great deal of it at the end of *Othello*. Shakespeare there seems deliberately to exploit pathos as much as possible, as appropriate (apparently) to the nature of the tragic story. So much so that critical readers in our time have suggested that he is just putting it on, and that the real story is a brilliant examination of a certain kind of histrionic and egocentric personality. This brings us again to the question of divided discourse in the tragedies, and I shall return to it, but in this connection it seems evident that the death of Desdemona is pathetic but not painful, not 'real', even though to Dr Johnson it seemed something 'not to be endured'. Her death is not stylised as Hamlet's is, or Julius Caesar's or Brutus', but it is, by other means, just as much of a stage death.

So much so that she hardly seems to die at all but to fade away, like the heroines of Dickens. Having revived once, and uttered suitable sentiments, why should she not revive again? Lear believes Cordelia may still be alive, and is frenzied by the failure of the bystanders to help him revive her, or at least not distract him from the attempt at it. His frenzy shows how dead she is, and the wordlessness of the bystanders confirms it, whereas any suggestion that Desdemona might be revived would – in that context – only draw attention to the obvious fact that she is not really dead at all. Othello the soldier has seen plenty of dead men, and women too, in his time, but it would not be in his tragedy to say, as Lear does, 'I know when one is dead and when one lives.' It is no part of tragic propriety, and the atmosphere appropriate to his story, that he should say Desdemona is 'dead as earth', even when he finds out what he has done. When he does, his attitude is an exaggeration, suited to himself and to his story, of tragic community in death, the protagonists being all in it together. There is no ultimate divide between the one who is dead and the one who lives. And Othello has a special reason for regarding Desdemona as still, so to speak, 'active'.

> Now how dost thou look now? O ill-starred wench.
> Pale as thy smock. When we shall meet at compt,
> That look of thine will hurl my soul from heaven,
> And fiends will snatch at it. Cold, cold, my girl,
> Even like thy chastity.
>
> V. ii. 275–9

'Now how dost thou look now?' is both touching and dreadful in its simplicity. It suggests that Othello does not consider her as dead at all but as capable of change in her appearance as a living person. Her body is growing cold but that declares to him something that he should have known all along.

Kinds of literalness are always coming through the kinds of atmosphere and feeling that are appropriate to each separate case of tragedy. Othello's conviction of a continuing relationship with Desdemona is a case in point. It may show that he is in one way madder than Lear, that Iago's deception has deranged him, and this comes through – or rather appears beside – the kinds of pathos that are suited to the end of this story. Emilia's death has the same blend of the tragic-conventional ('I will play the swan/And die in music') and a similar sort of literalness:

> So come my soul to bliss, as I speak true;
> So speaking as I think, I die, I die.

Othello also speaks as he thinks. And it is appropriate both to his own nature and to the nature of the story as tragedy that he thinks of Desdemona as still there, to judge him, perhaps to forgive him and love him again; and of his own suicide as one of the 'moving accidents by flood and field' that fill his life. He continues to live with Desdemona in a manner which the nineteenth century well understood, as Browning shows in 'Porphyria's Lover'. Lodovico's understanding of this is conveyed in his line: 'You must forsake this room and go with us'; and Emilia has already expressed her intuition of disaster in opposite terms: 'Perchance, Iago, I will ne'er go home.' Othello does not forsake the room, his last strongpoint, to be held as Cyprus was to be held against the Turks. Important here that Othello's sense of things is not a delusion but an estimate, which we accept in terms of the tragic experience of the play – granted Othello and Desdemona, and their love, and Iago, all that follows is right and proper. There is, so to speak, in *Othello*, no true death to recall us to our senses: indeed this is part of the normal effect of tragedy, but in *Othello* the effect is particularly specialised and all of its own.

And so Othello's suicide, falling on the bed and kissing her, is an act of love, and one that seems to make their relationship perpetual, not ended. As with *Hamlet*, only even more so, the deaths exist to give a permanence of life to the characters, their story existing as a result of it. Othello's finale – 'I kissed thee, ere I killed thee. No way but this,/Killing myself, to die upon a kiss' – is the crudest possible effect of 'feeling', in terms of the atmosphere of the play, so much so that austere critics like H. A. Mason find it too impossibly revolting – or it would be if we were attending any more. ('The nerve of nausea has ceased to throb,' he says.) But nothing in Shakespeare is just empty sentiment, of the kind that eighteenth- and nineteenth-century audiences in search of 'feeling' were quite content with. Othello's death and death-words have the same combination of literalness with romantic sentiment as Emilia's have: the deaths of both show us something very important to the play, the kinds of human consciousness out of which its special kinds of tragical fantasy and logic proceed. We see both in Othello's case and Emilia's how naturally literalness and down-to-earthness go with romantic sentiment, in Othello's case sentiment of the most high-flown kind. That they should and do so go together is precisely the condition of the play's romance, and tragic outcome.

Othello is by nature given to romantic love and sentiment, just as he is to the romance and mastery of war. Emilia is given to it too, and is very romantic about Desdemona and her new husband. Clearly at one level she lives in a world of women's magazines. But this goes with an extremely down-to-earth attitude towards sex and marriage, and a common sense that blazes forth in a crisis. Everyone knows the kind of person. And so, in another way, with Othello; but here the common,

the almost universal, combination shows its disastrous potentiali-
ties. Othello's down-to-earthness is of the kind that hates to be
reminded of the fact. He would rather not contemplate the facts of sex
and sexual possession which he depends on. Reminded by Iago of
nakedness in bed, of keeping a corner in his wife for others' uses, of
gendering and slime, he recoils passionately to the world of romance
and romantic sentiment.

His progress is the opposite of Emilia's: she recoils on the literal
down-to-earth world when crisis arrives. As no doubt Desdemona
would if she could: her sentiments about Othello and his tales of war go
perfectly well with her wifely and housewifely instincts – feeding him
on nourishing dishes – and the determined realism with which she cuts
adrift from her father and family. She is quite at home with the down-
to-earth jokes and chat of the two officers; especially with Cassio, who
has the same sort of temperament – in his case the matter-of-factness
which goes with his prostitute friend, and the romantic idealism which
goes with his attitude towards his profession, Othello his general, and
to Desdemona herself.

Iago is the one exception to this normal human pattern, a particular
emphasis on which produces the tragic stuff of *Othello*. The aesthetic
manipulation needed may be excessive, but it is certainly true that
death in the play forms a part of the fantasy on which it is based. Iago
has no part in it, and in its sense he cannot die. 'I bleed, Sir, but not
killed,' and as the for once impotent Othello says: 'If that thou be'est a
devil I cannot kill thee.' Death for the other characters is a part of that
unstable mixture of literalness and romance on which their lives are
based. Othello's 'Now how dost thou look now?' confirms in the most
literal way his repossession of Desdemona, which he asserts by falling
on her as he expires. His exclamation is at the change in her, now she
is dead, but that is itself an indication of continuity, of the same kind as
he envisaged for himself when he exclaimed at their meeting in Cyprus
– 'If it were now to die/'Twere now to be most happy.'

Othello is a virtuoso piece – Shakespeare's great feat of casting
tragedy as romance. His creative powers found this the way to treat the
story, engendering disaster out of the most ordinary and widespread
human attribute: the oscillation of the normal mind back and forth
between romantic dream and illusion, and down-to-earthness. For
Othello the process is poisoned and turned inside out – 'the seamy side
without' in Emilia's words. Emilia turns from romance to reality at the
crisis – the normal human response. Othello goes the other way.

Inevitably, because Iago has persuaded him that fantasy – the invention of Desdemona's guilt – is literally and vilely true, and that the romance by which he lives has no truth and substance whatever. The literal and the sentimental have changed places in his mind, become totally at cross purposes, and no doubt their relationship for him has never been a natural one. This goes with the audience's sense of him as a great romantic portent, his blackness, his exoticism, his wonderful and formidable attractiveness.

An ideal audience should be charmed by Othello. That is essential to the tale, a tale of fantasy and faerie. For the success of his project Shakespeare must succeed in that, but being Shakespeare he also makes Othello, as he made Shylock, fully and comprehensively human. The Moor of Venice, like the Jew of Venice, is a figure of outlandish romance, but he is also instantly recognisable as one of us. And in the case of Othello, protagonist of a tragic fantasy, the bold paradox involved has caused resentment and irritation to intellectuals – from Rymer onwards – though not to a sympathetic audience. Such an audience is more at home in the reaction of 'It's wonderful but we don't believe a word of it,' which in a sense is a proper response – even if an unconscious one – to the magic and pathos of the theatre, as it is to the magic and pathos of Dickens.

We can cry over Desdemona because we don't believe in her death: we are shocked by Cordelia's because we do. That would be one way – and perhaps the most decisive – of putting the difference between the two tragedies. *Othello* achieves its particular kinds of isolated reality by being as much and as obviously an artistic invention as Iago's terrible invention inside it. The story from the Italian source may have been 'true', but it ceases to be so in Shakespeare's art. It is lifted to a level of grandeur and romance, and this is inevitably compromised with the romantic aura with which the hero is most deliberately and splendidly endowed. T. S. Eliot's feeling that it contains 'a terrible exposure of human weakness – of universal human weakness' says what many a thoughtful reader may feel, but it ignores the way in which the play actually works. That 'exposure' is taken for granted, as are Othello's jealousy and murderous impulses, for the tragedy is concerned with what is in reality a much more difficult task: leaving romance, sentiment and pathos – one who was 'great of heart' – intact and triumphant inside the magic circle formed by art.

That art secures its tragic effect by arranging – to put it very schematically – the triumph of romantic sentiment over down-to-earthness;

and that apotheosis should occur in the reaction of the audience. But of course such a triumph does not mean the extinction and removal of that down-to-earth aspect of things. In one sense the germ of the *Othello* formula, hatched in the 'quick forge and working house' of what was most instinctively congenial to Shakespeare's creative powers, can be found in *The Merchant of Venice*.

TUB. One of them showed me a ring that he had of
    your daughter for a monkey.
SHY. Out upon her! Thou torturest me Tubal!
    It was my turquoise. I had it of Leah when I
    was a bachelor. I would not have given it for a
    wilderness of monkeys.

III. i. 102

This is certainly echoed, it seems to me, in Othello's words:

> Nay, had she been true,
> If heaven would make me such another world
> Of one entire and perfect chrysolite,
> I'd not have sold her for it.

V. ii. 146–9

Undoubtedly Othello as an exotic paradigm had many predecessors, in Shakespeare himself and in other plays. Not only Shylock but Aaron the Moor and the Prince of Morocco and Marlowe's Barabbas, with other lesser-known figures, are in the background. (Sometimes indeed Shakespeare seems to forget – so hallowed is the formula – that the Moor of Venice is not for his romance and tragedy supposed to be fantastically *rich* as well as romantic. A suggestion of great wealth drifts in, whether absent-mindedly or not, as in Othello's orders for his coffers to be brought up from the ship; and Gratiano in the last speech of the play is bidden to 'seize upon his fortunes'.)

Both Shylock and Othello become fully 'human' under Shakespeare's art, but Othello must, and does, become more than that. He persuades us that his sentiments are true and noble, however merely 'human' his impulses and awareness may be, and he shows us that the romance men live by does not always expose their weakness: it can also reveal virtue and strength. Yet at the same time the romance of the Shakespearean formula has taken over tragedy and death. The outburst of Emilia against her master – 'O gull! O dolt! As ignorant as dirt. . . . Nay, lay thee down and roar' – brings us smartly down to earth, but does not affect the atmosphere of *liebestod* that follows, in which Emilia herself takes part. In this tragedy death is, as it were, on the side of Othello, who does not *really* seem to have killed anybody, even the turbaned Turk, even himself. Which brings us back to the point that the degree of make-believe involved is assured to us, much more obviously than in most tragedies, by our relationship to the pair in death. As a work of art *Othello* has death well inside it. And anything down-to-earth in the formula has ultimately to defer to this state of affairs.

Everything in *Othello* is more obviously inside the play than is the case with any of the other tragedies. *King Lear* in particular is quite different, Cordelia seeming not to take part in the play, and her death not being a part of its tragedy. As it ends we seem to be outside the play altogether. An achievement in art, of course, and yet the impression is that the art of the play has been done with; while the art of *Othello* can be seen to rally itself at the end for an obvious final effort. All the resources of an actor are needed for the last climax, and an actor would be cheered by the anticipation of rising to it, while an actor has nothing to look forward to at the end of *King Lear*. The dead Cordelia has subdued any possible initiative of the theatre. The theatre can always fight back, even against Shakespeare, and an effective theatrical device – at least demonstrating the kind of difficulty that performance is up against – might be if Lear entered bearing in his arms not a live actress at all but some sort of dummy.

Cordelia and the Fool

For different reasons both Cordelia and the Fool are on the outside of the play. Cordelia gives this impression chiefly because we know nothing about her, as we know nothing about such a person met in life. Her reserve is actress-proof. Mrs Jameson, the highly intelligent author of *Characteristics of Women* (1833), perceived this and remarked of her that 'anything like mystery, anything withheld or withdrawn from our notice, seizes on our fancy by awaking our curiosity.' But, in the case of Cordelia, as we also apprehend, our curiosity is awakened in vain: there is nothing about her to be curious about. Desdemona we know at once, by the same instant genius which reveals the past and the personality of any character in the plays, even those to whom we are barely introduced.

The Fool is not like that. But both Cordelia and the Fool are brought together by being outside the play. Their relation and non-relation show again how different, and how indifferent to each other, the elements of the work are. And again one must emphasise that this is not a question of incongruity. Incongruity, especially in dramatic art, is the great unifier. *Othello* is a signal instance. I commented on the importance to the magical fabric of that play of idealised magnificence as a vision of life contrasted with a very down-to-earth view. That view stems from Iago but is emphasised in all the characters, most in Othello himself. It is vital to the strategy of a piece which needs a very dominating approach in order to pull things off, and a cast whose function is wholly identified with that of the drama.

The 'clown' in *Othello* is not quite as feeble as is usually taken for granted. He comes out to see off the musicians whom Cassio has paid to play in front of Othello's lodgings.

CLOWN If you have any music that may not be
heard, to't again. But, as they say, to hear music
the general does not greatly care.
1 MUS. We have none such, sir.

III. i. 14–18

And the play has none such either. All the *Othello* music can and must be very distinctly heard, even down to the part of the ephemeral 'clown' himself. (Though the company clown took the part and is so named in the part, the character he plays must actually be one of Othello's servants.) Feste in *Twelfth Night* similarly conducts and presides over a wholly audible music. By seeming outside the play's preoccupations he actually dominates and controls them.

Played originally by the same brilliant actor, Feste comes closest in point of dramatic function to the Fool in *King Lear*; but his function is to vindicate the part by playing it with effortless effectiveness, whereas the Fool in *King Lear* has the stage on which he should play withdrawn from under him. Cordelia has no awareness of her part; the Fool is deprived of his. The unsettling of the area in which the work operates upon us is all the more radical in consequence, because at the beginning of the play the Fool is outside the action by reason of the formal definition of his part. The Fool's function is to comment on the events and passions of the play, above all to comment on the action in so far as it is being created by *actors*. The Fool makes deflationary comments on the part that Lear is playing, the outraged father, the angry monarch banishing one of his subjects. When he comes on in the fourth scene, at Goneril's palace, he discharges his exterior part as effectively as Feste did his, and hence has the same status in relation to the action.

But that action does not remain within the compass of an ordinary play, with its plot of conspiracy and contrivance, the sort of plot action that a Fool, with his candour and witty home truths, can be his own kind of master of. The turbulence of *King Lear*, seeming to develop in natural showers and scourges of wind and rain, pushes the Fool out literally into the cold. Made to play his part on the stage of the court, the Fool shrivels into a wretched little human being on the soaking heath and in the teeth-chattering chill of the hovel. Ingratitude, villainy and conspiracy are diminished into a world that is merely dark, cold, and wet. ('How dost, my boy? Art cold? I am cold myself'.) Carrying on as it can in these conditions, the mechanism of the play appears comically artificial and self-absorbed, as in Kent's speech to the Gentleman.

> For confirmation that I am much more
> Than my out-wall, open this purse, and take
> What it contains. If you shall see Cordelia,
> As fear not but you shall, show her this ring,
> And she will tell you who the fellow is
> That yet you do not know. Fie on this storm!
>
> III. ii. 44–9

This is bound to seem as beside the point as Lear's furious rhetorical speeches – 'Blow winds and crack your cheeks. . . .' and 'Let the great gods/That keep this dreadful pudder o'er our heads/Find out their enemies now. . . .' That they should seem so is largely owing to the presence of the Fool, who has lost his role as an effective commentator on human folly and self-preoccupation, together with the stage on which he played it. A Fool completely out of his element is, and remains, a unique figure in the handling of drama; just as 'Poor Tom's a'cold' is a strange cry to hear in tragedy. When Flamineo in *The White Devil* says 'I have caught an everlasting cold,' he is making a conceit out of his imminent demise, as Hamlet might do. But that is very different from a character in tragedy catching cold and gradually succumbing to it, being pushed further and further in the process from the role he should be playing, which he knows how to play. (The role of Mimi in *La Bohème* is to *play* a dying consumptive at the opera's climax.)

The Fool is not playing an 'ordinary person', as he might be in a piece by Beckett, nor is he a development of the convention of melancholy and detachment, mocking to hide a wounded heart, etc. He seems to have wandered into the world of wind and rain, as if it had sucked him in from the stage where he was at home. He tags along in a state of increasing exhaustion. No play of the period, or of any other period, manages to give an impression like this of prolonged discomfort, and the way we are made conscious of this is by its effect on the Fool. He is unnerved by the apparition of the disguised Edgar and calls out to Lear, 'Help me! Help me!' – not the sort of appeal that a Fool is expected to make. He falls silent in the face of Edgar's vigorous acting of the part of a mad beggar, a part well inside the plot of the play, whose devices have compelled it; and suitably overdone in consequence.

And so Edgar's crude performance overshadows the Fool, who can no longer take any part in the sort of drama that this is becoming. Its nightmare naturalness makes him natural too; that is, cold, afraid, subdued, dependent as a child. In response to Edgar's flourishes of pseudo-madness he can only say, as any anxious and miserable citizen in such a predicament might say, 'This cold night will turn us all to fools and madmen.' He has no further comment to make on Lear's raging obsession, and it is left to Kent to supply one when his master demands how Edgar's daughters have brought him to this pass. Kent's patient reply – 'He hath no daughters, sir' – is a moment of unintended humour, not the kind of humour which the disguised Edgar or the eclipsed Fool can supply.

Instead their comments take on that air of irrelevance and inadequacy to the situation which is the hallmark of most speech in *Lear*. The Fool does his best to rally in the mock-trial scene, but his part is a passive one. All for him is cheerless, dark, and deadly; and his final comment, while failing to rise to the situation, gives his sense of the upside-down world through which he is being hurried. His master will have supper in the morning, and he will go to bed at noon. But there is no end for him on this stage that has ceased to be a stage. Roused again for the flight to Dover he disappears into the night, urged on by Kent: 'Come, help to bear thy master;/Thou must not stay behind.' Edgar's speech which follows – 'When we our betters see bearing our woes' – seems to emphasise plot business, the need of the play to get back to the norm of assertion and sentence. But the Fool has been consigned to silence, that silence out of which Cordelia's sense of things began, and in which she too will end. In the whole dimension of *King Lear* these areas of silence have reassurance and freedom in them as well as loss. The joy of Dover cliff and the desolation of Cordelia dead are both outside the tragedy as such, and so is the fate of the Fool.

The man and the fate

To contain such gifts of art, free satisfactions both of delight and sorrow that seem unrelated to its tragic necessities, is the supreme quality of *King Lear*; and Shakespeare's greatest manipulation of the form and concept of tragedy. I have laboured the fact that while there is plenty of purpose and technique expended on the tragic material as such, the further sets and kinds of art in *King Lear* seem unaccounted for in its specification, and unaccountable in terms of meaning and idea. All we can conclude is that the core of the tragic material – a family situation – made a deep, a very deep, appeal to Shakespeare's temper and convictions. So much so that it unconsciously began to form areas and depths of effect, independent of the tragical events contrived and enacted.

A family situation, the fate of 'whatever is begotten, born and dies,' is in one sense all the tragedy human beings know or need. But that does not get us far. A tragedy addressed solely to this fact would be merely pretentious, or at best starkly reductive, as so many modern plays have been. The clue may be the unadmitted and undefined contrast in *King Lear* between the necessities of family behaviour and the aesthetics of play behaviour – the gusto in roles, the practice of perception and intrigue, soliloquy and rhetorical hesitations, humorous detachment, self-advertisement, self-scrutiny and self-pity. Families may play at being fathers and mothers, sons and daughters, and this may be beneficial, but it never goes very far. Family life reveals the natures and drives of the participants in a manner that is so predictable as to be usually merely boring. And in a way Cordelia and her sisters *are* boring: their natures as they are, and as the family situation reveals them, would make no sort of a play without external help.

Cordelia is as she is, and so are her sisters: only a man who has played king and father so long would not know this, and the fact that Lear does not is an entirely convincing opening to the special kind of tragedy which the story tells. But behind that is something older, more inevitable, more unending. It is the unrelenting human reality of a family situation, which cannot be acted up to or acted out of. The Fool, who is inside this family, knows all about it, even when Goneril is still acting the part of a reasonable and much-put-upon daughter: 'Yes, forsooth, I will hold my tongue. So your face bids me, though you say nothing.' The directness of silences and the unspoken is at one with the family feeling in *King Lear*, and the directness of Cordelia herself, which cannot be glossed in terms of 'love'. Shakespeare's understanding here seems unexpressed in the play, but to come out in the unsuitability for acting of the family emotions, somewhat in the same way – to take a much slighter and more measurable instance – the physical misery in the unhoused scenes of Acts II and III appears through the gradual silencing of the Fool.

Shakespeare's instinct, in a tragic setting, seems always to be to work through characters who in one way or another are unsuited to the action, its conventions, its atmosphere. Their natures in fact declare themselves through this unsuitability; it is by this means we get to know them and to feel intimate with them. There are two ways in which this can happen, though it is only the first that develops our impression of intimacy. It is obvious enough that a man as sensitive and imaginative as Macbeth is not well suited to the tasks he sets himself, and that Hamlet has not the temperament for an effective revenger. The part of a romantic lover, or of 'one that loved not wisely but too well,' is not ideal for Othello, who is black, middle-aged, and possessed of the strongest animal passions. 'Character' in Shakespearean tragedy is mainly a matter of our discovering in what ways the individual and the action fail to get on, whereas in other tragedies the two are designed to coincide.

But the further way in which this occurs is more radical, more disturbing to the play as a unit, and it is this that happens in *King Lear*. Though the tragedy depends on the family situation, that situation gets behind the tragedy, leaves it standing on its own. For here the leading characters are not suited to play in a drama at all: as I suggested, they are, in their various ways, too boring to do so, too boring to be effectively taken over by actors. Lear himself belongs to that class of person whom it is not interesting to read about, and to hear, see, or talk to. A moment arrives in the play when everything he says is tedious in itself. In this he is like Timon of Athens, and one of the most interesting things about both characters is the way in which the play does not depend on our relation with the leading figure. In the case of *King Lear* success is complete, because Lear's and Cordelia's comparative vacancy as characters is the truest and deepest aspect of the family situation. And that wholly real situation, offset to and proof against the artifices of tragedy, is none the less able to go along with them on a basis of the separateness embodied by Cordelia. That separateness focuses into a sharper, more effective relief the manifold other pursuits and dimensions of the play – its evil, excitement and intrigue, its sobriety of detail (hut, farmhouse, great house with stocks in the courtyard), the co-ordination of meetings and journeyings, the strangely vulnerable and isolated pronouncements of individuals, their several convictions that Nature and the gods are organised in accordance with their own advantages and their own schemes of morality.

The contrast between the two ways in which a tragic hero can be un-suited to his situation is very important. Brutus, Antony, Coriolanus, Othello, Macbeth and Hamlet, all rise to the occasion, in their various ways. To be histrionic is for them the natural mode of thought and feeling; it brings them before us; it makes us intimate, or at least inward, with them. Even with Othello? Certainly. The first sentence he utters – ' 'Tis better as it is' – suggests in the actor's mouth a per-sonality that at once arouses our interest, and this is fully confirmed in his next speech to Iago.

> I fetch my life and being
> From men of royal siege, and my demerits
> May speak unbonneted to as proud a fortune
> As this that I have reached. For know, Iago,
> But that I love the gentle Desdemona,
> I would not my unhoused free condition
> Put into circumscription and confine
> For the sea's worth.
>
> I. ii. 21–8

Who is this man? What is the source of his power, the power that emerges a moment later in the command to Brabantio and his follow-ing: 'Keep up your bright swords, for the dew will rust them.' It is clear that the writer aims at making us want to know, as he does in the case of Hamlet and Macbeth. One thing these three have in common is that we always want to know what they will say next. A speech like 'O what a rogue and peasant slave am I' has this common with 'She should have died hereafter,' or 'It is the cause, it is the cause, my soul.'

These are 'characters' in the fictional sense. They interest us as

human beings, and the sense of suspense that attends them is in themselves, not in the necessary unwinding of the plot. It is the peculiarity
of their natures, in the context in which these have to operate, which
arrests our attention. But Lear and Cordelia are not like this, nor – in
their variously different ways – are Timon and Troilus, Cressida and
Cleopatra. All are a more simple matter: they do not possess the
dimension in fiction common to those three 'characters', who –
because they are native to the fictional world and its interests – are also
in Shakespeare's art natural denizens of the world of acting and drama.

Lear, Timon, and the others, do not belong to that world. With them
there is none of that questioned correspondence between what they are
and what they seem to be, between the impression they make on us
and the way they must behave in order to be actors in their proper
drama. It is this above all that follows from the unsuitability, as tragic
protagonists in that drama, of Macbeth, of Hamlet, and of Othello; and
it is this that gives to each of those plays its particular depth of perspective. It seems most unlikely that Shakespeare moved from one kind of
play to the other in any purposeful way. It is usually supposed that
King Lear is the tragedy that comes next after *Othello*, yet it is followed
by *Macbeth*, a play more essentially like *Othello* than it is like *King
Lear*. Both are preceded by *Hamlet* and *Troilus and Cressida*, two plays
again essentially dissimilar, although with certain superficial resemblances. But it would seem that the three tragedies that follow –
Antony and Cleopatra, *Coriolanus*, *Timon of Athens* – all more or less
belong to the class of tragedy quite different from the three which give
us a hero unadjusted to his situation, and for that reason making a
theatre of speculation and query based on the hero himself. The
audience's imagination is as much involved in this type of drama as if it
were going on in their own minds. In that private area of fiction and
possibility the acting of the heroes becomes at one with the individual's
acting of his own part in life. And in that area of his own being the
individual at all given to introspection instinctively feels that he is not
'suited' to whatever part he is playing, a part that none the less he
has to play as best he can.

The contrast, then, is between the tragic hero who in various ways is
intimate with the audience's response, and the hero or protagonist who
represents to the beholder a kind of detached spectacle, case or
problem. In both cases it may seem that the hero is miscast, which is
why the distinctions I have been trying to make get blurred very easily.
Lear, we might say, does not know how to play the part of an old man,

since he does not grasp that he is one. Few old men do, no doubt, which is why Goethe remarked on the universality of the Lear condition. None the less there is a difference between Lear's inability to be an old man and Hamlet's to be a revenger, Macbeth a murderer, Othello a great lover. In the latter cases we are involved with them because they are they themselves and not another person; because the process of their mind and being is compelling in itself, and comes close to our unique selves because it is their unique experience. There is nothing compelling about Lear's mind, nor about Timon's, Antony's and the rest. And indeed in the case of Lear his lack of singularity is especially apt and needful, for it expresses the nature of Cordelia's relation to him, a relation which puts both of them, as I have been suggesting, outside the tragic occasion, its contrivance and setting.

Lear is not a 'case', and yet there is much in the play that treats him like one. This is why Lear is in one sense in the same possible category as Timon, Coriolanus and the others. But there the case of the hero *is* the play, its justification, its point and its pattern. What makes *King Lear* the remarkable exception is the absence of the exclusive in it, of the purposeful coherence that defines the other plays in terms of a given fate. Lear's commonplaceness puts him outside his own play, or at least to one side of it. It also makes it impossible for the play to be 'about' anything, as the plays with case or fate heroes so manifestly are. *Timon* is about riches and ingratitude, *Coriolanus* about power and the ego, and these topics subordinate all action to themselves and the key player.

The reasons for *Timon of Athens* being, comparatively speaking, a fiasco, now become clear. What it is 'about' swallows the entire action. Assuming – which seems the most probable explanation – that the play is in an unfinished state, it is likely to have been put aside by Shakespeare before completion because it was not coming out right. The state it is in – for example the failure to co-ordinate the activities of Timon and Alcibiades – may give some indication of the fact that Shakespeare's extremely meticulous and brilliant handling of scene liaison, seen at its best in the movement of *King Lear*, is something that may have been organised by him at quite a late stage of the play-making process. However that may be, he may have seen no chance of making the process come alive in the case of *Timon*.

And if Shakespeare was dissatisfied with it this suggests something important about his instincts in relation to plays, and the sort of thing his own tragedies did best. They depend on a variety of scenes and

persons, heterogeneous interests, different styles of discourse and
approach. And they depend on these things not only because of their
intrinsic effectiveness when handled by such a poet and scene maker,
but because the leading figures emerge both more clearly and more
ambiguously as a result of them. For example, when Hamlet meets the
players we see another Hamlet, surprising in his excited vitality,
touching in his absorption:

> One speech in't I chiefly loved: 'twas Aeneas' tale to Dido; and
> thereabout of it especially, where he speaks of Priam's slaughter.
> If it live in your memory, begin at this line: let me see, let me
> see. . . .

For the time the prince becomes like any other theatre-buff or hi-fi
man. And this makes Hamlet the son, the revenger, the expectancy
and rose of the fair state, that much more of a reality. When Hamlet is
describing to Horatio his shipboard ventures, and the outwitting of
Rosencrantz and Guildenstern, there is a brief flashover to the incisive
and opinionated man of the arts, for whom ruthlessness is simply a
function of fastidiously high standards. Those who fall below them, as
Rosencrantz and Guildenstern have done in the moral sphere, by
'making love to their employment', are removed from the critic's consideration as if they had failed in their parts.

This dramatisation of wholly different moments in the consciousness
of an individual, moments which none the less may flash out unexpectedly at one another, deprives the drama as a whole of that striking but
overbearing simplicity which makes the hero and the action naturally at
one with each other. Tragedy has always sought that simplicity, never
more so than when, as in the case of Euripides, it was simplicity of a
startling and novel sort. Its great advantage is to make hero and action
naturally suited companions, and to eliminate precisely those vagaries
of the inner life which Shakespeare's art sets such store by. *Timon* is
the instance of Shakespeare, at the height of his powers, attempting
such simplicity in what might have seemed a very tempting and suitable subject for it, and failing to bring the thing off. *Timon* secures
neither the grand certainties of a simple tragic theme nor the equivocations that illuminate a complex one; and it does not make of Timon
himself a moving and effective 'case' either, as occurs in the other late
tragedies. In his early days Shakespeare had made a simple and unified
tragic story – a *Pyramus and Thisbe*, as it were – out of *Romeo and
Juliet*, with a hero made to be 'writ in sour misfortune's book', but he

also filled the play with youth and pleasure, childhood and cheerful age, which have no part in the tragic events.

Macbeth may seem simple enough, but it is also in fact the play with the clearest and most terrifying discrepancy between inner consciousness and action. How can a human 'self', with all that entails, do this deed in cold blood? Macbeth never gets over his amazement that it can, and has. The free vagrancy of a human consciousness, which would have enjoyed the most simple and engaging of human pleasures – wearing battle honours in their newest gloss, enjoying 'troops of friends' – is now wholly condemned to a single situation, that of having 'done the deed'. Macbeth turns the norm of tragedy, the formal partnership of protagonist and action, outside in. The pysche is shown to be unfitted for the role that tragedy requires of it. That is to say the mind at its most active and most inward looking – the place where other minds can meet and commune most easily with it – is shown in its most seductively open context – 'as broad and general as the casing air' – and shown so clearly because of the imprisoning tragic neighbourhood.

What the forms of tragedy take for granted – that Clytemnestra should kill her husband Agamemnon, and Orestes avenge his father by killing her – is shown in *Macbeth* to be impossible in terms of an individual human consciousness. And yet it happens. The Greek tragedians saw the paradox not in the private consciousness but in terms of social propriety, and the Furies are a manifestation of group disfavour, based on law and divinity. The house of Atreus must be cleansed in the same way that the Kingdom of Scotland must be cleansed. But Shakespeare, as so often, has it both ways. Duncan's murder produces portents and disasters, affects the natural as well as the social order of things until the proper state of affairs can be restored. But it is more pertinent to *Macbeth* as a work of art that the inner man is revealing something about the mind, the freedom of consciousness which can be broad and general as the casing air, and its nightmare servitude to an irrevocable act.

This interior intimacy and the vulnerability of the inner man is suggested above all by that most private function, sleeping: the power of sleep – 'balm of hurt minds' – is as insistent in *Macbeth* as the rain and cold is in the middle part of *King Lear*. Moreover, a strange thing about the inner man in this most intimate of tragedies is his power to demoralise those who live entirely on the outside of themselves. The self that is fitted for the deed can do it without a second thought or subsequent qualm, and in showing the fitness of Lady Macbeth for it Shakespeare may well have had Clytemnestra and Medea at the back of his mind, as they no doubt were – in their vulgarised Senecan versions – when he created Tamora, the Queen of the Goths, in *Titus Andronicus*. With Aaron the Moor for a husband, or someone like him, Lady Macbeth might well have lived happily ever after and never spared another thought for Duncan's end. She would always have been proud of having helped her husband to a throne. It is often said that she realises too late what murder means, that she experiences after the deed all the horrors that Macbeth had gone through before. The truth is surely much less tidy, and more psychologically true, as well as touching. It is because she loves her husband that Lady Macbeth is destroyed by him; because she loves him she is open to the inner man and can see what has happened to it. It is the transformation of Macbeth, not her own sense of the murder, that deprives her of the life-giving will to scheme and fight on his behalf.

Once it is accomplished, Macbeth is in one sense no longer incongruous with his deed – he has become 'the deed's creature'. The phrase is that of the hero-villain, De Flores, in Middleton's *The Changeling*, a tragedy obviously influenced by Shakespeare's. In *The Changeling* the young Beatrice-Joanna, who has made use of De Flores to murder her official suitor so that she can marry the man she loves, finds herself in consequence irrevocably bound to De Flores and to his desire for her. Having no conscience herself she finds herself – with a difference – in Lady Macbeth's position. But unlike Lady Macbeth she is incapable of love; and De Flores, who tells her exultantly that she has become 'the deed's creature' and hence belongs to him, is totally lacking in Macbeth's innerness of mind. All he can do, and it is a common kind of accomplishment among Elizabethan hero-villains, as we can see from Edmund and Iago, is to make sport of other people by defining their predicaments and shortcomings.

Macbeth and Lady Macbeth, the one through her love, the other through his conscience, are quite unfitted for their drama. Her love and his consciousness, and the intimacy between them that is shared by the audience, are more important than the drama, or at least as important: they constitute precisely that space, distraction and variety which Shakespeare's tragedies can scarcely do without. Othello's consciousness offers the same kind of distractions, and, like Hamlet's, the same kind of unconnections that none the less flash across to reveal the beginning of a personality, which in turn draws us in as much as with

Macbeth or Hamlet and – for the sake of *Othello* the play – even more necessarily.

Nothing involves us in a consciousness more than its moments of relaxation, however bitter, dejected or exhausted these may be. And there is a kind of sad relaxation, of exhaustion of spirit, in Othello's words after Iago has been at work on him:

> This fellow's of exceeding honesty
> And knows all qualities, with a learned spirit
> Of human dealings. . . .

All – and it is much – that is plain and literal in Othello's nature responds to that of Iago, for about that nature itself Othello is not deceived: Iago *is* a species of truth-teller, in the sense of the candid friend. The distinctions here are very odd and very equivocal ones. Shakespeare was always intrigued by the psychology of 'plainness', even a slight sketch like that of Nym in *Henry IV* shows that, and he puts his own kinds of truth into the Elizabethan stage convention of the blunt soldier, with his false reticence and mock modesty. Iago is the kind of person who discredits plainness, as many plain speakers do (Katherine Mansfield remarked of Middleton Murry that at his frankest he was most insincere), none the less there is a kind of bond between the two men, based on their military psychology of directness. (As his aide of long standing, Iago is closer to Othello than Cassio is, however much Othello may value Cassio as colleague and friend.)

Othello's plainness appears in his crisp ' 'T is better as it is,' in response to Iago's home-thrusts about Roderigo ('With the little godliness I have I did full hard forbear him'). But the bond between them takes us back to another bond, forged in very different circumstances, when Othello was induced to speak of his adventures to Desdemona. What fascinated her was clearly the obvious and literal truth of the account, a truth she divined as vouchsafed especially to her, and which her natural instinct would interpret as a kind of love-offering. Othello was not romancing: it would not have occurred to him to do so, and if he had been she would have known it and not been impressed as she was. The truth-teller responded to the person who fully recognised the truth of what he was saying:

> She loved me for the dangers I had passed,
> And I loved her that she did pity them.
>
> I. iii. 167–8

In the immediate truth of this encounter there were none the less the usual stratagems. Desdemona had recourse to an artless device to show what she was feeling:

> she thanked me
> And bade me, if I had a friend that loved her,
> I should but teach him how to tell my story
> And that would woo her.

I. iii. 163–6

Othello himself must have perceived the effect his words were having, and 'upon this hint I spake.'

Othello responds to the 'truths' Iago utters with the same fullness of recognition with which Desdemona had once responded to his; and as if this too was something for which he had been waiting all his life. Since Othello lives by the truth, he believes its utterance to be as simple as it is uncompromising. He knows nothing of what Henry James called 'the drop to directness which is thereby the voice of insincerity.' Were he in any sense a fraud he would know how to identify it; were he even a romanticiser, with the romantic's ability to worship the woman of his imagination, he would not have leapt at the literal truth as Iago presents it.

Othello's literal and truthful view of Desdemona could easily become Iago's view, for truth has a special and peculiar role in the play. The play conveys that the characters are all in it together, and we with them. The flashover points in Othello's speeches help to involve us in what is going on in a way that could not occur if we were watching a 'case', as we watch Antony or Coriolanus or Timon. They are all concerned, as Othello is not, with the business of being themselves, and this gives them a certain kind of invulnerability, the kind that Lear too has, in his own way. The 'case' is bound to be more apt to his role than Hamlet, Macbeth, or Othello are, because he is able to adjust the sense of the self that he lives by, in one way or another, and in accordance with the demands of the action.

> Would you have me
> False to my nature? Rather say I play
> The man I am.

That claim of Coriolanus would be unthinkable in the case of Hamlet, Macbeth or Othello. The inward and intimate nature of their plays *diffuses* them, as it were, not only among the tones suggested and the questions raised in their different speeches, but among the other characters and among the audience too. We are all in it together, and that is the form composed by these three plays in their representation of consciousnesses unsuited to their destiny, and yet transformed by it into the *anima* and spirit of the play.

All speech in *Othello* is shot through with truth and falsehood, opposed but closely related in opposition, as the characters themselves are. 'I am your own for ever,' Iago says to Othello; and Desdemona appeals to Iago as to an old friend: 'What shall I do to win my lord again?' He concludes his reply with words of intimacy and comfort that in comedy would be spoken by a friar: 'Go in and weep not: all things shall be well.' The atmosphere of deception is also the atmosphere of intimacy, which in *King Lear* is wholly lacking. Lear addresses the blinded Gloucester like a public meeting ('I will preach to thee: mark. . . .') and, as Emrys Jones has pointed out in *Scenic Form in Shakespeare*, the recognition scene that seems about to take place at the end of *King Lear* disappears into apathy and incomprehension. Lear 'knows not what he says, and vain is it/That we present us to him.' There is no intimacy for us here, and none between those who are present in the scene – one cannot say taking part in it.

I have been trying to suggest, then, that the incompatibility of the protagonist with the situation gives a vital clue to Shakespeare's development of a tragic theme; and that it can occur in several ways. To sum up, so far as the idea allows, there are three plays – *Hamlet*, *Macbeth*, and *Othello* – in which the function of incompatibility is to bring us as far as possible into a world of consciousness, that of the protagonist expanding into our own, and that of the play as a whole. There are four – *Julius Caesar*, *Antony and Cleopatra*, *Coriolanus*, and *Timon of Athens* – in which incompatibility declares itself as something from which a moral can be drawn, a case can be studied: we can appreciate a 'character' from whom we remain, comparatively speaking, detached. *Romeo and Juliet* and *Titus Andronicus* show signs of the feature later developed. It is irrelevant to *Troilus and Cressida*, which works in quite a different way. Its operation in *King Lear* is particularly radical and strange, producing discrepancy between different parts of the play, and moving its two central figures outside it, or at least to one side. Lear and Cordelia have no 'consciousness', but we are not detached from them either.

CHAPTER 3

THE BIG IDEA
Timon of Athens

Admirers of *Timon of Athens* have responded to it in rather the same way. Timon is not someone whose consciousness can be entered, as Coleridge and so many since felt they entered that of Hamlet, but any Romantic wishing to cultivate the persona of misanthrope could take Timon as an exemplar. Noble generosity, followed by virulent disgust with the world: in the first half of the nineteenth century such an identification was too tempting to be missed. And the valuation of the play in our time has depended on a rather similar kind of admiration for the conception of Timon, as symbol and prototype of the Renaissance spirit, endeavouring to realise in an earthly context its bounty and aspiration, and finding that the earth is no place for such an ideal of magnificence. Such a subject would certainly be impressive, and its impressiveness as a subject has made Wilson Knight proclaim *Timon of Athens* to be Shakespeare's greatest and most comprehensive tragic achievement.

But the 'big idea' does not go with Shakespearean tragedy. At least it does not go with the kinds of effect that I have been trying to formulate, the very different but always elusive effects found in *King Lear*, in *Hamlet* or *Othello*. There is nothing in the least elusive about Timon. He is the centre of his play and his point and function are equally unmistakable. An aspect of the difference which I have been suggesting between the two kinds of tragedy in Shakespeare is that, if one is a matter of consciousness, the other exhibits the powers of construction – of what, for instance, can be constructed out of Plutarch. An impression of structure, of construction, would be suited to plays that come from classical sources, but in the plays other than *Timon of Athens* the appropriate construction seems at some stage of the play to give way before a natural pressure of life, the life that cannot be kept out of the events in Shakespearean drama. Thus it is that Cleopatra's doings begin to surprise us; while even in *Julius Caesar* the relation of Cassius and Brutus, the friendship that seems unrelated to their personalities and philosophies as the play structures them, absorbs and moves us more than the official winding-up of the play.

In *Timon*, however, the idea seems so tyrannical that the construction process has to be continued all the way. Two 'states', of generosity and misanthropy, are necessary for displaying the point and drama of Timon: he moves from one to the other, and that is the end of the matter. Whether Shakespeare could have made matters different if he had gone back to the play, or whether he abandoned it because idea and construction prevented any further natural access of variety, is impossible to say. An obvious but striking point is the lack of female interest, and this is the odder because an earlier *Timon* play contained a reasonably promising female character, Callimela, to whom Timon was betrothed in the days of his seeming prosperity and who threw him over when his money and credit were gone. His discovery of gold in the woods brought her back to him, as the Poet and Painter come to visit the Shakespearean Timon, and she is savagely repudiated by him. Not, perhaps, a character who might have become one of Shakespeare's great female parts, and yet something unexpected and attractive would almost certainly have resulted if Shakespeare had brought her in and started to write about her.

It is of course possible that he had no knowledge of this fairly obscure and academic play, though, as well as in Plutarch, he may have read of Timon the Misanthrope in Lucian's 'Dialogues of the Dead', which would be the common source. The earlier play, written twenty years or so earlier and perhaps performed by London schoolboys, was of the naïvely academic type, and this could have a certain importance. For Ben Jonson had set himself to transform that engagingly clueless academicism, whose enthusiasm Shakespeare himself had made a source of charm and amusement in *Love's Labour's Lost*, into something dynamic and authoritarian, a fusion of drama and Renaissance learning that would be as formidable to the critics of the stage as to men of scholarship and letters. And there is reason to suppose that Shakespeare, who had himself acted in *Sejanus* and *Volpone*, would have been impressed by, prepared to have a shot at, this tough and

thoroughgoing treatment both of classical themes and of social lessons
that might be drawn from them.

Though it is difficult to judge from the state of a probably uncom-
pleted script, the poetry of *Timon* has none the less all the marks of late
Shakespearean mastery – it is terse and elliptic, leaping between word
and idea with arbitrary and yet persuasive power. But whereas in the
other plays of the same probable period – *Coriolanus* and *Antony and
Cleopatra* – this cryptic economy is the servant of high matters, world
crises, the emotions of rivalry and regret, jealousy, pathos and fantasy,
with *Timon* it can be devoted only to the same obsessive and monotonous states of mind. In terms of dramatic poetry such a 'state of mind' is
the opposite of 'consciousness': the words of Macbeth or Hamlet or
Othello have a transparency even at their most eloquent and complex,
so that we seem less taken up with the poetry itself than with the
changeable stuff of reflection and reaction to which it serves as utterance. Style in *Timon* cannot help drawing attention to itself, because
the speaker is not thinking, or expounding in the manner native to his
present mood, as Antony, for instance, expresses his sudden vigour and
resolution about present events:

> Hear me, Queen.
> The strong necessity of time commands
> Our services awhile; but my full heart
> Remains in use with you. Our Italy
> Shines o'er with civil swords.
>
> I. iii. 41–5

Timon seems to be choosing language carefully in order to continue
making the same old point with more striking effect:

> The learned pate
> Ducks to the golden fool. All's oblique;
> There's nothing level in our cursed natures
> But direct villainy. Therefore be abhorred
> All feasts, societies and throngs of men!
> His semblable, yea, himself, Timon disdains.
> Destruction fang mankind!
>
> IV. iii. 17–23

When Timon, alone in the woods, finds gold, his reaction is merely
accentuated:

> Why, this
> Will lug your priests and servants from your sides,
> Pluck stout men's pillows from below their heads.
> This yellow slave
> Will knit and break religions, bless th'accursed;
> Make the hoar leprosy adored; place thieves,
> And give them title, knee and approbation
> With senators on the bench. This is it
> That makes the wappened widow wed again:
> She whom the spital-house and ulcerous sores
> Would cast the gorge at, this embalms and spices
> To th'April day again.
>
> IV. iii. 30–41

Timon's speech gives the impression of marking time between good ideas. 'This yellow slave/Will knit and break religions, bless th'accursed,' is just water under the bridge before something really venomous occurs to him. And the effect of this reliance on words is the opposite of the way the language works in the other tragedies, both those of construction and those of consciousness. The impression is disconcerting in ways it seems the play can hardly intend. Timon is left with nothing but words, rich in them only, and this is all the theatre and the actors have. The play reminds us involuntarily of that fact, which is one reason why it seems so much less of an invention and separate world than any of the others, more of a recitation, or opera in concert performance.

Its affinity here is more with *Troilus and Cressida* than with *King Lear*. When Timon has done he says 'Lips, let sour words go by and language end.' In the same way *Troilus and Cressida* eats up itself in terms of language, and the taste left of nothing but words is sour, bequeathed to us like diseases, as Pandarus says in the last line of the play. Both *Timon* and *Troilus and Cressida* are plays in the sense that both draw attention to the fact that they are nothing else. They use words and rhetoric openly and deliberately. But there the resemblance ends, for while *Troilus and Cressida* suggests a whole world of triviality and absurdity, of wars and lechery that figure nothing but instant emotion and instant advantage, Timon is constructed as a symbolic portent whose generosity and misanthropy show 'how this world goes': and yet, because Timon is so overbearing a presence, the world remains elsewhere, fundamentally untroubled by his view of it.

And an audience (assuming the play had been performed) would
hardly know whether to take Timon's side or not. Clearly they would
enjoy, with a self-indulgence Shakespeare rarely permitted them, the
suggestion that things are rotten to the core. But only an inferior play,
in any age, would allow them to indulge this common human gratifica-
tion without suggesting something more subtle or disturbing, less
comforting and commonplace. Lear's vision of how this world goes is
received by the audience as it is by the other players, with a certain awe
and deference due to such age, affliction, and madness in a king; but
also without prejudice to the sense of what he is saying. Lear's state
produces such manifestations, and anyone can see why, but the
reaction of Timon is both more generalised and more commonplace.
Ingratitude and false friends are common phenomena to which everyone can take exception, and Timon is doing so with a satisfying degree
of rhetorical intensity.

But is there more to it than that? Probably not much, or Shakespeare
would have gone on to round out and complete the play. But not only
are there wonderful things in *Timon*, for all its schematic quality, there
are also suggestions of a kind of tragedy as different from all the others
as all the others are different from each other. The kind of situation
that might engender unusualness – for Shakespeare, the route of the
individual to tragic experience – might in Timon's case lie in a particular kind of self-centredness, which, not so much unlike that of Lear,
is compelled to adjust itself to a nightmarishly different set of circumstances. Timon is different. Like Richard III he lives – or as the contour
of the existing play gives it us, seems to live – for himself alone. His
steward and servants love him, but that is no doubt because he has set
himself to be loved by them by the same exaggeration of his own good
nature that he has shown to false friends. His steward Flavius understands this in his own way, as appears from what he says to the
senators who come searching for Timon in the fifth act:

> he is set so only on himself
> That nothing but himself, which looks like man,
> Is friendly with him. . . .
>
> V. i. 115–17

A senator replies.

> At all times alike
> Men are not still the same. 'Twas time and griefs
> That framed him thus. Time, with his fairer hand,

Offering the fortunes of his former days,
The former man may make him. Bring us to him,
And chance it as it may.

V. i. 119–24

Such a speech serves a dual purpose, rather too obviously perhaps, but a certain heaviness where dramatic indications are concerned is typical of *Timon*, as it is of Jonson's satirical and classical touch. Suspense up to a point is kept alive – will Timon relent? – but there is also the suggestion that the senator is a shrewd man, and inclined to think, as the cynic Apemantus shows signs of doing, that Timon likes to arrange his own *scènes à faire* in his own way, whether these are designed to exhibit his own bounty, the monstrous ingratitude of others, or – as now – a possible transformation scene of forgiveness. In hoping for something of the sort, the senators were in fact relying on a well-known classical (and Renaissance) paradigm of the great man who organises demonstrative happenings to reveal different aspects of his own greatness – Antony does something of the kind after Actium when he calls all his 'sad captains' around him for a carouse, a scene the playing of which nearly goes wrong and has to be hastily modified when the captains show signs of taking the ceremony of gloom too seriously and becoming demoralised in consequence.

Naturally Timon does not relent. He prefers to play a cat-and-mouse game with his visitors, and this gives the play chances both of satire and suspense. But they are of a Jonsonian kind – this is the way Volpone and other of Jonson's heroes behave – and the audience's impression near the end of the play is bound to be that Timon is not so wholly miserable as tragedy requires him to be. Perhaps Shakespeare thought so too and felt the play to be a failure in consequence. Certainly by his standards the state of Timon is not properly brought home to the audience. Compare him with Antony, or with Brutus or Coriolanus. All are in their different ways desperate men, whose state of desperation is totally conveyed. It does not travel into our consciousness in the way that Macbeth's final sense of things does, or Othello's. Timon's state in fact is almost entirely schematic and depends on being physically acted (which Wilson Knight has himself done in productions, to some effect).

Timon's lack of desperateness is perhaps not difficult to account for, given the fact that Shakespeare probably had not much sympathy with the character but thought he could do something fairly spectacular with

it in terms of a play. Three kinds of treatment which could to some
extent coexist, as they do in the multiple discourse of other tragedies,
might have emerged out of the Shakespearean handling. A Jonsonian
treatment is the most obvious, and is the impression of the play that
most strikes one in relation to the other tragedies. Jonson's plays, like
those of the other Elizabethan tragedians, have no deep world inside
them. But they are far more robustly competent in terms of what they
can do than is *Timon* in terms of what it seems to be trying to do.
Jonson's satire is more authoritative, detailed and penetrating, the ugli-
ness and stupidity of human calculation more down-to-earth, the
'trials' and demonstrations of human behaviour more vigorously
dramatic. *Troilus and Cressida* is far more vigorous in this manner than
Timon, and indeed may well be the first play of Shakespeare's in which
the Jonsonian method was deliberately tried out, however much transformed by the versatility of Shakespeare's genius.

Alcibiades' soliloquy after his banishment by the Athenian Senate is
a good example of the difficulty of getting the tone. Tone in Shakespeare, like impression, is usually instinctive and immediate in the
reception, whether complex or simple. The hearer's sympathy seems to
reach out instantly to that of the writer. As Maurice Morgann put it in
his Falstaff essay, in our understanding of the world of the play 'the
Impression is the *Fact*'. But in *Timon* it is difficult to receive any
coherent impression. The play is either too obvious or too far off.

> I am worse than mad. I have kept back their foes
> While they have told their money and let out
> Their coin upon large interest; I myself
> Rich only in large hurts. All those for this?
> Is this the balsam that the usuring senate
> Pours into captains' wounds? Banishment!
> It comes not ill: I hate not to be banished.
> It is a cause worthy my spleen and fury,
> That I may strike at Athens. I'll cheer up
> My discontented troops, and lay for hearts.
> 'Tis honour with most lands to be at odds:
> Soldiers should brook as little wrongs as gods.
>   III. v. 106–17

One does not ask for the kind of reflection, in which ideas of value
change from line to line as new thoughts strike the speaker, which, for
instance, Hamlet expresses when he sees the army of Fortinbras.

Alcibiades is a soldier with a grievance, a man of action in a state of bitter disgust. But even the disgust, like much of Timon's, is merely signalled by the words and not felt through them. Is it satire of a kind directed at Alcibiades himself? If so, such a use of it would be very rare in Shakespeare, where dramatic speech usually co-operates with the speaker in giving a picture of himself. This appears in the speech of Henry V, as prince and king, in Falstaff's, in that of the braggart soldier Parolles of *All's Well That Ends Well*, who is both well aware of his own nature and engagingly complacent about it:

> if my heart were great
> 'Twould burst at this. Captain I'll be no more;
> But I will eat and drink and sleep as soft
> As captain shall: simply the thing I am
> Shall make me live.

IV. iii. 307–11

Parolles is the opposite of Alcibiades and Timon, and this in itself shows something unusual about the *Timon* play, for character in Shakespearean tragedy is usually just as volatile as in comedy, and as able to surprise itself and us. There is very little chance of Alcibiades or Timon doing so, but perhaps they were not intended to? Jonson's classical tragedies have comedy scenes in them, but their heroes are as straightforward as Alcibiades or Timon, as seemingly two-dimensional.

There are an unusual number of rhymes and couplet-endings in the verse of Timon, almost suggesting the idea that Shakespeare in an early draft found it quicker and easier to block things out in such a formal fashion – effects of complexity and informality perhaps came as after-thoughts or took a little longer. Prose, though, has the feel of instant mastery, spare and colloquial in the Jonson manner, but with Shake-speare's own unmistakable hallmark on it. It is illuminating to compare that speech of Alcibiades with the prose dialogue succeeding it between the false friends of Timon who have been invited to his last banquet.

1 LORD. The good time of day to you, sir.
2 LORD. I also wish it to you. I think this
    honourable lord did but try us the other day.
1 LORD. Upon that were my thoughts tiring when
    we encountered. I hope it is not so low with him
    as he made it seem in the trial of his several
    friends.

2 LORD. It should not be, by the persuasion of his
new feasting.
1 LORD. I should think so. He hath sent me an
earnest inviting, which many my near occasions
did urge me to put off: but he hath conjured
me beyond them, and I must needs appear.

III. vi. 1

Such prose is as satisfying as it is subtle: the judicious self-approval of
that 'I should think so' can be exactly heard. It would have been easy
to convey the hypocrisy and pomposity of these men of the world, but
an exchange like this does something more – it makes their habitual
mode of exchange intimate to us, makes them as familiar as if they
were being accurately and sympathetically delineated in a society novel.
More than that, it echoes Timon's own earlier speech, with something
of that flashover effect we noted in the tragedies of intimacy and shared
consciousness. Though Timon in his earlier bounty and courtesy
speaks in verse, the tone is recognisably the same:

Commend me to him. I will send his ransom;
And, being enfranchised, bid him come to me.
'Tis not enough to help the feeble up,
But to support him after.

I. i. 108–11

This is Timon's own elevation of the idiom of the great, the manner
in which they understand one another. And it may be that the play
itself never manages to accept – and therefore to make us accept – the
transformation of this Timon into *misanthropos*, the hater of man-
kind. Shakespeare took up the story, but did he – in the true sense of
his creative powers – really believe it? This is what I meant by saying
that there is a lack of desperation in the fate of, and the end of, Timon.

Shakespearean tragedy seems to depend on the arbitrariness of the tale
being married with a total psychological probability, of the kind that
Shakespeare could discern and supply without, in the modern phrase,
'reinterpreting' his story. Cleopatra and Coriolanus are paramount
examples, in the same probable period and genre as Timon. *Othello*
could be said to have presented Shakespeare with a problem of a
comparable kind, and there it is solved not only by making us intimate,

in an unusual way, with the hero, but by giving a particular kind of disturbing bluntness to that intimacy. We instantly identify the truth that Othello's romantic nobility about war and love goes with the male instinct of possession; and that Desdemona, a maiden never bold and opposite to marriage, accepts this because she loves him: she had no taste for the idea of it in an upper-class Venetian suitor, of the kind to which she was accustomed.

This instinct for the probable seems involuntary with Shakespeare, his sense of it something that develops in the handling of the play without conscious volition. If in the case of *Timon* he was pursuing a Jonsonian idea, a picture of society with the types and humours that abound in it and give it vices and virtues, he may have deliberately refused himself interest in the Timon personality. But his inability not to be realistic about it, which gives so much subtlety and power in other tragic contexts, only lends unreality to Timon's situation. We keep expecting Timon to 'come off it', and we wonder if that is indeed what we are supposed to think.

The case of Timon not only shows us much about the complex and disparate nature of successful Shakespearean tragedy; it also shows the difficulty for Shakespeare of simplifying things. It may be that *Timon* points the way to the later plays, where something of the arbitrariness of the Timon situation (the jealousy of Leontes, the wickedness of Cymbeline's queen) is a natural part of the magic, and where the rapidity and telegraphic brilliance of the verse carries few, if any, deep psychological echoes, echoes of a consciousness within that a whole life has produced. Timon has no life in this sense, which means no past. We have no intuition of any specialness in him which would produce this result, and if we had the result would automatically be a more complex thing.

So the effects that are most impressive in *Timon* – one can hardly say most moving – are almost wholly impersonal. That they are so may paradoxically be the reason for the Romantic, nineteenth-century use of him – Romantic and Byronic stereotypes are equally impersonal – and for the admiration of readers who, like Wilson Knight, value Timon as a paradigm of generosity and disillusionment, splendid ideals doomed to failure in a world like ours. But the most moving moments do not concern Timon at all. Flavius, his steward, and his servants love Timon, and this again is one of the many 'facts' of the play which require mere acceptance. Their faith is a parallel to Timon's bounty. They are 'All broken implements of a ruined house'.

> Yet do our hearts wear Timon's livery,
> That see I by our faces; we are fellows still,
> Serving alike in sorrow. Leaked is our bark,
> And we, poor mates, stand on the dying deck,
> Hearing the surges threat: we must all part
> Into this sea of air.
>
> IV. ii. 17–22

The image and its power with us is like the actual sea scenes of *Pericles* and *The Tempest* – a fellowship on the verge of dissolution, of being cast away. And this seems virtually unrelated to Timon and his story. The fragility of the episode is emphasised by the fact that very little is afterwards made of Flavius, the good steward, even though the play seems well aware of his importance in its social and moral framework. The play at this point (the end of the fourth act) seems aware in a fatigued way what further might be expected of its matter, and Flavius' soliloquy (IV. iii. 457–71) makes a wholly predictable effort to say the proper thing. The first lines – O you gods!/Is yon despised and ruinous man my lord? – are obviously both perfunctory and provisional, and the rest of the speech falls easily into a sing-song with rhymed ends. It is a good example of how the Shakespearean imagination loses interest in a tragic context when there is nothing for it but to go through the motions of tragic piety. Compare the invigorating surprises implicit towards the end of their plays in the speeches of the Bastard Faulconbridge, Othello about to commit murder, Macbeth reacting to the fulfilment of the prophecies. *Timon* depends on a predictable decorum, based on rhetoric, whose upshot is 'sour words' followed by the end of language.

The servants, who in their metaphor suffer shipwreck together, are echoed by Timon himself, at what is scenically the climactic moment of the play. The audience must still want to know if anything will cause Timon to relent. And apart from the proper operation of suspense such a relenting might have that truth to psychology which in a Shakespeare tragedy is the ally and senior partner of suspense. The defeat of Coriolanus by his mother is an obvious example, and so is the behaviour of Cleopatra after Antony's death. Timon's obduracy is a given fact, just as his bounty was: nothing can be done about it. 'We speak in vain,' says a senator, as they realise that nothing will move him to help save Athens. Timon is writing his epitaph: he is dead to them already.

> My long sickness
> Of health and living now begins to mend,
> And nothing brings me all things.
>
> V. i. 184-6

As they turn hopelessly to go they are startled by a most unexpected phrase:

TIM. But yet I love my country, and am not
  One that rejoices in the common wrack,
  As common bruit doth put it.
1 SEN.   That's well spoke.
TIM. Commend me to my loving countrymen.
1 SEN. These words become your lips as they pass thorough them.
2 SEN. And enter in our ears like great triumphers
  In their applauding gates.
TIM.   Commend me to them;
  And tell them, that to ease them of their griefs,
  Their fears of hostile strokes, their aches, losses,
  Their pangs of love, with other incident throes
  That nature's fragile vessel doth sustain
  In life's uncertain voyage, I will some kindness do them.
  I'll teach them to prevent wild Alcibiades' wrath.

> V. i. 189–201

The echo of Hamlet's 'To be or not to be' speech – 'The pangs of dis-prized love, the law's delays' – is evident, and the topic makes it natural at such a moment, but more important is the sense of delicacy and vulnerability conveyed in the speech. We have no real inkling of the uncertain voyage of Timon's life – the play has seen to it that he is presented in a different context of seeing and feeling – but here he utters words whose sensibility indicates more than a commonplace and brings briefly into view the kind of consciousness we are made free of in *Hamlet* and in *Measure for Measure*.

This makes Timon's next speech all the more of a contrast.

> I have a tree, which grows here in my close,
> That mine own use invites me to cut down,
> And shortly must I fell it. Tell my friends,
> Tell Athens, in the sequence of degree
> From high to low throughout, that whoso please

> To stop affliction, let him take his haste,
> Come hither ere my tree hath felt the axe
> And hang himself. I pray you, do my greeting.
>
> V. i. 203–10

Again it is a question of tone. The lack of it in *Timon* makes us realise
how easy and rapid it is, despite all their complexities, to pick up the
tone in the other tragic plays. The grating deliberation of Timon's
speech here reveals nothing, except that the idea of 'easing' the spirits
of his countrymen by this offer is now what Timon accounts a love for
his country. The tenderness in his former words was a trap, if anything
so obvious can be called a trap. Like the senators the audiences have no
more to say, or even to think or to feel.

In Shakespearean terms that flat finality is a dramatic disaster, however little it matters in the world of Ben Jonson. But, as I suggested
earlier, there are two other ways of looking at *Timon*, which, in the
context of its queer atmosphere, means two other ways of interpreting
the tone. One, the Wilson Knight way, is to read it as a majestic and
moving allegory. After the world has treated Timon in the way it has,
his total rejection of it and determination to die have a noble logic
about them. Such a rejection, after such a giving of magnanimous,
open-handed confidence, is on this view of things a tragic epiphany on
the grandest scale.

Quite commensurate with this could be the feeling that Timon is in
fact a 'case' – of a special sort – but a sort that Shakespeare's sympathy
can make us see and feel with. Wounded and enraged, Timon would
then be like someone who sucks a sore tooth for the hurt that it gives
him, a hurt that he exacerbates in the ideas that are most horrible to
him, and most gratifying for that very reason.

> Pity not honoured age for his white beard;
> He is an usurer. Strike me the counterfeit matron:
> It is her habit only that is honest,
> Herself's a bawd. Let not the virgin's cheek
> Make soft thy trenchant sword, for those milk paps
> That through the window bars bore at men's eyes,
> Are not within the leaf of pity writ,
> But set them down horrible traitors. . . .
>
> IV. iii. 111–18

On this view of Timon his raging would be a special version of that standard sort of Elizabethan tirade of which Shakespeare's poetry, in its wonderfully virtuoso way, commands all kinds of mastery. When Hamlet does it, we see into aspects of his life that are all the more arresting because of the play's apparent indifference to them. When Lear does it, we understand too, though understanding is less intrigued, more resigned.

But with Timon we have nothing to go on. What is his relation to usury, to parents, wives and children? Has he any distinct one, and if not why not? With other Shakespearean heroes we infer these things, and such inference seems the way the play works on us. Here the exercises of inference meet a blankness; all that appears in this human sense in Timon is the wish to be loved by his peer group. To be loved by all he is prepared to go to any lengths, and when he finds what happens his disgust is equally childish. Lear exhibits the same childishness, but there is a vital difference; with Lear every sort of inference can be drawn because he is in the centre of a family situation (so in a different way is Coriolanus). Shakespeare understood the childishness of men, the nature and motivation of Timon as much as that of Lear, but in the latter case he finds ways of making us feel what the issue involves, expands it into multiple plot and treatment.

What survives here in *Timon* is something *hurt*, and that is touching. But how to relate it to the human scene? One of the interests of *Timon* is that it does bear out the curious law of Shakespearean tragedy that the tragic fate should be quite incongruous with the human being, as if – to approach from another angle a position already stated – the unspoken comment of Shakespeare on the literary form was that tragedy would be an excellent thing if human beings were capable of it. That is why Timon's violence is never quite convincing, never rings true. Those qualities of the 'off-key' in *King Lear* are comparable, but there they are firmly placed in the many-sided dimension of the play. Yet by not ringing true, Timon's violence can sometimes in an obscure way touch us, by suggesting some tender creature who yearns for the things he hates and calls down hideous curses on – girls, boys, mothers and fathers,

> peace, justice, truth,
> Domestic awe, night-rest and neighbourhood,
> Instructions, manners, mysteries and trades,
> Degrees, observances, customs and laws. . . .
>   IV. i. 16–19

But out of this muffled apprehension of the true child in Timon
nothing else much can emerge. The blankness of the play forbids it.

It suggests, however, another question which does not, like so many
happy questions in Shakespeare, rise spontaneously out of the play in
the plays, their poetry of grace and intelligence. This query has to be
dragged to the light of day, where it joins the limbo of other rather limp
hypotheses – the Jonsonian intention, the allegory of magnificence, or
the all too human case of the man who wanted too much to be loved.
The query relates to Timon's actual ethical and business dealings, and
whether Shakespeare wishes his audience to bear them in mind. This
goes with another way in which Timon, for all his 'flyting' and retort-
ing capacity, essential to an audience in the absence of other dramatic
business, none the less touches us, and quite simply. As he bitterly
reminds Apemantus he is not doing this for fun nor out of principle.
He is not, like Apemantus, a professional cynic and misanthrope, well
accustomed to penury: he is one who knew

> The sweet degrees that this brief world affords
> To such as may the passive drugs of it
> Freely command
>
> IV. iii. 252–4

and in this exchange he can be seen as more simply destitute, miserable
and forlorn, than either he or his opponent in wrangling will openly
admit. Apemantus suggests first that he is doing it for show, to impress
his former flatterers who in fact 'have forgot/That ever Timon was,' or
to impress the natural world itself, which will certainly remain
unmoved:

> Shame not these woods
> By putting on the cunning of a carper. . . .
>   What, think'st
> That the bleak air, thy boisterous chamberlain,
> Will put thy shirt on warm? Will these moist trees
> That have outlived the eagle, page thy heels,
> And skip when thou point'st out?
>
> IV. iii. 207–8, 220–4

To these odiously knowing arguments Timon replies, in substance,
that what matters is that he has been reduced to wretchedness: 'I, to
bear this,/That never knew but better is some burthen.' The argument
is too haggled by each scoring points against the other for us to take
this simply and be put on Timon's side by it, but between the lines a

bankrupt is saying plaintively: 'Don't you realise what I have to put up with?'

And of course Timon is a bankrupt. The fact he is not enjoying himself means that others are in the same boat as a result of his actions. And again the play leaves us in the air here, just as it does in relation to Alcibiades and his plea for the friend who has killed a man. Further work on the play might have given these questions a usual degree of interest and complexity, but as it is we can barely even derive a Maurice Morgann style 'impression' from them. Flavius the steward, who knows all about Timon's business deals and credit, is a partial witness, however movingly eloquent.

> O the fierce wretchedness that glory brings us! . . .
> Who would be so mocked with glory, or to live
> But in a dream of friendship . . . .
> Poor honest Lord, brought low by his own heart,
> Undone by goodness! Strange unusual blood,
> When man's worst sin is, he does too much good!
>
> IV. ii. 30

Here any allegory of bounty can only be said to be at odds with the facts of the case. There is a parallel in what the First Senator says to Alcibiades, pleading for the life of a killer, his friend:

> You undergo too strict a paradox,
> Striving to make an ugly deed look fair. . . .
>
> III. v. 24–5

and·

> You cannot make gross sins look clear.
> To revenge is no valour, but to bear.
>
> III. v. 38–9

Timon doing good on credit and Alcibiades exonerating a crime – the one may be a gloriously fallen and the other a dashingly splendid figure ('That great rogue Alcibiades,' as Yeats fondly called the latter) – but we are again brought back to that very unShakespearean predicament: What to think about it? A common reaction to a modern play, where we are evidently supposed to think something, but not to Shakespeare. There is something facile in the implication that a spendthrift and a racketeer may yet be noble large-hearted men: it is not at all the kind of paradox that makes Othello a noble soul and a merciless killer, or Macbeth a power schemer with an incomparably subtle imagination.

The problem is again the same: we lack the inwardness in the play to give us room to think and to feel. And the element of debate and demonstration involved lacks the fierce clarity that Jonson would have given it.

Was Shakespeare himself 'sincere' here, in the sense of ragingly unbalanced? A surprising number of sensible people have thought so. One of the most judicious and sceptical, E. K. Chambers, thought the play showed symptoms of mental disturbance, that 'during the attempt at *Timon of Athens* a wave broke, an illness followed, and that when it passed the breach between the tragic and the romantic period was complete.' Chambers typically added that this could be only 'a personal whimsy' of his, but contemporaries of his and later critics took something like it more or less for granted, though there was always reasoned and scholarly dissent, like that of O. J. Campbell and John Danby, and most notably by C. S. Sisson in *The Mythical Sorrows of Shakespeare*. William Empson, though, has called the play 'an outpouring of personal agony'.

All very confusing, but one reaction to the play – I myself have it – is not that it is agonising, but, on the contrary, it is not agonising enough. It is too cheerful in the sense of being too perfunctory. Oddly enough this goes with the general instinct to relate the play to the author himself. It might be a subject that Shakespeare thought he might do well in what Falstaff calls 'King Cambyses' vein', the manner in which the player describes the death of Priam in *Hamlet*. Like all great artists Shakespeare was probably quite unmoved by what he was writing, personally unmoved. And the more he was absorbed in his subject the more unmoved he would be – the theme in creation would preoccupy him completely, as the family theme preoccupied him in *King Lear*. But that does not mean he shed any tears over Cordelia: on the contrary. Pushkin – another such artist – understood this very well. When he tells us how fond he is of the hero and heroine of *Eugene Onegin*, how moved he is by the heroine's plight, this is a way of saying that he is in fact engrossed in his art, 'the products of my fancy and device'. Personal agony does not get into such art, either on behalf of oneself or one's characters.

But the flatness of *Timon* suggests that Shakespeare is not far away; he is not an artist engrossed in the depth of a play as Pushkin was engrossed in his poem (and pretending he was living it). The speeches of *Timon* give the feeling of the artist, but the artist who is directly indulging his own pleasure in the virtuosity of writing powerful verse, terrific denunciations, ingeniously elaborate disgust. This is the artist who, as W. H. Auden said, loves describing battles, shipwrecks, and thunderstorms, loves showing what his exuberance and skill can do. The immodesty of art in this sense is part of its charm, and it is this that gives a kind of ineluctable cheerfulness to the *Timon* panorama; but Shakespeare's engrossment – as everyone knows – is usually such that it seems to be the characters themselves who are producing the art, not the author.

That the author is the artist is overwhelmingly evident in *Timon*, just as it is in Jonson's plays. Indeed, in this sense, the play seems to be both unlike Shakespeare and close to Shakespeare, unlike his works that is to say and close to the work-sheets of a brilliant poet, performing as a brilliant poet. Except for words themselves there is an unreality about everything in *Timon*, and this is because the words are setting out to do their job with such obvious virtuoso muscle power. Words and the poet are so important that the natural objects referred to – trees, roots, gold, jewels, caves, water – seem in utterance to become stage properties, as if they were the auditory equivalents of the cardboard substances which a stage Timon would be cursing and swearing about as he acted his part, and handling in view of the audience. When we think what it is like to see Dover cliff, or the apothecary's shop in *Romeo and Juliet*, or the sentry-ways at Elsinore, this stage-property aspect of everything in *Timon* becomes all the more curious, suggesting not only the norm of Elizabethan, non-Shakespearean, tragic atmosphere, but also the possibility that Shakespeare's plays may have begun thus in his head, before expanding out into what seems the natural world with all its sights and doings.

Lear being absurd in his rage is moving, boring, embarrassing; but his rage and absurdity seem to belong wholly to him, while in Timon's case they seem supplied by the author.

> Common mother, thou,
> Whose womb immeasurable and infinite breast
> Teems, and feeds all; whose self-same mettle
> Whereof thy proud child, arrogant man, is puffed,
> Engenders the black toad and adder blue,
> The gilded newt and eyeless venomed worm,
> With all the abhorred births below crisp heaven
> Whereon Hyperion's quickening fire doth shine.
>
> IV. iii. 176–83

Timon's apostrophe has no flavour of his own in it: it is a good piece of work by the poet. Isabella's calling on 'Man, proud man, drest in a little brief authority' does seem an utterance of her nature, probably because the drama of *Measure for Measure* has already brought that nature home to us. Timon's poetry is not factitious, but sounds sometimes like a parody of Shakespeare.

> Rascal thieves
> Here's gold. Go, suck the subtle blood o' th' grape,
> Till the high fever seethe your blood to froth,
> And so 'scape hanging.
>
> IV. iii. 426–9

The parody lives not in falseness but in the absence of a full tragic world to make it true. It may be significant that Walter de la Mare, an excellent poet, successfully caught something like this effect in the pseudo-Shakespearean verse of his small fantasy play, *Heresy*; and also that a speech of Timon's was a favourite with the novelist Nabokov, who borrowed a phrase in it for his own fantasy novel, *Pale Fire*:

> I'll example you with thievery.
> The sun's a thief, and with his great attraction
> Robs the vast sea. The moon's an arrant thief,
> And her pale fire she snatches from the sun,
> The sea's a thief, whose liquid surge resolves
> The moon into salt tears.
>
> IV. iii. 433–8

All this points to a Shakespeare who, far from being a suffering soul, was enjoying a particular degree of freedom, taking a subject and writing 'strong' poetry for it as he pleased. As an increasingly prosperous and settled man, secure in his growing fame and the fellowship of the most successful theatre, it may have given him pleasure to write about this idea, to cast filthy lucre metaphorically aside and revel in the presentation of a man disgusted with it, and the world it breeds in. Art presented its picture, very different from the life of comforts which the artist at the time was probably more than content to have a chance to live. It may indeed be that increasing prosperity made Shakespeare more of a poet and less of a dramatist, and that *Timon* does represent some end to the full creative engrossment of the tragic period, and the beginnings of the more detached and aesthetic world of tragi-comedy. It is just as possible that the subject of *Timon* had failed to engross Shakespeare's deepest powers, either in a drama of a case or of consciousness, and was for that reason set aside at a time when some of the later tragedies were still unwritten.

But the real significance of *Timon* is to reveal more fully to us the nature of the other tragedies. Its anomalies are revealing, and in a negative way so is the disconcertingly faceless exuberance that informs it. That energy conceals a kind of absurdity, here never fully humanised, and situate in the figure of Timon himself. Comedy was present in Lucian's account of Timon, and in a true Jonsonian treatment it could have been firmed into something tough and farcical, with a Timon related to Volpone, even a kind of grand relation of Morose, the gull of *Epicoene*. That ugly and derisive word occurs in the senator's Jonsonian reflection:

> When every feather sticks in his own wing,
> Lord Timon will be left a naked gull
> That flashes now a phoenix.
>
> II. i. 30–2

The gull, an unfledged bird, a human target for hard derision, can also be a creature of the air, and the phoenix dies and is reborn in its own funeral pyre. But these allusions that would echo in the perspective of another tragedy have no resonance here. Othello too is a gull in the mind of Emilia, and that brings us sharply up against the kinds of intimacy we have with him: the senator's comment arouses no comparable reactions in us on behalf of Timon.

But what peeps through the anonymous exuberance of the play is an anomaly of odd gentleness that has nothing to do with absurdity, but much to do with the Shakespearean instinct for the unsuitable hero. Timon is unsuited to be *misanthropos*, as wildly unfitted for the role of easy lordship, the all-adored and all-giving, as he is for the role of power and action which the repentant senators at the end vainly and implausibly urge upon him. What he is suited for is to be loved. The anomaly is a sufficiently tragic one. For there is no one to love him, except his steward, and an exchange with him gives a very brief glimpse of the face of the anomaly: also the most moving speech of the play.

FLAV. The gods are witness,
        Never did poor steward wear a truer grief
        For his undone lord than mine eyes for you.

TIM. What, dost thou weep? Come nearer. Then I love thee
      Because thou art a woman, and disclaim'st
      Flinty mankind, whose eyes do never give
      But thorough lust and laughter. Pity's sleeping.
      Strange times, that weep with laughing, not with weeping.

FLAV.I beg of you to know me, good my lord,
      To accept my grief. . . .

                                              IV. iii. 479–88

It is easier for a man to accept grief and solicitude from a woman. The
absence of one to care about Timon is never more evident, and though
there is no other echo of it in the play, there is mute point in the
distinction he indicates here between man and womankind. Though
there are so few of them, there are moments in the play when truth
seems about to break through, as it does so dramatically for Coriolanus
outside the gates of Rome. Similarly, Timon's suicide can be seen as a
kind of surrender to the mute female understanding, absent in his days
of grandeur and striving generosity.

              Then Timon presently prepare thy grave.
              Lie where the light foam of the sea may beat
              Thy gravestone daily.

                                              IV. iii. 375–7

'Lie where the light foam of the sea may beat. . . .' The phantom of
feminine consolation could hardly be more achingly conveyed. As in
the other objective tragedies we perceive this, here very fragmentarily
and darkly, but it is not the sort of knowledge we seem able to share
with Timon, thereby increasing our own knowledge of things, or with
the overall personality of the play. By Shakespeare's standards such a
personality hardly exists, and in any case it is the *donnée* of the play
that Timon himself has moved off the scale of the personal. As the
First Senator says, 'His discontents are unremoveably/Coupled to
nature.'

  To be human for Timon has become intolerable; perhaps in some
odd way it always was so? But there the play lets us down, for we
cannot look back into Timon's life or see past the figure that the rigid
construction of the piece had initially to set up. It is ironic that
Timon's fate is in one sense the most tragic of all – he is too good for
this life, or at least too extreme for it – and that is no doubt why critics

like Wilson Knight, who take a lofty view of Shakespeare's meta-physical status as a tragedian, set such a high value on the play. But a tragic figure in this sense is hardly suited to Shakespeare's empirical view of human beings: no doubt he knew it. So does Apemantus, who says of Timon: 'The middle of humanity thou never knewest, but the extremity of both ends.'

CHAPTER 4

LONGING AND HOMESICKNESS

Troilus and Cressida

Troilus and Cressida is the other tragedy in which Shakespeare neither offers the tragic study of personality nor creates the mind that personifies the play. Unlike *Timon* it is too early to have been influenced by Jonson's major new-style plays, though it refers to *The Poetaster*, the satiric play of Jonson's performed in 1601. That year or the next is the probable date of *Troilus*, making it one of the earliest tragedies, excepting *Romeo and Juliet*, written six or seven years earlier, *Julius Caesar*, and *Hamlet*, produced probably the year before.

In many ways it is as baffling as *Timon of Athens*, as apparently un-Shakespearean. That the poetry is Shakespeare's there can be no doubt at all; both plays contain some of his finest and most vigorous verse. And in both plays the verse looks all the finer in a way for being at the service of virtuoso performance, not closely engaged with and controlled by the natures of the speakers, or their situations, but wheeling about in dazzling displays of weightless emotional vigour or extended rhetoric. This is even more true of *Troilus* than it is of *Timon*. But *Troilus* also presents a well-coordinated plot based on an exciting story of love and war, and a complex social and national situation. On the face of it we might expect *Troilus* to be as much a play of public reality and private consciousness as *Hamlet*, or a display of political behaviour, and the individual's role in it, as comprehensive as *Julius Caesar* or *Coriolanus*, or even the English history plays. Perhaps all the more so because *Hamlet*, together with *Macbeth* and *Othello*, has so much in common with those plays, and their grand climax in the Henry and Falstaff sequence.

But in *Troilus* Shakespeare took another way altogether, and produced a unique kind of play, a unique tragedy. As with *Timon* there are all sorts of reasons why this might have happened, none of them necessarily connected with a theoretical or artistic idea, on Shakespeare's part, of how the play should go. It may have been intended for a special kind of audience, clever young people under whose patronage plays were put on at the Inns of Court, or at Cambridge as the Parnassus plays were. The evidence is more than usually conflicting and indeterminate, but it seems likely at least that the play had a different kind of acting history from the normal; it may have flopped on the public stage or never been performed there, it may have been performed at court. An epistle attached to the 1609 Quarto stated that it had never been 'staled with the stage or clapper-clawed with the palms of the vulgar'.

Such as it is this evidence suggests a piece designed to appeal to intellectuals, perhaps to exploit in those circles the popularity of *Hamlet* while leaving out the simpler elements that had helped to make *Hamlet* a popular stage success. *Troilus* has, and was no doubt intended to have, the perennial appeal of a 'debunking' work of art. There is no better way of pleasing those who think themselves clever, as Shakespeare was no doubt well aware. For clever youth a heroic view of things is almost always old-fashioned, slightly ridiculous. It is not unlikely that Chapman's version of Homer, part of which had appeared in 1598, was in some sense a target. Chapman's orotund 'fourteeners' had an outlandish magnificence about them which to new appetites for poetry – Donne's poetry, for instance – might seem worth teasing, even though the translation was admired. In any case 'the matter of Troy' did not depend upon Homer. It was already known to an audience, even a popular audience, through medieval tale and ballad; and the fate of Cressida, in her descent from infidelity to the lazar-house, was proverbial.

Shakespeare, then, was taking a topic already determined as he had done for *Timon of Athens*, and in much the same way. It was both predictable and inconclusive. Timon rises to no tragic moment: he simply dies like an animal in a trap, unseen: the violence of his emotions runs down and comes to an unspecified end. *Troilus and Cressida* ends with the two characters still alive, but their situation too has come to an end. The rest of their lives, as the audience know, will be an afterthought and anti-climax, the one killed in some obscure scuffle with Achilles, the other ending up as a leprous beggar.

The way the story is treated could thus be said to be the natural,

almost the inevitable, way to do it. But Shakespeare provides one
important surprise: the manner of Hector's death. Here it seems to me
probable that he ingeniously ran together the end of the *Iliad* with a fact
noted almost in passing in the bleak conclusion of the traditional
Troilus story. In terms of an ending that story takes the break-up of the
famous love affair. In Chaucer it has endured for three happy years
before Criseyde is sent over to the Greeks; in Shakespeare for one night
only. Chaucer refers in an aside to the subsequent fate of his hero –
'Despitously him slew the fierce Achille' – in an aside because, for the
reader of his poem and by its conventions, the tragedy of Troilus is
already completed by the defection of Criseyde. His death is a postscript, and this element of the story almost certainly gave Shakespeare
the hint which transferred the death of Troilus to Hector himself. The
play virtually ends on that postscript, rather than anything in the
nature of a climax.

The sense of desolation with which not only Chaucer but all the
medieval narrators of the Troilus story conclude it, thus comes
naturally to Shakespeare and is converted to dramatic ends. Indeed the
play shows a very sharp sense of these – uncharacteristically so,
perhaps, if we feel that growth rather than design seems to determine
the plan and movement of most of the tragedies, perhaps even of
Timon, though there the growth is aborted. The betrayal and desolation of the Troilus story, made more aching in Chaucer by the slow
and miserable fade-out and the adjuration to the reader to turn to God
and the consolations of the Christian religion, consolations not available to pagan Troilus – these are deftly changed into a kind of instant
moral and spiritual bankruptcy. The demoralisation brought about by
the tale's action, by chance and fate and the absence of any inward
sureness and faith, become in the momentary world of the play its own
condition of brief existence.

And yet like all the tragedies there is no one mood in it. This is very
important. In one sense it is a delightful, cheerful, comical play, and
much of the comedy is far from black. The sense of enjoyment in the
first act is overwhelming, the exchanges, both rhetorical and colloquial,
more exultantly masterful than almost anything else of their kind. In a
way the thing is almost too free and easy, the indulgence of style giving
an impression of relaxed and confident genius more open than in
Hamlet, far more open than in *Julius Caesar* or the later history plays.
Shakespeare here seems to indulge himself, free to indulge, to parody a
bit, to summon up without effort the ripple of laughter and guffaw, as

of keen intellectual enjoyment and amusement. The doleful tale at first seems to liberate him completely, while a few years later the tale of Timon seems to call out his virtuosity against the odds, then to narrow it and to cage it.

This appearance of a reductive process is visible also in *Troilus and Cressida*, but in a quite different way that aids the naturalness of the tragic declension and seems a part of it. Soulless geniality is delightful, as an effortless style exhibits it, but it has both its jovial and its ugly empty side, and the second comes to take over. The role of Thersites is an index of the process. In Act I he is an odd, defiant figure, the victim with no weapon but his tongue, and with an inexplicable but not wholly unendearing pride in being there at all. For obvious reasons he stands up to the blockish Ajax – 'I would have peace and quietness but the fool will not' – but injured dignity comes out in one reply and makes him human.

ACHIL. What's the quarrel?
AJAX. I bade the vile owl go learn me the tenor
  of the proclamation, and he rails upon me.
THER. I serve thee not.
AJAX. Well, go to, go to.
THER. I serve here voluntary.

II. i. 86ff.

But Thersites is he who plays the Fool, in one of the Fool's many variations, and as the play goes on he plays a more and more conventional role as the obscenely sardonic commentator who reduces all to his own level. And the play allows itself to be so reduced. What is fresh, natural, and vivacious in the early part turns increasingly into stereotype, the figure of Thersites emphasising the change most markedly, and the process has its formal inception at the moment when Pandarus has brought Troilus and Cressida together, and the three formally identify themselves in and as their traditional roles.

It is this process which seems to have a mysteriously deadening effect; indeed it could be said to turn the action towards tragedy, in the unique and peculiar sense in which this play presents it. Nothing has really changed – the nature of the tale will not let it do so – and yet the possibilities of the world are inexorably reduced – reduced to *the fashion*, the thing that is always there and the same – to wars and lechery. The freedom that seems possible in the opening has vanished, along with the play of zest and intelligence that animated it, and the characters in whose mouths it was found.

Troilus seems a tragedy of intelligence, of the impersonal quality that animates the will, the sense and the intellect. The animation that can appear, under the wing of poetry especially, as so lively and fresh, is also at the same time restrictive and predetermined, repetitive and dull. It is often so with Shakespearean tragedy: an analysis of what is characteristic and remarkable about any particular example has to take into account the possibility that what seems at deep level effective and meaningful may be just the result of carelessness, haste, inadvertence, or even, where *Timon* and *Troilus* are concerned, the working over at different times of different scripts, and materials supplied by another hand. And yet the life of the play seems unmistakably conscious, amused in a sense, relishing the vigour and vitality of those who pursue power and love, but conscious of their limitations, of the stupidity that dwells alike in *raison d'état* and *raison d'amour*. 'This is the monstruosity in love, lady,' says Troilus, 'that the will is infinite and the execution confined, that the desire is boundless and the act a slave to limit.'

The play conveys this notion throughout its general tenor. Desire, intelligence and 'spirit of sense' end up as stereotypes. But there is nothing bitter in the process, as conceived in Shakespeare's effortless good nature: it is the way things are. The act of poetry is itself a slave to limit, and in the act of fulfilling itself divides what it says from the freedom of unvoiced apprehension. We label ourselves by utterance, by the very act of intelligence, and in the impulse to know and to label others. The labour of wit, its touching conscientiousness, appears in every exchange.

PATR. Then tell me, I pray thee, what's
    Thersites?
THER. Thy knower, Patroclus. Then tell me,
    Patroclus, what art thou?
PATR. Thou mayst tell that know'st.
                    II. iii. 43ff.

The wit is designed to hurt. As a licensed railer Thersites has an interesting variation of the Fool's part: 'Good Thersites, come in and rail.' He angers by his pretension to be a knower but he also fascinates;

and he is vulnerable himself. He calls Patroclus Achilles' 'brach', that is 'bitch' – Elizabethan slang for 'boy-friend' in the sexual sense – and Achilles is delighted:

THER. I will hold my peace when Achilles' brach
  bids me, shall I?
ACHIL. There's for you, Patroclus.

Yet he is powerless against Ajax, the most delightful stupid man in all literature, whose insensate rage ignores the rules of the game and takes to its fists.

THER. That fool knows not himself.
AJAX. Therefore I beat thee.

The stupidity of Ajax causes Thersites to lose his cool and indulge in wild vituperation. In juxtaposition, the 'stirring' of wit seems as futile as stupidity. To Thersites' protest – 'I serve here voluntary' – Achilles points out that 'no man is beaten voluntary. Ajax was here the voluntary, and you as under an impress.' And there is something exquisitely ludicrous about the illiterate Ajax enslaving Thersites to 'go learn me the tenor of the proclamation.' The stirrer of wit is not superior to the man who 'wears his wit in his belly': he is not even independent of him.

Troilus, Cressida, and Pandarus label themselves in a different way. By doing so they abdicate as characters, just at the moment when they might have begun to show more of the individuality implicit in the zest of the opening. But the poetry that has decided to demarcate them in their legendary roles is no more superior to them than Thersites to Ajax. Nothing in the style of the play looks down on its situation. Poetry and the stuff to make paradoxes might seem at first sight to be lords of all here, and to use the material as Thersites claims that the Greek leaders use the beefwitted lords like Ajax and the 'princes orgulous' like Achilles, to 'plough up the wars' like draught oxen and be 'bought and sold among those of any wit, like a barbarian slave.' But the charm of the play, though charm may seem an odd word to use, is made by poetry being as much engulfed in the situation – the 'present eye' praising the 'present moment' – as are the lovers in their roles, Thersites in his railing, the men of power in their wiles. Poetry is a slave of the moment and its exigence, just as the rest of the cast are.

This modesty of course is characteristic of Shakespeare, but it shows up all the more in a play which superficially could be said to be in the same class – for patronising brilliance – with Marston's Antonio plays, and *The Malcontent*, a play speaking over the heads of the groundlings to the wits on the stage.

Much that is in the play, and its general tone, is a reminder to the wits for whom it may have been produced that poetry and paradox eat themselves up no less than do wars and lechery. They seem here at the service of the characters, as the characters themselves are at the service of the roles they portray. Cleverness is gently and amusedly revealed, in the context of war and the context of love, as usually neither gentle nor amusing. The famous 'bitter' tone of the play, always noted by editors and critics, is really an illusion begotten by this process. As in *Timon*, but in a different way, the style is the reverse of bitter: indeed the concept means nothing in relation to such a functional marvel – there is nothing 'bitter' about a tiger or a kingfisher. This marvel removes all dramatic transparency and anonymity, makes the characters and theme its puppets and subordinates.

Subordination shows itself in several different ways, making a play of statements, somewhat in the modern manner. 'Tragedy' in Troilus has the impact and the quality that one would expect it to have in a modern play. There is nothing grand, pitiable, or terrible, but just this is the way things are: a good man (but he is not so good perhaps) is butchered in a hole-and-corner way by some thugs, themselves manipulated by cynical men who enjoy power. Meanwhile a girl has betrayed her lover, but perhaps in any case his love did not deserve her faith? These are events looked at without either tragic dispassion or tragic sentiment, in the plain way that we like to think we look at them today. The effect of objectivity is produced by the play seeming to be detached from its characters and their situation and to be merely making use of them; and again this is something we associate with modern drama.

The word 'modern' frequently signified in Elizabethan usage what was modish, temporal and ephemeral, just arrived and therefore not long lasting. 'Full of wise saws and modern instances.' Or – alternatively – something always present at the latest moment. Ross, in *Macbeth*, speaks of Scotland under the tyranny of Macbeth as a country 'almost afraid to know itself', 'where violent sorrow seems/A modern ecstasy,' that is, a distraction continually with us. In this sense *Troilus and Cressida* certainly treats its theme in a modern manner, with – as I have already suggested – an imperturbably two-faced suggestion that modern people, clever people, like things to be done this way. Poetry and style oblige, and by obliging acquire not so much a neutral as a venal air. Like the most skilful of mercenaries they are at the service of modernity.

Detachment is at the service of the characters, as poetry itself is, and their employment of both defines their own existence and function.

> If I be false, or swerve a hair from truth,
> When time is old and hath forgot itself,
> When waterdrops have worn the stones of Troy,
> And blind oblivion swallowed cities up,
> And mighty states characterless are grated
> To dusty nothing, yet let memory
> From false to false, among false maids in love,
> Upbraid my falsehood. . . .
>
> III. ii. 180–7

The beauty of Cressida's declaration seems quite deliberately to draw attention to the several separate aspects of itself, like a brilliant lawyer striking his fingers into his palm. The only thing it tells us nothing about is Cressida herself, and that indeed is a part of its forensic effectiveness: the private life, so to speak, of the person swearing in court is not at issue, only the question of oaths, action, evidence, verdict. The plain irony is that Troy will not be worn away by waterdrops but destroyed by fire and sword. Everyone knows that, even the speaker herself it seems, and the knowledge presents to the court of the audience two kinds of tragic action and idea. One is the paradox of swearing faith, when time takes the nature and character out of all things; and the other, a malicious and invisible attendant on the first, is the catastrophe that blots out all transactions irrespective of the slow process of time. By means of the speaker the poetry draws our attention to both notions, and then to herself as an illustration of the unimportance of either: the point of art is to entertain ourselves with the idea of them.

Like Troilus and Pandarus, Cressida is thus the vehicle here for a complex kind of frivolity. Her previous exchanges with Pandarus, robust and humorous, could have given her the lively promise of a Beatrice, or even the capacity of a Desdemona to jest in the atmosphere that calls for it, while holding her love and its preoccupations and anxieties concealed in herself. Cressida claims indeed that this is exactly what she has been doing.

> Boldness comes to me now, and brings me heart.
> Prince Troilus, I have loved you night and day
> For many weary months.
>
> III. ii. 110–12

So she asserts a little earlier, when Pandarus brings Troilus to her. The existence of such a state of affairs, and its declaration at the right dramatic moment, would, in either Shakespearean comedy or tragedy, confirm the reality and the being of the speaker, and cause the poetry to vanish into this reality, which would engage all the audience's sympathy and attention.

> That I did love the Moor to live with him
> My downright violence and storm of fortunes
> May trumpet to the world. . . .
>
> I. iii. 248–50

When Desdemona makes her statement the paradoxes in it relate entirely to herself. She is a modest girl, for whom a moment in love has come to speak out. The rhetoric in her speech makes her case, because her feeling appears to create it, and in so doing to establish her bona fides as an actual person. That actuality relates very straightforwardly to Othello's own. They are similar in what they say and feel: naturally, because they are in love, and because the heart of the play is concerned to give them their authenticity in feeling and being, the authenticity which is the play's own point. Othello is close to, at one with, Desdemona when he vows vengeance against her:

> Never, Iago. Like to the Pontic sea,
> Whose icy current and compulsive course
> Ne'er feels retiring ebb, but keeps due on
> To the Propontic and the Hellespont. . . .
>
> III. iii. 457–60

Both exist for us by feeling the same way. Cressida and Troilus have no such affinity. Her assertion that she loves him seems to lose her any power of being and becoming someone, in the way that Desdemona and Othello gain this power. She has a good moment, which any teasing comedy heroine who knows her own heart – a Beatrice, Rosalind, even a Juliet – might have had, when Troilus marches past in the excellent comic sequence earlier on, Pandarus and his niece watching. 'What sneaking fellow comes yonder?' she says, knowing quite well who. It's a nice moment, that goes with the fussy preoccupation of Pandarus, but inside it there seems an uneasy blankness. It is a scene in a variety show, tailor-made for the right actors, and the fact that we can hear it so perfectly only seems to increase the puzzlement and unease about what uncle and niece are actually feeling. 'Here comes more,' she says, after Troilus has gone by, and the acoustic perfection of that should mean something, but doesn't; or rather it means just the right phrase for an actress to get a laugh by saying coyly, with an up-from-under look.

The teasing quality of Cressida personifies the teasing quality of the play at large. Its tragic atmosphere or personality seems to depend on the treatment itself. If life itself is merely as contingent and perfunctory as this, with nothing behind it; if art and poetry are themselves only the slaves of this superficiality, then we need look no further for what amounts to a tragic sense of things. Tragedy is inherent in presentness and consumes itself from moment to moment, as all other things do. Youth's a stuff will not endure, nor its cleverness, its powers of response, the expectations that whirl it round. In one sense Cressida's speech is like one of Shakespeare's songs, in its impersonal performance, its enactment of 'What is love? 'Tis not hereafter.' Yet it is not impersonal, because of the teasing personal intonation she gives it, the sound of that 'When time is old and hath forgot himself.' Time is senile, even in the 'extant moment' that Agamemnon conjures up, the moment in which the play and all in it have their lives. In Cressida's speech we know that the future will not take place, Troy's stones will not be slowly worn away; and, by the same inversion of meaning, time, which she archly imagines as one day being so old that he has forgotten who he is, in fact forgets himself in the world of the play from moment to moment.

A process of misplacement teases and disturbs, not by launching heavy irony, bitter sarcasm, disillusionment at us – though such effects are usually relied on by producers and accepted eagerly by an audience – but by transpositions of tone like those in this scene between the watching Pandarus and Cressida, between Pandarus and Troilus, or when the three of them are together. These are cheerful, romantic, ardent, sensual, happy: but as they make each impression of this kind, poetry and language slip away successively into limbo. The behaviour of Pandarus in the hero-watching scene is as exquisitely ludicrous as the behaviour of Ajax enraged.

> That's Antenor. He has a shrewd wit, I can tell
> you, and he's a man good enough. He's one of
> the soundest judgments in Troy.

But again the fun is not exactly in Pandarus himself, as it is in Shallow
or Silence or Falstaff or Menenius. The incongruity of possessing one
of the soundest judgments in Troy is comedy for the clever, but Shakespearean comedy of this sort is not normally for the clever. The genial
thing would be for some owl to be called one of the soundest judges in
Warwickshire: then we should all know where we were. 'Judgment', in
Troy, is too disturbingly unreal a notion. This extant moment of fun is
placed in a world of invisible nightmare, and any chance of Pandarus –
or any of the others – becoming a coherent character is forfeited to the
tragic implications of that nightmare.

In the free flow of Shakespeare's world, motivation is never analysed
or presented for inspection but inferred by us instinctively, as we might
infer that of real people around us (the most deliberately observed
motives are those of Brutus and Macbeth). But in *Troilus and Cressida*
motivation is simply not bothered with. To be sure, Ulysses and Nestor
have the automatic instincts of those who live by power and the
manipulation of others, but the others behave, if not exactly on the
spur of the moment, with a dislocated vigour which at the same time
seems aimless. Iago brings the question of motive incessantly before us
by telling us why he is doing what he is, and through those comments
there appears the real obsession. In *Troilus* we seem suddenly pushed
into a society in which a lot is going on we cannot understand; we are
not in the swim, though it is as if we are doing our best to go along
with the general vivacity. This is a highly realistic impression to
receive, but an uneasy one. It is instructive to compare the atmosphere
of the gathering at Helen's, where Pandarus clowns and sings, with the
party on Pompey's galley in *Antony and Cleopatra*, assuming that – as
the audience – we are fellow-guests at each.

It has often been noted that Shakespeare repeats, in a transformed
context, parts of scenes and the beginnings of scenes, but it has not
been remarked, I think, that the opening of *Troilus and Cressida* bears
a remarkable resemblance to that of *Othello*, which was quite possibly
the next play that Shakespeare wrote. In both cases we infer that the
younger man is hopelessly in love, and the elder is going to help him to
do something about it. In both cases this 'love' is a simple matter, however tormenting and distracting, and one which Donne and the young
men at the Inns of Court knew all about:

> Whoever loves, if he do not propose
> The right true end of love, he's one that goes
> To sea for nothing but to make him sick.

Roderigo longs to possess Desdemona; Troilus desires Cressida. And this possession is what their love is all about, however much and however genuinely they may suffer. 'I will incontinently drown myself,' says Roderigo; and Iago replies: 'If thou dost I shall never love thee after.' When Troilus and Pandarus enter at the opening of the play, Pandarus is going through the motions of washing his hands of the whole business: 'Well, I have told you enough of this. For my part I'll not meddle nor make no farther. . . . Faith, I'll not meddle in't. Let her be as she is.' This pretence resembles the seeming bluntness of Iago, who has also been 'reluctantly' helping Roderigo for some time when the play opens.

But Pandarus' motive is merely his name, his label, his vocation. And Troilus is at the service of poetry, as Cressida is in her fidelity speech.

> The Greeks are strong and skilful to their strength,
> Fierce to their skill and to their fierceness valiant,
> But I am weaker than a woman's tear,
> Tamer than sleep, fonder than ignorance,
> Less valiant than the virgin in the night,
> And skilless as unpractised infancy.
>
> I. i. 7–12

No play of Shakespeare's has more beautiful poetry at its commencement, poetry more happily assured of itself and its function. Compare the first scene of *Hamlet*, probably the play before.

> But look, the morn, in russet mantle clad,
> Walks o'er the dew of yon high eastward hill.

It is typical of *Hamlet* that this flicker of gratuitous beauty – Horatio's comment to his fellow sentinels – is interposed between speeches and exchanges whose poetry we take wholly for granted because it is so well adapted to what it works in, 'digested' – to use Hamlet's own phrase for well-made dramatic entertainment – by the activities it accompanies. At the beginning of *Troilus* poetry has no such digestive function; it can cheerfully work the other way, producing incongruity of effect. Troilus is hopelessly 'in love', like a young man in *Love's Labour's Lost*. He is also a classical hero, and a mythology is lightly suggested to go with this, split into prismatic rainbow hues like the ones to which Ulysses compares Achilles' helmet – 'his crest that prouder than blue Iris bends.' The virgin of the zodiac becomes the comedy figure to whom Troilus ruefully compares himself in his first speech, and Pandarus completes the suggestion of mythology even in his jocular apostrophe: 'Had I a sister were a grace, or a daughter a goddess, he should take his choice.' This poetic classicism is the converse of the comic classicism which finds its expression in Pandarus' remarks: 'And her hair were not somewhat darker than Helen's – well, go to – there were no more comparison between the women. . . . I would someone had heard her talk yesterday, as I did. I will not dispraise your sister Cassandra's wit, but——'. The idea of Cassandra's wit is as engagingly absurd as Troilus' smile 'becoming him better than any man in all Phrygia', or Antenor having 'one of the soundest judgments in Troy'. The peak of this manner is of course in reference to Helen herself. When Hector left for the field in the morning, Helen was 'not up' yet, like a lazy hotel-guest; and her husband Paris excuses his own lack of enthusiasm for fighting with 'I fain would have armed today, but my Nell would not have it so.'

A third note is struck in the Prologue, the most accoustically sonorous speech of its kind in Shakespeare. Like Troilus and Cressida themselves the 'Prologue armed' is at the service of poetry and the play, and what he says has the same sort of disingenuous detachment. Yet the speech is magnificent in itself:

> From Isles of Greece
> The princes orgillous, their high blood chafed,
> Have to the port of Athens sent their ships,
> Fraught with the ministers and instruments
> Of cruel war.
>
> Prologue 1–5

The Trojans and their city have an equal splendour:

> Priam's six-gated city,
> Dardan, and Timbria, Helias, Chetas, Troien,
> And Antenorides, with massy staples,
> And corresponsive and fulfilling bolts,
> Sperr up the sons of Troy.
>
> Prologue 15–19

But the magnificence is disingenuous, as all poetry by its function and nature is in this play.

> Now expectation, tickling skittish spirits,
> On one and other side, Trojan and Greek,
> Sets all on hazard.
>
> Prologue 20–2

The Prologue may promise 'hazard' and 'the chance of war', but the audience know the story and its outcome as well as he does.

> Our play
> Leaps o'er the vaunt and firstlings of those broils,
> Beginning in the middle; starting thence away
> To what may be digested in a play.
>
> Prologue 26–9

Nothing will be 'digested', in the sense that Hamlet praises a play for being, but everything will be eaten up, which is rather a different matter. 'He that is proud eats up himself,' says Agamemnon, and that sound comment is disingenuous too, for it is addressed in flattery to the blockish Ajax whose plain-man queries ('Why should a man be proud? How doth pride grow? I know not what pride is'), have all the conceit of stupidity. 'What's become of the wenching rogues?' asks Thersites of Diomedes and Troilus, who are contending for Cressida's favour pinned in the latter's helmet, 'I think they have swallowed one another. I would laugh at that miracle. Yet, in a sort, lechery eats itself.' He calls it lechery but it is what Troilus felt as love, and it is the same with desire and contention of all kinds, on which the play itself is based. Poetry is in the same case, and can stand apart and take a pride in it.

The styles and aspects of the play eat each other, instead of settling down together. The intrigue of Pandarus is devoured in this manner. The point of his long comic dialogue with his niece (I. ii. 40ff.) seems to be – and it is a good dramatic ploy – to needle her by constant reference to Helen and to Helen's sentiments about Troilus. 'I swear to you, I think Helen loves him better than Paris.' 'Then she's a merry Greek indeed,' retorts Cressida pertly, but the impression is that she begins to be irritated by the idea. That all women are jealous of one another is one of the all-predictable elements in the play. But there is no liaison here with Cressida's statement that she has loved Prince

Troilus for many weary months. Those months belong with time being old and forgetting himself, and with Cressida's own comment on Pandarus' tedious recital of an infinitely trivial event:

PAN. And all the rest so laughed, that it passed.
CRES. So let it now, for it has been a great while
    going by.

It is in the context of a comic story that love passes. Troilus' fear, when he is at last within sight of the possession of Cressida, is that he will lose distinction in his joys. That is the last thing the play loses. Each effect is very distinct. 'She was beloved, she loved: she is, and doth.'

What is Cressida's own feeling about the business of love? In Chaucer she is an experienced lady, a widow, and she distrusts the whole business deeply. She is won over very gradually, and when sent out of Troy she as gradually realises she must adapt herself to the new situation. Shakespeare must do everything at speed. He leaves Cressida's status, whether maid or widow, uncertain, but implies a degree of experience, the temperament of 'a daughter of the game'. For the Chaucerian timidity and distrust he substitutes a complete awareness of what love, for a young man like Troilus, really amounts to: that he wants her, he must have her. She goes along with that, but she is not deceived, except in so far as she wants to deceive herself, as Troilus does.

His treatment of the tale gives Shakespeare a unique opportunity to show indeed the monstrosity in love, and what is, depending on the viewpoint, both comic and tragic in it. Flirtatiousness acts reluctance because it is genuinely reluctant: the onlooker assumes it to be merely an act to cover a decision already reached, and he is right; and yet the reluctance is truly there. 'Yet hold I off': she knows that when Troilus has possessed her he will not feel the same. Her advantage will be lost, and yet there is nothing else for it.

> My thoughts were, like unbridled children, grown
> Too headstrong for their mother. See, we fools!
> Why have I blabbed? Who shall be true to us
> When we are so unsecret to ourselves?
>   III. ii. 119–22

The tone is intimate and distraught, yet tender. These soft feelings are in her, as in everyone; and hard feelings too.

TRO. What offends you, lady?
CRES. Sir, my own company.
TRO. You cannot shun yourself.
CRES. Let me go and try.
    I have a kind of self resides with you,
    But an unkind self that itself will leave
    To be another's fool. I would be gone.
    Where is my wit? I know not what I speak.
                     III. ii. 140–7

What is most affected is also affecting. Her starts and hesitations are the equivalent of Troilus' love-speeches: in one sense not to be believed, in another sense wholly true to the immediacy of the feelings. These brilliant and touching exchanges make visible the two levels of such an emotional relation – the hidden level of privacy, calculation and the will, and the open assertions of faith and truth, of innocency, of undying love. Each is necessary to the other for without falsehood there would be no loving:

> Therefore I lie with her and she with me
> And in our faults by lies we flattered be

as Sonnet 138 puts it.

    Troilus and Cressida enact their own variation of the falling-in-love theme also found in *Romeo and Juliet* and *Othello*. To be in love, and to find the loved one is also mutually in love – emotionally and dramatically the situation is one to which an audience would be sure to respond. In *Romeo and Juliet* and in *Othello* it is presented as the happiest of ideals, a feeling that finds itself wonderfully and amazingly reciprocated, a marriage or true minds and hearts, eclipsed only by external fate and evil. There is no doubt that Ford, the Jacobean dramatist who most often paid Shakespeare the sincere compliment of imitation, borrowed the concept for *'Tis Pity She's A Whore*, a tragedy in which brother and sister discover to their joy that each has been secretly in love with the other. It is a characteristically Jacobean perverting and sensationalising of the idea of mutual love, though moving none the less. But in *Troilus and Cressida* the mutual love theme is set in a thoroughly equivocal and ambiguous situation, which is both legendary and in a social way highly realistic. Is love eclipsed solely by the external factor of separation, or is it already compromised

– not necessarily fatally – by being an affair, and an affair of the moment?

Nothing in the play asks that question or wishes it to be answered. There is no code involved: momentariness has its own logic and solution. The actors' sentiments consume themselves in performance, and no inner suggestion of mind enables them to become characters. The parallel and the contrast with *Othello* is again obvious. At the beginning of *Othello* Iago is assisting Roderigo to get what he wants, but the real action – solid, invisible, productive alike of growth or of catastrophe – is the marriage of Othello and Desdemona which has just taken place. *Troilus and Cressida* presents love, as it presents war, wholly in relation to activities and feelings that have no prospects or future but abolish themselves in expression. The rhetorical machine, so superbly deployed by Ulysses, reiterates the argument that nothing done in the past has any continued existence, that achievement must be constantly renewing itself. Like so many brilliant arguments this one seems unconscious of its own implications: if there is no past there can also be no future. 'Faith and troth', which Agamemnon in greeting Aeneas treats as matters for, and conveniences of, the moment, make no more sense for the future in love than they do in war. The immediate engagement is the thing, just as in love 'joy's soul lies in the doing.'

Gruesomely effective in *Troilus* is the seeming marriage relation between Paris and Helen, a relation as unreal as that between Troilus and Cressida themselves and having a special kind of sickliness all its own. Paris and Helen live in 'love' as Ulysses and Nestor live in statecraft and intrigue, and Paris' 'Sweet, beyond thought I love thee' seems to parody the brittleness in the exchanges of the two main lovers. One must emphasise again how misleading it is to say that the atmosphere of *Troilus* is 'cynical', intent on exposing 'life for what it really is' etc. It is in its own way much worse than that, or much better; the kind of tragi-comic mix-up that Shakespeare always presents, but here given a metaphysical limitation in its strict confinement to the present, which denies it any saving growth or further potential. The relations of Troilus and Cressida, their uncertainty about each other's feelings, distrust, will to possess and instinct to withhold, could well be the accurate and moving prologue to a positive, a 'happy' dénouement, like the courtship of Levin and Kitty in *Anna Karenina*. There Levin realises with something like joy that Kitty's 'love' for him is a highly equivocal affair, compounded, amongst other things, of relief and pleasure that he wants to marry her, and relief and pleasure that she will then have attained the status of a married woman and need no longer feel anxiety and the restlessness of looking for something.

Troilus and Cressida are in the same state and behaving with the same mixture of desire and duplicity, but their relation has no place to go. Once they are out of bed their relation is already 'distasted', at least for the moment, and as it turns out the moment is all there is. Before the news of their separation arrives they are already separated, and the relation between what it is necessary to say in love, and the way in which you are actually feeling, is now more evident than ever: but again this is as touching as it is droll and inevitable; there is nothing harsh or deliberate about it. Indeed the most salient, if also the most unease-making, aspect of the art of *Troilus* is how little deliberate the effect of the play is, given the story and given the timing. There is a disconcerting naturalness about the whole business, which outraged Dryden, for whom the whole point of art in a play is to make the dénouement as ingenuously conventional, as nobly unlifelike, as possible. In rewriting *Troilus* he made the supposed infidelity a misunderstanding, and caused a distraught Cressida to perish on the battlefield, seeking Troilus to convince him of her continued faith and love.

The perturbing naturalness of the moment in Shakespeare proceeds in great part from the way in which the different styles consume each other without, as it were, seeming to notice the fact. Thus the morning-parting of the pair starts in a realistic and not unengaging vein as a relief to them both:

TRO. Dear, trouble not yourself: the morn is cold.
CRES. Then, sweet my lord, I'll call mine uncle down:
    He shall unbolt the gates.
TRO.   Trouble him not.
    To bed, to bed. Sleep kill those pretty eyes,
    And give as soft attachment to thy senses
    As infants' empty of all thought.
CRES.   Good morrow, then.
TRO. I prithee now, to bed.
CRES.   Are you aweary of me?
TRO. O Cressida! But that the busy day,
    Waked by the lark, hath roused the ribald crows,
    And dreaming night will hide our joys no longer,
    I would not from thee.
CRES.   Night hath been too brief.
                          IV. ii. 1–11

Troilus is tender, but it is the tenderness of an achiever; his possession,
like a child, must be put back to bed. Her query shows a hint of her
perception of this, and calls forth the appropriate declaration of the
lover at dawn, to which she makes the demurely correct reply. Romeo
would not have mentioned ribald crows; he was embarking breathlessly
on a romance where Troilus is conscious only of having won his prize,
and of the need for security and discretion. Troilus' exclamation when
the bad news arrives parallels that of Romeo but is of a different kind.
'How my achievements mock me!' is instantly followed by the
necessary reminder to Aeneas – 'We met by chance: you did not find
me here.' The outbursts of Pandarus and Cressida are proper to their
roles, and those roles contradict the wry yet moving genuineness we
have just seen between the lovers at their own personal and untypical
dawn song. Now poetry comes forward to take over, with the complete
and deadpan assurance its function demands of it in this play. Cressida
exclaims:

> Time, force and death,
> Do to this body what extremes you can;
> But the strong base and building of my love
> Is as the very centre of the earth,
> Drawing all things to it.
>
>   IV. ii. 100–4

At the opening of the scene they were about to part on the terms
appropriate to their relation: now something more forceful must be
added, and this eclipses what has gone before, as the new style and
convention of courtly rivalry that enters with Diomedes ('I have
chastised the amorous Trojan/And am her knight by proof') blots out
the enigmatic intimacy of the pair's early relation, the relation that
Cressida could seem to free herself into with 'Prince Troilus, I have
loved you night and day/For many weary months.'

The alternating task of poetry, officialising what is dubious and
uncertain, takes haste as its cue, as well as reason of state. As in
Chaucer there is no arguing with the exchange arrangements.

CRES.   Is't possible?
TRO. And suddenly, where injury of chance
      Puts back leave-taking, justles roughly by
      All time of pause, rudely beguiles our lips
      Of all rejoindure, forcibly prevents

Our locked embrasures, strangles our dear vows
Even in the birth of our own labouring breath.

IV. iv. 31–7

The crisis seems to give love a further dimension, and one which would hardly have been recognised in the scene a little earlier, when Pandarus gave himself the pleasure of twitting his niece, as her lover himself does.

CRES. Who's that at door? Good uncle, go and see.
My lord, come you again into my chamber.
You smile and mock me, as if I meant naughtily.
TRO. Ha, Ha!
CRES. Come, you are deceived. I think of no such thing.
How earnestly they knock! Pray you, come in.
I would not for half Troy have you seen here.

IV. ii. 35–41

It is this atmosphere which is roughly put by, swallowed up as the separation gives a new appearance of poignancy and expression to their love, before this too is displaced by something else. It is because time moves so fast and so unpredictably in the play that it also seems to stand still: helplessness is both a physical and a psychological condition. Achilles, like all the others, is borne from one state of mind and activity to another. 'My mind is troubled, like a fountain stirred,' he says helplessly, 'and I myself see not the bottom of it.' His murder of Hector seems scarcely done of his own volition, nor does the man that commits it appear the same as the one we met earlier. In war men find themselves doing these things, as women do in love.

The element of tragedy in Cressida's consciousness spreads out through all the play, and her gaiety and high spirits does the same. 'This is and is not Cressid' – she is not to be recognised in one personality. The element of tragedy in *Troilus* concentrates itself into the uncertainty of being that the protagonists display. It is a torment to them if it involves love, the torment Troilus comes to feel in relation to Cressida, that she is aware of in relation to her own self, the self that 'itself would leave'. Achilles has it, and Hector too, 'whose patience as a virtue fixed' is none the less wholly vulnerable to unreason and dissension, the demands of the extant moment.

It is deeply interesting that Shakespeare's feel for the subject and the way to handle it warned him off attempting, as Chaucer did, a 'defence' of Cressida. It could have been done: a few strong speeches, more comments on her own predicament: Shakespeare's women are not usually behindhand with these, making us aware of themselves and sympathetic to their situation. But in this metaphysical hiatus of a play, chopped out, discontinuous with its elements, a play in which 'violent sorrow seems a modern ecstasy,' it is right that Cressida too should be discontinuous with any notion of personality. She is doubly betrayed, by the legendary label she wears and is required to endorse.

> Ah, poor our sex! This fault in us I find,
> The error of our eye directs our mind. . . .

Also, and much more realistically, by the dislocation of moods and circumstances which hurries the play along. In using her, Shakespeare often contrives things both ways. The dawn scene suggests her lover's readiness to be gone, and the ensuing separation scene her own corresponding readiness to leave Troy, which, in the proper conventions of love and parting, she protests against too much. With Diomedes in the Greek camp she has little choice: she is trapped by the persona which is easiest for a girl like her to wear when she goes into a society like this. The scene in which Troilus watches her in an anguish of jealousy is no more a conventional betrayal scene than their parting that morning had been a conventional *alba*. Cressida is exasperated by her situation ('O Jove! *do come*. I shall be plagued'), but she cannot afford to antagonise Diomedes. This is no more a betrayal of love than love itself, as we see it in the play, corresponds to any ideal of it.

There is a suggestion here of Timon, and of his nameless longing. The inexhaustible vulnerability of Timon gives us some moving speeches, as when he sees his steward weeping:

> What, dost thou weep? Come nearer. Then I love thee
> Because thou art a woman, and disclaim'st
> Flinty mankind, whose eyes do never give
> But thorough lust and laughter. Pity's sleeping.
> Strange times that weep with laughter, not with weeping.
>
> IV. iii. 82–6

Both Troilus and Cressida give us hints of the same longing. They see in each other something ideal, which life, as the play presents it, hurries into a bewilderment of expectation, lust and laughter. For Timon it is easy to treat the two Athenian courtesans as he does, bidding them hold up their 'aprons mountant', which he fills with his unwanted gold. He despises them, as he does the poet who writes for him and the gold that might work for him; but his speech to his steward shows a different idea. The extreme realism of *Troilus* is similarly transformed with longings for the ideal, which the presentness of life devours and leaves as left-over scraps, 'the bits and greasy relics'. Troilus and Cressida disappear into limbo like that, but the ideal remains and has been there for both of them: in Cressida's 'Prince Troilus I have loved thee night and day'; in Troilus'

> O that I thought it could be in a woman –
> As, if it can, I will presume in you –
> To feed for aye her lamp and flame of love;
> To keep her constancy in plight and youth,
> Outliving beauty's outward, with a mind
> That doth renew swifter than blood decays.
>
> III. ii. 154–9

This is a vision of the time that in *Troilus* is never available, the time that Desdemona on her arrival in Cyprus looks forward to with Othello. But there is no way in which sensation and ideal – the raw experience and the dream that brings responsibility and fruition – can come together in *Troilus*. Love needs poetry and deception, the ideal and the chivalric, and so does war. In general, humanity mingles and muddles all together, must do if human decency and civilisation is to survive, but in *Troilus* the fact of experience and the saving ability to cherish it, change it, build upon it, are kept apart.

CHAPTER 5

DETERMINED THINGS
THE CASE OF THE CAESARS

In *Troilus* the poet is invisible. But in a sense he is there, no less surely than the real poet whose art is at the disposition of Timon of Athens. Poetry in *Troilus* is at the disposal of the story, which it serves in no less a deadpan way than the appetite for wit and brilliance of a probably select audience. It is the same in *Timon*, and there may well be a certain deliberate irony in the fact that the Poet in his dialogue with the Painter in the first scene enlarges on the emblematic tale he is inventing under Timon's patronage, a tale apparently similar to the story which the tragedy itself will unfold for us:

POET. I have, in this rough work, shaped out a man,
      Whom this beneath world doth embrace and hug
      With amplest entertainment. My free drift
      Halts not particularly, but moves itself
      In a wide sea of wax. No levelled malice
      Infects one comma in the course I hold;
      But flies an eagle flight, bold and forth on,
      Leaving no tract behind.
PAIN. How shall I understand you?
POET.   I will unbolt to you.
                                        I. i. 46–54

The Poet goes on to sketch out a commonplace of tragical pattern:

      Sir, I have upon a high and pleasant hill
      Feigned Fortune to be throned: the base of the mount

Is ranked with all deserts, all kinds of natures
That labour on the bosom of this sphere
To propagate their states: amongst them all
Whose eyes are on this sovereign lady fixed,
One do I personate of Lord Timon's frame,
Whom Fortune with her ivory hand wafts to her;
Whose present grace to present slaves and servants
Translates his rivals.

PAIN.   'Tis conceived to scope.
This throne, this Fortune, and this hill, methinks,
With one man beckoned from the rest below,
Bowing his head against the steepy mount
To climb his happiness, would be well expressed
In our condition.

POET.   Nay, sir, but hear me on.
All those which were his fellows but of late,
Some better than his value, on the moment
Follow his strides, his lobbies fill with tendance,
Rain sacrificial whisperings in his ear,
Make sacred even his stirrup, and through him
Drink the free air.

PAIN.   Ay, marry, what of these?

POET. When Fortune in her shift and change of mood
Spurns down her late beloved, all his dependants
Which laboured after him to the mountain's top
Even on their knees and hands, let him slip down,
Not one accompanying his declining foot.

PAIN. 'Tis common.
A thousand moral paintings I can show,
That shall demonstrate these quick blows of Fortune's
More pregnantly than words.

                                        I. i. 66–95

The story of Timon is pictured and drawn in words, foreordained by
the dialogue of the pair, whose existence depends on exploiting this
kind of situation in art, a situation which the play will show us to the
life. There is in this the usual Shakespearean interplay between shadow
and substance a lengthy variation in one sense of the device of talking
about plays within the play, as if it not only counterfeited but was itself
reality ('How many times shall Caesar bleed in sport?'). But more

important is the feeling of flatness, of two-dimensional representation, which is implicit in the exchange between the pair, and associates not only with their status but with their attitude to what they present.

This flatness is panoramic, bold and magnificent: it does not suggest defect. None the less, art discussing itself always carries an overtone of the comic, and in Shakespeare this becomes a delightful levity, both discreet and inspiriting. His poet is himself, who can doubt it? His free description of how Shakespearean verse tragedy works is inimitably true. The dramatic movement goes where and does what it wants, traversing as easily as a stylus on a waxen tablet: nothing is aimed at with that lust for definition which is art's pitfall and temptation: no tell-tale trace is left behind to show how and with what intention it has been done, and to catch at the words that have been used. But who can doubt that the final irony in the lines, and the most significant in terms of our interpretation of Shakespearean tragedy, is the gap between the fall of a great man as commonplace, and the actual figure of Timon that we have, a figure wholly vulnerable and wholly unfitted for the 'common' notion of Fortune and her tragic victims?

There is a parallel with two of Pushkin's lighthearted miniature dramas, *Mozart and Salieri*, and *Egyptian Nights*. The former concerns the gaiety and irresponsibility of a musical genius, for whom a plodding composer feels both passionate admiration and passionate disapproval. *Egyptian Nights* is more specifically Shakespearean. A poor, greedy, and rather absurd Italian mountebank, who can improvise superlative verses, is asked to produce something on the theme of 'Cleopatra and her Lovers', and duly obliges. Pushkin also uses the metaphor of the eagle, the noble free-soaring bird associated with the needy poet in reduced circumstances. Shakespeare's poet magnificently describes the working of his own genius, as Pushkin's also does, and then goes on to sketch a very ordinary theme for tragic commonplace, as commonplace in its own way as the theme of Cleopatra and her Lovers.

Poetry affects amusement at itself and its situation, but in so doing is also glorying in its own almost superhuman powers. The amusement parallels and identifies itself with the hidden amusement Shakespeare seems to show in *Troilus and Cressida* at the attitudes of his audience, with their taste for rhetoric and for the sophistication of the moment. Amused art, whether it expresses itself in parody or in self-parody, is always two-dimensional and self-conscious. Both characteristics are present in the flat brilliance of *Troilus* and *Timon*, but – as if it rose out of that impression – we also receive another one: the yearning and,

as it were, homesickness, that lies below the monotonous and turmul-
tuous surface of *Timon* and the gay ephemeral surface of *Troilus*.
Something in the way both plays are written seems to affect their
principal characters with a longing for a world of another kind: for
Timon a world of woman's tears, and forgiveness and love; for Cressida
a world in which love meant something more than backstairs transactions, cautious lusts and rivalries.

These impressions, if they exist for us, are born out of the method
which the unremitting effectiveness of poetry imposes upon the play.
Poetry is identified both with the cursing of Timon and with the
rhetorical wit and energy in *Troilus*, and the very impact that it makes
persuades us that poetry is not the end of the story. Its total integration
with the dramatic world of Macbeth, Othello, Hamlet; its unique and
unhoused residence in *King Lear*, where it seems to lend itself to
separate egos, not as poetry but as self-justification; to escape from itself
entirely with Cordelia, and to become itself entirely on Dover cliff: this
means that we do not consider it as bearing a specific burden, as
keeping the play going. In *Troilus* and *Timon* it does just that; and
there is also a sense in which it does it in the Roman tragedies. In all of
them, though in various ways, poetry has a detached, slightly deferen-
tial quality, the handmaid and lieutenant of formal tragedy; sometimes
here too the role suggests amusement at, or pleasure in, itself.

Dramatic poetry seems in these plays to study its subject, and sometimes itself as well. In doing so it enhances the splendour, formality and
weight of the Roman tale, appearing equally as cheer-leader, sardonic
bystander, or committed enthusiast at a Roman triumph. When
Enobarbus takes on the mantle of eloquence 'The barge she sat in, like
a burnished throne,/Burned on the water. . . .' it is in a different way
from that of Nestor and Ulysses, and yet there is a similarity: they all
employ fine words as if deliberately in keeping with the status and
nature of the performance. I suggested that what is really most moving
in the 'tragedy' of Timon and of Troilus is not the official subject – the
betrayal of Troilus or Hector, the ingratitude that drives Timon to the
wilderness – but a disturbing sense of longing, apprehended through
the behaviour of the leading characters, for something *outside* the play,
and thus outside the art that has made it what it is. Such an impression
is certainly not to be felt in the Roman plays, where everything is hard
and clear and external. There are no hidden worlds here, no longings
for experience or stability outside the society the play presents.

In that sense the Roman tragedies resemble the English history plays.

But the possible dimension of the English histories is in fact wider – it includes heaven and hell, and the kinds of aspiration and damnation that go with them. It is about another country, in all senses, that the Bishop of Carlisle in *Richard II* speaks in his reference to Norfolk's banishment:

> Many a time hath banished Norfolk fought
> For Jesu Christ in glorious Christian field,
> Streaming the ensign of the Christian cross
> Against black pagans, Turks, and Saracens;
> And, toiled with works of war, retired himself
> To Italy: and there at Venice gave
> His body to that pleasant country's earth,
> And his pure soul unto his captain Christ,
> Under whose colours he had fought so long.
>
> IV. i. 92–100

When Coriolanus is banished, and proclaims 'There is a world else-where,' we feel at once that the opposite is the case. There is no other world for Coriolanus, even in Corioli, in fact particularly not in Corioli, his ironically titular home, where he will continue the same obsessive and determined activities as before. Bolingbroke in exile has 'sighed my English breath in foreign clouds,' but Corioli is for its new champion Rome by other means.

This total acceptance of the world they know as the only world there is distinguishes the characters of all the Roman plays. It is the legacy of Plutarch, but, in this particular Shakespeare's imagination out-Plutarchs Plutarch. As his imagination presents it, the ancient world is as flat and bright as a painted board, not so unlike that Mediterranean world which Flaubert imagined in his novel *Salammbo*. The plays make us realise how greatly tragedy, and its imagination, are elsewhere for Shakespeare spiritual matters. And of course not only tragedy but comedy too.

> Look how the floor of heaven
> Is thick inlaid with patines of bright gold.
> There's not the smallest orb which thou behold'st
> But in his motion like an angel sings,
> Still quiring to the young-eyed cherubins;
> Such harmony is in immortal souls.
> But whilst this muddy vesture of decay
> Doth grossly close it in, we cannot hear it.
>
> V. i. 58–65

Platonic-Christian imagery comes as naturally to Lorenzo in *The Merchant of Venice* as to Hamlet or Macbeth. But tragedy is by far the greater beneficiary of the two worlds which give fullest expression to the duality of body and soul. Soul, in the effortless and mysterious Shakespearean sense, is absent from the Roman plays, naturally absent. In *Timon* and *Troilus* it is absent by default.

This may strike us when Timon, and Antony in *Antony and Cleopatra*, seem, as it were, to be attempting the language of another world, and the longing for it. Poetry at such moments seems itself to be doing without a soul and the characters that goes with it, to be executing on its own behalf a beautiful but mechanical task. Antony's sense of his own dissolution has a wonderful detachment about it, but the beauty that in *Timon* seems to suggest another world is here doing the opposite and conveying the absence of one:

ANT. Eros, thou yet behold'st me?
EROS.   Ay, noble lord.
ANT. Sometime we see a cloud that's dragonish,
        A vapour sometime like a bear or lion,
        A towered citadel, a pendent rock,
        A forked mountain, or blue promontory
        With trees upon't, that nod unto the world
        And mock our eyes with air. Thou has seen these signs:
        They are black vesper's pageants.
EROS.   Ay, my lord.
ANT. That which is now a horse, even with a thought
        The rack dislimns and makes it indistinct
        As water is in water.
EROS.   It does, my lord.
ANT. My good knave Eros, now thy captain is
        Even such a body. Here am I Antony,
        Yet cannot hold this visible shape, my knave.

IV. xiv. 1–14

In the tragic context and atmosphere of the Roman plays it is singularly appropriate that the hero should dissolve and dissipate in the bright air like a cloud. Impossible to imagine the metaphor of such a fate for Macbeth, or for the sturdy Bolingbroke, who remains inalienably himself under foreign clouds. In the tragedies of consciousness the tragic hero's self is absolute, the body and soul of his being becoming the more intense and concentrated the more the experience of his fate is heaped upon him. But Antony has never had that kind of reality. He cannot hold this visible shape, although, as for all the Romans – witness Brutus and Cassius and the constancy of the Northern Star that Julius Caesar claims for himself – to do so is the only great and proper ideal. In the tragedies of consciousness inner being grows and intensifies: in the Roman tragedies the external self stands up to the end, until it is struck down or strikes down itself.

Charmian's words to her distracted mistress are accurate because they are contradictory. 'The soul and body rive not more in parting/Than greatness going off.' The parting of soul and body is a sudden thing, like a Roman suicide, but Antony's dissolution is pro-tracted, like his own death-agony. Unable to hold this visible shape he attempts to do the Roman thing, and botches it. 'Eros, thou yet behold'st me?' has great pathos, the desire for reassurance that he still has existence of some kind. And yet Antony's dissolution is not really an affair of pathos: the 'blue promontory' of the Mediterranean makes a detached picture beside which his greatness going off and his dying can take place. The lines stand apart from the stunned exhaustion with which he now sees himself, contrasting with the burst of hysteric violence after the last battle, when he called on his reputed ancestor, Hercules, to teach him a proper rage:

> Let me lodge Lichas on the horns of the moon,
> And with those hands that clasped the heaviest club
> Subdue my worthiest self.
>
> IV. xii. 45–7

Antony invokes his great ancestor only, by implication, to reject him. His worthiest self is the self that loves Cleopatra, whom his hands are now seeking to kill. This frenzy has spent itself before Mardian enters with the false news of Cleopatra's suicide. Instead of the madness of Ajax and the strength of Hercules there now descends on Antony a dreamy lethargy which welcomes its own dissolution. The un-Romanness of it is singular and apt: Antony joins Timon here in exhibiting that most subtle and persistent of Shakespearean truths about the tragic character – his unsuitability for the role. No more than Timon's do Antony's ravings carry any ring of conviction:

> Nay, weep not, gentle Eros: there is left us
> Ourselves to end ourselves.

The name of Eros and his noble behaviour seem to receive the ruined
Antony more tenderly and absolutely than Cleopatra herself. His
collapse is extraordinarily touching, as realistic as it is pitiful. Though
there is no further world of the spirit and the consciousness in *Antony
and Cleopatra*, no more than in the other Roman plays, there is a great
contrast. It is not between Egypt and Rome. It is between the figure
one puts on ('Eros, thou yet behold'st me?') and the dissipation of that
rigid persona which comes with death and catastrophe and yet is unexpectedly welcome and gentle. Antony played the lover as much as he
played the Roman: now both parts can be given up; he can sink into
non-individuality.

The process involves both parts. Antony desires to die like a Roman
and a lover. But the formal Roman suicide, done with such propriety in
the case of Brutus and Cassius, is here botched by Antony to the extent
of being, in artistic terms, wholly naturalised. In the final exchange
with Eros we can feel the tension of impatience and stoicism, like the
moment before having a tooth pulled out.

EROS. My sword is drawn.
ANT.   Then let it do at once
        The thing why thou hast drawn it.
EROS.   My dear master
        My captain and my emperor, let me say,
        Before I strike this bloody stroke, farewell.
ANT. 'Tis said, man: and farewell.
EROS. Farewell, great chief. Shall I strike now?
ANT.   Now, Eros.
EROS. Why, there then. Thus do I escape the sorrow
        Of Antony's death.   [*Kills himself.*
                                         IV. xiv. 88-95

Antony endeavours to do the job himself and fails; and his failure in the
Roman part is soon to be followed, most touchingly, by his last débâcle
as a lover, heaved laboriously aloft to his mistress instead of bounding,
as it were, into her bed. The two episodes are brilliant in terms of stage-
craft – the suspense before Eros stabs himself, and the laborious
business of raising the dying man aloft to the monument – but they are
also the most signal instance of how Shakespeare naturalised Plutarch.

CLEO. Here's sport indeed! How heavy weighs my lord?
        Our strength is all gone into heaviness.

> That makes the weight. Had I great Juno's power,
> The strong-winged Mercury should fetch thee up
> And set thee by Jove's side. Yet come a little.
> Wishers were ever fools. O come, come, come!
>   *They heave Antony aloft to Cleopatra.*
> And welcome, welcome. Die when thou hast lived.
> Quicken with kissing. Had my lips that power,
> Thus would I wear them out.
>
> IV. xv. 32–40

The Folio reading, before being modified to the standard text by succes-
sive editors, gives that question mark after 'How heavy weighs my
lord?' and also '*when* thou hast lived', which editors change to *where*,
transposition of *n* and *r* being a common printer's error. This seems
quite likely, for *where* is equally good in terms of the general idiom and
feeling of the play, but 'Die *when* thou hast lived' gives a finer
impression both of Cleopatra's sense of her own enlivening power, and
– more profoundly – of the world accepted by Antony and exploited by
him. As A. E. Housman put it,

> he that drinks in season
> Shall live before he dies.

Antony has drunk; he has lived; and it is now time for him to die. The
clear light of all the Roman plays provides a total definition of their
characters, and it is this simplicity which defines Antony. What makes
him moving, too, is the contrast between soldier and lover and the
suffering burden that now 'makes the weight'.

That is a most memorable observation of Cleopatra, coming as it
does from the wholly 'non-poetic' side of her, the side that does not in
the least aspire to speak and act the Roman part with her lover, in her
emulation of, and passion for, him. The tenderness in the words she
babbles here seems wholly unacted, as if her lover had now become
simply her child, an object to be weighed and dandled. But in the same
speech she gives vent to the appropriate idiom in which they had
indulged together the picture of themselves as creatures of mythology,
followers of the gods. Both are equally suited to accompany the
audience's participation in what is being done, its interest in the
mechanical side of the business, mentioned by Plutarch and probably
copied from Shakespeare by Daniel in his *Cleopatra*. Shakespeare has
made completely natural and integral with the atmosphere of the play

the way in which Antony tried to kill himself, and the way in which his still-living body is heaved aloft to his mistress. The slow-motion clumsiness of both operations is very much of a part of its world of living and dying, whose simplicity underlies the grandeur, the politics and the passion, and the self-presentations appropriate to all these.

Cleopatra is here the twin of Antony: they have either come to resemble each other or they have always done so. Like him she aspires to be Roman, and in her own way succeeds as little as he does. The effect would be much less moving if Cleopatra was, as it were, wholly 'Egyptian'. Fine sentiment and psychological truth enrich each other here without effort, for Cleopatra's passionate adulation of her dead lover echoes what Antony himself had pronounced about Brutus – 'This was the noblest Roman of them all' – and what, with an effect of great pathos, he gasps out about himself in his last moments:

> the greatest prince o' th' world,
> The noblest, and do not now basely die,
> Not cowardly put off my helmet to
> My countryman, a Roman by a Roman
> Valiantly vanquished. . . .
>
> IV. xv. 54–8

Antony, as Plutarch tells us, had taken lessons in the art of rhetoric; most great Romans would have done the same, probably with a schoolmaster from Asiatic Greece. This makes the reference now to his 'countryman' particularly poignant. And the tone of the last speech, so wholly different from that of any other Roman, is transparent in its affirmation of, and release into, weakness. Rhetoric is more subtle in *Antony and Cleopatra* than in any other play, based as it is on the invisible but highly meaningful divisions between official strength and individual weakness. Antony's reference to his countryman, his assertion of a tired child going to sleep that he has done everything that could be done – these are assertions that produce their own kind of sympathy with us, and intimacy. They contrast with rhetoric in full flow, making its points, as Antony's earlier did, with a still dynamic accuracy:

> All length is torture. Since the torch is out,
> Lie down and stray no farther. Now all labour
> Mars what it does; yea, very force entangles
> Itself with strength. Seal then, and all is done.
>
> IV. xiv. 46–9

The metaphor of force, duration, entanglement, need only that of weight and sleep to complete it, and these are provided – with an effect the opposite of rhetorical – by Cleopatra herself and by Antony at the end.

Just like her 'Husband I come' – and the word as she uses it touches in the same way as Antony's 'countryman', only more deeply – Cleopatra alternates between assertions of her Roman temper and spirits and the self-revelation of endearing natural weakness.

> and then, what's brave, what's noble,
> Let's do't after the high Roman fashion
> And make death proud to take us.
>
> IV. xv. 86–8

Such sentiments reveal to us their opposites, as does 'and I have nothing/Of woman in me. Now from head to foot/I am marble-constant.' Against these dualisms, and claims that come out as confidences, the rhetoric of Octavius Caesar is in clearly deliberate contrast. Its generosity is not false but has nothing inside it, no confusion of impulses, and that in this play is as damning as the most leaden insincerity. Where for Antony he was 'countryman', Caesar's eulogy describes Antony as

> my brother, my competitor
> In top of all design, my mate in empire,
> Friend and companion in the front of war.
>
> V. i. 42–4

The words are moving but the tone is not. Caesar as usual is eminently reasonable. It was him or me, he begins:

> I must perforce
> Have shown to thee such a declining day
> Or look on thine. . . .
>
> V. i. 37–9

And yet Agrippa is right when he says 'Caesar is touched.' It is the function of the narrative eye in the Roman plays to 'look quite through the deeds of men', as Julius Caesar said that Cassius can do. Looking with that eye we see them steadily and whole: there is nothing of that extreme of intimacy in *Hamlet*, *Othello*, or *Macbeth*, the plays in which the same consciousness seems to enfold us and the protagonists. Caesar *is* touched, and his entourage make appropriate comments on the fact, but he turns his feeling, like everything else, to good use. The narrative eye is wholly fair, especially in noting how incongruity makes 'human' the least obviously human of men. Caesar speaks from the heart, and makes at the same time an official statement to his staff – the press, as it were – about his record and policy. As he is getting going – 'Hear me, good friends' – the Egyptian messenger appears, and he returns at once to unfinished business:

> But I will tell you at some meeter season.
> The business of this man looks out of him:
> We'll hear him what he says.
>
> V. i. 49–51

His uncle Julius was seen with the same eye and noted in the same way, though not with such seasoned and unemphatic skill. But there is a family likeness in the way Julius Caesar spoke to his friends.

> Such men as he be never at heart's ease
> While they behold a greater than themselves,
> And therefore are they very dangerous.
> I rather tell thee what is to be feared
> Than what I fear, for always I am Caesar.
> Come on my right hand, for this ear is deaf,
> And tell me truly what thou think'st of him.
>
> I. ii. 208–14

Talking about Cassius to his henchman, Antony, Julius Caesar was as shrewdly official as his nephew, and at the same time – where the play-goer is concerned – as transparent. We look quite through the deeds of these men. Seen in clear light, Caesar and his nephew can both be clearly understood, as clearly as Antony and the Queen of Egypt. Like all the characters in the Roman plays they are full of preoccupation, not with themselves but with business and duty – Antony's pleasure is itself a kind of duty to him – and this reveals them all the more clearly. Shakespeare follows Plutarch but sharpens the focus, so that the characters unknowingly present their good and bad qualities together to us on a scale of intimacy rather than in the wider perspective of the historian. It is probably a sign of his lack of experience in this new kind of treatment that Shakespeare plays it safe with Julius Caesar. He uses the rhetoric appropriate to a great man, as Tamburlaine might have done, usually referring to himself in the third person as 'Caesar'. 'Yet Caesar shall go forth' echoes, or perhaps is echoed by, Marlowe's play *The*

Massacre at Paris. From Shakespeare's point of view here, it was the readiest way to do a great man, so that his greatness would be taken for granted by the audience, whose closer attention would be on what was revealed about the conspirators.

From the point of view of tragedy, the treatment gives birth to a kind of originality, although one that was not necessarily fully intentional on Shakespeare's part. The great man and his fall are not the centre of attention; that is reserved for the more domestic matter of the conspirators, and particularly of Brutus and his wife Portia. And because of the fact that friendship and domesticity – the daily basis of living – bulk so large in the play, the rigidity of Caesar's pose seems not so much a convention for conveying his greatness as a means for the audience of coming close to his position and understanding it. The fabulous achievements, that have at last brought peace to the immense territories of which Rome is now master, have no way of being their proper selves in the domestic hugger-mugger of Roman politics. Caesar's behaviour veers between displays of comradely and demagogic solidarity, like those of the popular leader which he still depended on being, and the official rhetoric which his position required for his role in the play:

> Good friends, go in and taste some wine with me;
> And we like friends will straightway go together.
>
> II. ii. 125–6

In the Roman plays there is never any question of dissembling. Caesar is as frank in friendship here as he is in regard to his own status, the great man of whom he speaks in the third person.

In so far as it has regarded Caesar as a subtle portrait, criticism has tended to see him as a man whose greatness is slipping and who is conscious of the fact, needing to remind himself and others all the time of what a great man he is. This impression comes from the perhaps rather simplifying policy that Shakespeare adopts. But in terms of the play there is no doubt whatever about the effectiveness of the man, just as there is none about that of his great-nephew in *Antony and Cleopatra*. Like the other characters in the three Roman plays Caesar is inherently uncomplicated: he is what he is just as much as Coriolanus is. His desire for power and a crown is as direct as his affection for Calpurnia, his desire for comradeship. The historical Caesar was well aware of the risks he was running but preferred to run them in order to remain in touch, on terms of apparent equality with friends and colleagues in affairs of state. 'Let me have men about me that are fat,' which is taken from a report in Plutarch of Caesar's conversation, should be delivered with a slight smile. But it is undeniable that Shakespeare makes no attempt to render the terseness implicit in Plutarch's Caesar and probably in the real one. (His comment when signing despatches at the dinner table, when the others were speaking of the best kind of death to have, is rendered by North as 'Death unlooked for'. 'A sudden one' would probably be closer to Plutarch's sense.) Shakespeare's instinct was to make a contrast between the measured utterance of the great man and the sudden fate that overcame him; and so this terseness had to be sacrificed and becomes

> Cowards die many times before their deaths;
> The valiant never taste of death but once.
> Of all the wonders that I yet have heard
> It seems to me most strange that men should fear,
> Seeing that death, a necessary end,
> Will come when it will come.
>
> II. ii. 32–7

The naturalness of human incongruity and inconsistency, so effortlessly presented in the Roman plays, is less effective in relation to Caesar himself. In Plutarch he is normally superstitious, and particularly struck by Calpurnia's fears because she was not given that way. This is changed by being put into words spoken by Cassius:

> For he is superstitious grown of late,
> Quite from the main opinion he held once
> Of fantasy, of dreams and ceremonies.
>
> II. i. 195–7

This is typical of Cassius' attitude and his compulsion to put down Caesar, as Iago desires to put down Othello. We learn about Cassius from his attitude, not about Caesar. But Cassius' speeches have another function, which is to mark Caesar out as the great man destined to be sacrificed. Our knowledge of what is to take place – the most famous of all historical 'tragedies' – rightly separates Caesar from anyone else in the play, makes him a different sort of being, a being who can walk only in one direction, and that is towards death. Caesar's speeches are dramatically perfect, in that they are those of a man who is marked out for sacrifice, whose tone and speeches proclaim the fact while he himself is necessarily unaware of it.

This solitary and anomalous position of Caesar separates him from the other people in the Roman plays. But these plays also indicate something that is curiously disconcerting, accustomed as we are to the received idea that the political portraits in them are expertly and authoritatively done. Are they? I would say only in *Coriolanus*, where the relation of Menenius and the tribunes, Coriolanus and his mother, is as perceptive in terms of politics and power as anything in the English history plays, as well as being licensed to complete objectivity. Henry IV and his son, as Prince Hal and as king, positively benefit as studies of people in power from the fact that they must be praised and admired as archetypes of the right sort of establishment people. Such official praise sharpens and gives its own kind of point to the criticism of them that is both secretly and obviously at work. Without the need for such praise, or the point of such criticism, the portrayal of the two Caesars is ultimately rather bland and perfunctory, as if they were too far away to excite the heat of creation in perception. Perhaps Shakespeare needed a spice of danger and diplomacy – the diplomacy that was always alert in his treatment of English historical figures – to give a secret and authentic bite to observation?

But the lack of secrecy is proper to the way the plays work. Both Cassius and Mark Antony, the rivals of the two Caesars, are exasperated by their inability to penetrate them and make them vulnerable in some way. The playwright puts himself into the same position. About the greatness of the two Caesars there is something banal, uninteresting – because so strong. Cassius' exasperation has something hopeless about it, which issues in his attempts to make Caesar appear contemptible:

> What trash is Rome,
> What rubbish and what offal, when it serves
> For the base matter to illuminate
> So vile a thing as Caesar!
>
> I. iii. 108–11

Cassius' obsession, like that of the revolutionary officer in Wordsworth's *Prelude*, seems to be with 'some uneasy place in his own body'. He assures Casca that he is a free man – 'Cassius from bondage will deliver Cassius' – because he can dismiss Caesar by killing himself – 'That part of tyranny that I do bear/I can shake off at pleasure.' But the impression is of a man infuriated by his own impotence. Antony comes to have something of the same attitude towards his rival, whom

he had at first patronised and then treated as an equal, and in his final
baffled rage makes attempts to attack personally in single combat. Like
Cassius, and like ourselves, he is rebuffed and repelled by the smooth
hard exterior of Caesar, and the realisation – which his soothsayer
merely confirms – that he can do nothing against this invulnerable
young man. Brutus and Cassius, for all the seeming result of their conspiracy, managed nothing against his uncle, except killing him. The
'natural luck' of the Caesars, as the Soothsayer calls it, is a smooth
impenetrable surface that Shakespeare's writing itself has to accept, as
its opponents do.

> If thou dost play with him at any game,
> Thou art sure to lose; and of that natural luck
> He beats thee gainst the odds. Thy lustre thickens
> When he shines by.
>
> II. iii. 26–9

Antony and Cleopatra is in the simplest sense the most determined
of all Shakespeare's tragic plays. The consciousness tragedies are by
contrast areas of infinite possibility: menace, relief, the untoward, and
the unlooked-for saving and mercy – all seem possible or imminent. In
King Lear the question of fatality does not even arise: neither the
expected nor the unexpected has any relevance in terms of the family
situation it involves us in. But in *Antony and Cleopatra* and in different
ways and degrees in *Coriolanus* and *Timon*, the notion of fatality is
wholly dominant. There is nothing overpowering about it; it is not the
moira of ancient Greek tragedy, the force which even the gods are helpless to control and which is constantly invoked by choruses with awe
and resignation. Nor does it in any way resemble the *Schicksal* of
German Romantic drama, a melodramatic affair which parodies the
classical realisation and turns it into a kind of luxury of doom. Fate in
this sense is also a flamboyant presence in Jacobean drama, personified
by hero, villain or revenger: 'Canst thou weep fate from his determined
purpose? – so soon wilt thou weep me.' In Shakespeare's tragedies of
consciousness the conceptualising of fate, stylised in the equivocation of
the prophesying witches who deceive Macbeth, is never situated inside
consciousness itself. When Othello exclaims 'Who can control his
fate?' it seems like an afterthought, a recollection of how the situation
he is in might be described from outside, and in the perspective of
literary experience.

But fate in *Antony and Cleopatra* has something almost good-natured about it, relaxed and familiar. The tone of the poetry, simultaneously terse and expansive, easy and strenuous, reinforces this impression. To give way to what is coming is the proper rule of life, most memorably expressed by Octavius Caesar himself:

> Cheer your heart!
> Be you not troubled with the time, which drives
> O'er your content these strong necessities;
> But let determined things to destiny
> Hold unbewailed their way.
>
> III. vi. 81–5

Such is the advice that Caesar gives his sister Octavia, and its tone is very like the 'advice' that floats before Antony's eyes in the form of the image of the 'cloud that's dragonish'. It seems not a stoical precept but an invitation to repose and tranquillity. Fate in this play comes in the image of the baby at the breast 'that sucks the nurse asleep.' It was the sentiment of this perhaps, as much as anything, that made Bradley feel that, in spite of 'a triumph which is more than reconciliation', there is something 'disenchanting' in the tragic story, which does not move us as do the love dramas of Romeo or of Othello. 'And the fact that we mourn so little saddens us.'

But the audience yields to the story in the same spirit as the participants. Relaxation goes deeper than Bradley's impression would suggest. Constantly the poetry ties itself into a tight knot that suddenly comes loose, the strands slackening apart from each other.

> The wife of Antony
> Should have an army for an usher, and
> The neighs of horses to tell of her approach
> Long ere she did appear. The trees by the way
> Should have borne men; and expectation fainted,
> Longing for what it had not. Nay, the dust
> Should have ascended to the roof of heaven,
> Raised by your populous troops. But you are come
> A market-maid to Rome.
>
> III. vi. 43–51

There are two things to notice about this passage. The phrase about 'expectation', recalls similar verbal effects, like the fans in Enorbarbus' account of the scene at Cydnus, which 'what they undid, did', and the air that went to gaze on Cleopatra and left a gap in nature. More important, the end of all the to-ing and fro-ing is the appearance of Octavia as a simple market-maid, as Cleopatra herself becomes

> No more but e'en a woman, and commanded
> By such poor passion as the maid that milks
> And does the meanest chares.
>
> IV. xv. 73–5

Efforts, like language, relax their strain and drop into simplicity, 'lie down and stray no farther', which is very different from the hero's rest at the end of tragic actions that have laboured to attain the hour. It is important that the sense of surrender, the drop from achievement into indifference, can come at any point in the play: it is not a gradual and cumulative process. Antony is the bellows and the fan at the beginning of the action, a phrase that though it undoubtedly means two types of cooling instrument – Shakespeare's frequent stylistic trick of putting two synonyms together – none the less suggests a to-and-fro, negative and positive indefinitely repeated, like the image of the fans that both cool and inflame Cleopatra's cheeks. The whole effect is one of sexual rise and fall, endorsing and yet also ironically contradicting the admiration of Cleopatra as making hungry where most she satisfies. In her last speeches Cleopatra herself calls up the idea in a concealed sexual reference – she must make haste and follow Antony, for otherwise Iras may meet him and he 'will make demand of her and spend that kiss which is my heaven to have.' The word 'spend' tells its own tale: Antony has spent himself in this homely fashion many a time throughout the play.

Oscillation – the 'swan's down feather' and the 'vagabond flag' upon the stream – fills the action, though interestingly it applies neither to Octavius Caesar nor to Cleopatra herself. It is Octavia who, as Antony tenderly says, shows it when she parts from her brother, looking both towards him and towards her new husband:

> Her tongue will not obey her heart, nor can
> Her heart inform her tongue: the swan's down feather,
> That stands upon the swell at the full of tide
> And neither way inclines.
>
> III. ii. 47–50

The current of the play is indeed tidal, bearing those who are at its

disposal forward and backward. Octavius is not like that, and he speaks
contemptuously of those that are:

> This common body
> Like to a vagabond flag upon the stream
> Goes to and back, lack'ying the varying tide,
> To rot itself with motion.

I. iv. 44–7

Octavia's hesitation is the same helplessness at a higher level – hers the
down feather to the water-flag of the populace – and though her brother
loves her he makes use of her, as of all others. But the action makes a
silent distinction between the power to feel emotion and the state of
helpless feeling. Octavius is no cold hypocrite, and the tears he weeps
as he parts from his sister are not crocodile tears. In their little aside
together Enobarbus and Agrippa make the point that both Antony and
Octavius are men of tears, and it is clear that this is not what makes
them different. Octavius' emotions simply accompany his will, while
those of Antony agitate him without progression, 'like to the time o'
th' year between the extremes/Of hot and cold'.

The structure of the play, then, expresses itself in the general helplessness of external and exterior life, willy-nilly subject to the alterna-
tion of action and passivity. Nothing less tragic in the usual sense can
be imagined, as Bradley clearly felt, but there is no usual sense in
which Shakespeare is tragic: the joys and fatigues of princely living, as
they appear in a story of dying, are as appropriate a subject as the fall of
princes. It is odd that Antony should come closest of any Shakespearean character to having what writers like Virginia Woolf have
made us think of as a 'stream of consciousness', which is clearly a very
different thing from what appears in those tragedies of consciousness,
Hamlet, *Othello*, and *Macbeth*. Antony is hurried, as Virginia Woolf
felt was the fate of consciousness, from one impression and reaction to
another; sensations and events fall on him: his death sequence itself is a
rich and confused accumulation of them. This appears in a most
striking way in the syntax of the passage after Antony has talked with
the Soothsayer and then dismissed him to find the officer Ventidius:

> He shall to Parthia. Be it art or hap,
> He hath spoken true. The very dice obey him –

II. iii. 33–4

The sense of consciousness vaguely flitting between one objective and
another is as graphic here as it is with Mrs Dalloway or Mrs Bloom,

and is expressed in the three different references of the same pronoun. *He* is Ventidius, also the Soothsayer, also Octavius. Dramatic inflection and pause would easily distinguish them, but Antony's awareness of things manufactures frustration and helplessness rather than distinctions, the decision which ends the speech seems a mere symptom of the vagaries of that awareness and its brooding in the toils of incongruous detail:

> His cocks do win the battle still of mine
> When it is all to naught, and his quails ever
> Beat mine, inhooped, at odds. I will to Egypt. . . .
>
> II. iii. 37–9

The sentence in Plutarch which clearly gave Shakespeare the clue for his treatment of Antony relates to the way in which Cleopatra had secretly bribed Canidius, Antony's general and commander of the land-forces, to recommend her remaining at advanced H.Q., as her withdrawal might demoralise the Egyptian fleet, a formidable and necessary part of Antony's total armament. 'For it was predestined', says Plutarch, 'that the government of all the world should fall into Octavius Caesar's hands.' The passive sense of determined things, so foreign to every other tragedy, finds imaginative expression in *Antony and Cleopatra* through the nature of the hero's consciousness. He makes no effort to 'take a bond of fate' or bid it, as Macbeth does, come into the lists and champion him to the utterance. Antony's mind acquiesces in what befalls him in the same way that the passive consciousness surrenders itself to passing experience, and it is incapable of that concentration and reflection that gives their individuality to Hamlet, Othello, and Macbeth. He evades such concentration as he here evades Caesar: and the incongruity between the lost games in a cock- or quail-pit, and the sudden impulse to set out for Egypt, indicate the process.

'No character is very strongly discriminated,' observes Dr Johnson of the play. Fate here seems to have leached out the kinds of individuality we are elsewhere accustomed to. Antony can only evade Caesar or be exasperated by him and dare him to personal combat, and again we are reminded of Cassius' way of escaping the elder Caesar's tyranny. But Cassius and Brutus, though their soldiership was not a patch on Antony's, seemed always to have an even chance of winning, a chance determined from the play's point of view by their whole mode of being and thinking. They are proper persons for conventional tragedy, working out their lot, heroically exposed to the shot of accident and dart of chance and the fatal misunderstanding which causes Cassius' suicide, in which his final words have all the recognition of appropriateness: 'Caesar, thou art revenged,/Even with the sword that killed thee.'

The lack of discrimination that Johnson noted is caused by two things – the mental processes in Antony and the lack of them in Caesar and in Cleopatra. Antony is unique in Shakespearean tragedy in being a lost man from the very beginning. The sense 'of what he has, and has not', is as emphatic in the first scene as it is in his demeanour before the final battle. The ominous precedent is that of Pompey the Great, in his dishonoured grave by the sands of Alexandria, driven to his death by the inflexible will and luck of the first Caesar. Cleopatra recalls him as she muses on her conquests when Antony is away:

> Great Pompey
> Would stand and make his eyes grow in my brow:
> There he would anchor his aspect, and die
> With looking on his life.
>
> I. v. 31–4

The same doomed paralysis is now to be continuously presented in Antony, but it gives us no sense of participation; no more does its opposite, the unmoved Caesar and the equally unmoved Cleopatra. Antony's self in the play engages with neither of them, and for the same reason, that both have such complete confidence in themselves and where they are going. One of the tactics of the piece is the simplification of Cleopatra, by a process that is analogous to the simplification of both Caesars. In all three cases Shakespeare abandons the indications of 'wheels within wheels' in the source, and forgoes the political dimension which it indicates. There is no depth in defence here, no jockeying for position.

For in reality Antony was involved in a complicated political power-game with his rival and his mistress, and Plutarch thoroughly enjoyed revealing the ins and outs so far as he had got wind of them or could embroider on what he had heard. He too is of course turning events into story and illustration. Cleopatra was for Antony a powerful political ally in his attempts to gain hegemony over the whole Middle East, an attempt that even before the break-up of the triumvirate had not been entirely successful. It was not only personally congenial to him but a part of Antony's political manoeuvring to 'go native', a move which though it made him popular in the East compromised his reputation in Rome and Italy. Shakespeare of course ignores such success as he had: what must have struck the playwright's imagination was the way in which the hero's luck had turned. Even the loyalty of Octavia to himself and his family became a political liability, because her dignity and forbearance could not but make excellent propaganda for the Roman side: a consequence on which her brother had no doubt calculated.

Cleopatra, for her part, had put her money on Antony as the best bet not only to retain her kingdom but to further her ambition to become mistress of the Middle East. Her decision to accompany Antony on the Actium campaign, which Shakespeare artfully transmutes into the eternally vacuous wilfulness of the eternal feminine, was in reality a pre-emptive move to ensure that her colleague did not do a deal of his own with Octavius, leaving her out. The treachery and defection of client kings which Antony's Eastern policies had already set in train, was no doubt her fault as much as his, but no more. Though his narrative purposes required him to show how Antony was ruined by Cleopatra and his love for her, Plutarch's narration also reveals them in the clearest fashion as *colleagues*. And colleagues they remained, even in their last days, which in Plutarch's account have something pretentious and repellent about them, as well as sinister, for such episodes occurred as the handing over of Seleucus' wife and children to Antony for torture and death. Seleucus was commandant of the frontier fortress of Pelusium, and Cleopatra committed this deed in order to clear herself of suspicion when the town fell easily to the forces of Octavius Caesar. Shakespeare gives the name to the comic treasurer, who gives her away when she makes a declaration of her assets to Caesar, and he smilingly reassures her: 'Nay, blush not, Cleopatra. I approve/Your wisdom in the deed.'

That seems indeed the extent of Cleopatra's 'naughtiness' in her comedy role. The change, and its significance, are clear. Cleopatra is to be as unremitting in her frivolity as Caesar in his pursuit of power. Between these two blank walls Antony's consciousness drifts to and fro. He can make nothing of them, and impose himself upon neither of them. And this pattern of course determines the general drift and image of the play. The hero is helpless in a unique sense, not like the conditions of any other tragedy.

The second clue which Shakespeare may have taken in his creative imagination of this process is Plutarch's comment on Antony's marriage in his young days, when he was a dissolute favourite of the older Caesar, to Fulvia. Plutarch remarks that in order to exercise self-control over his rackety existence Antony needed the help of a woman of character and strong personality.

> a woman not so basely minded to spend her time in spinning and housewifery, and was not contented to master her husband at home, but would also rule him in his office abroad, and command him that commanded legions and great armies; so that Cleopatra was to give Fulvia thanks that she had taught Antonius this obedience to women, that learned so well to be at their commandment.

Fulvia no doubt made a man of him in some sense, and loved him, for with the help of his brother she did her best to start a civil war in Italy to bring him home. But Cleopatra is a very different sort of woman. She may think herself powerful, and may have appealed to Antony because she seemed so, but in Shakespeare's presentation she is nothing of the sort. She demands attention; she affects authority and purpose; but really, and in her own robust way, she clings and vapours. She loves games and dreams and dressing up, and Antony's past makes him here the most congenial of playfellows. Their deep affection and love for each other here is undoubted, but she is not the woman to inspire him to action, as Fulvia was. Plutarch portrays her as a worthy successor to Fulvia, an enterprising if not altogether trustworthy colleague and comrade; but Shakespeare makes her a wholly different woman, not at all the sort that we may guess Fulvia to have been.

It is a part of Antony's helplessness that he never seems quite to find this out. She teases him, exasperates him, but fascinates him because he will go on against all the evidence in believing her to be stronger than he is. Her 'strength' is like Octavius' 'luck' – an impalpable thing whose influence is fateful to Antony because he so implicitly believes in it. If he is with her she is happy, and it matters not what is going on – peace or war. The latter seems to her a special sort of dressing up. 'I'll give thee, friend, an armour all of gold: it was a king's,' she tells Scarus, after Antony has praised his conduct in the last battle. She buckles on Antony's armour for him and he praises her: 'Thou fumblest, Eros, and my queen's a squire/More tight at this than thou.' This final desperate contest, nothing more than a forlorn gesture against an overwhelmingly strong and prudent enemy, seems in its excitement and innocence just like their Alexandrian revels, their inquisitive wanderings through the night streets together, the joke with the salt fish on the hook which Antony 'with fervency drew up.'

Shakespeare has of course introduced a degree of romantic simplification and stylisation here which is in keeping with the taste of the age. Samuel Daniel had portrayed a very similar Cleopatra in his tragedy of 1594, and Dryden in *All for Love* was to take the hint from Shakespeare and give a total passivity and helplessness to both lovers. Mars and Venus, the conventions of tapestry and emblem, are convenient to the change, and exercise a traditional influence in the scene. But behind it is our sense of the woman herself, and the presentation of her as fatal for Antony in a touching and homely sense. Shakespeare joins on romantic preconceptions of the part to his portrait of a weak woman with a strong personality. Such a woman could not be – as Plutarch's Cleopatra is – in constant communication with Caesar behind Antony's back: when Thidias (Thyreus in Plutarch) comes to treat with her, she behaves with a genuinely girlish naïvety, gratified to flirtatiousness by his courtesies, and professing respectful submission to his master. Neither means anything at all; they are merely symptoms of her instant, effortless way of dealing with every situation by being herself; the impression she gives is one of unbounded equanimity, whether she is giving audience to Caesar's representatives, mourning the fate of Antony, or ordering the asps *sotto voce* from Charmian while saying of Caesar; 'He words me, girls, he words me. . . .'

Shakespeare's sense of omission, and of timing, is perfect to this presentation of her. This Cleopatra could not be mentioned as experimenting on prisoners to see which death was the easiest, though we don't in the least mind hearing after her death that 'She hath pursued conclusions infinite/Of easy ways to die.' Nor could she have joined in the intellectuals' pact, mentioned by Plutarch as the *Synapothanumenon* – 'the order and agreement of those that are to die together' – which she and Antony used to celebrate in the last days with their friends. Our Cleopatra is no bluestocking, and neither cold-hearted nor methodical. Oddly enough the touch in Plutarch that Shakespeare would normally have delighted to use, and whose incongruity would not in the least have disturbed her self-possession, is that the soldier to whom she gave the golden armour, 'when he had received this rich gift, stole away by night and went to Caesar.'

The most moving thing about their relation is the sense of two people, who have, in the misfortunes they bring on each other, become inextricably close. It is a closeness easily ruptured, as so many knots of style are easily dissolved in the play, and death itself seems gentler and easier for being prolonged, the 'knot intrinsicate of life' insensibly untied. But the lovers are close rather than intimate. It is the only subtlety that can survive in their relationship, changed as it is from the sexual and professional intimacy of lovers and colleagues to Shakespeare's representation of the eternal feminine bewitching the grand captain, the greatest prince in the world. It is the only subtlety, I should say, that survives in the portrayal of the relationship, the most famous but also the most public love spectacle, not only in Shakespeare but anywhere in literature. The lovers are never alone together and there is no invitation to us to imagine them alone.

The role of Enobarbus, who hardly appears in Plutarch, is crucial here. Dramatically he is the confidant, unique in being the confidant of both lovers, as well as the candid friend and salty commentator. Typically, the role of confidant is naturalised by Shakespeare to the point where we feel that both lovers really do need him to inquire and consult with about each other. At the outset the matter is plainly put by Enobarbus, who is not, like most clever and cynical bystanders, seeing through the situation, but stating that there is no situation to see through:

ANT. She is cunning past man's thought.
ENO. Alack, sir, no. Her passions are made of
    nothing but the finest part of pure love. We
    cannot call her winds and waters sighs and tears:
    they are greater storms and tempests than
    almanacs can report. This cannot be cunning in
    her: if it be she makes a shower of rain as well
    as Jove.
ANT. Would I had never seen her!
ENO. O, sir, you had then left unseen a wonderful
    piece of work, which not to have been blest
    withal would have discredited your travel.
I. iii. 141ff.

'*Alack, sir, no. . . .*' That is just the trouble. If she were cunning past man's thought, as her original may well have been, and as in a distant and unamiable fashion she appears in Plutarch's account, there would, in one sense, be no problem. Antony would still be overcome by Caesar, but he would be overcome making use of her, and being used by her. Her not being cunning makes for the innocence and openness of their love that transforms the play. The play is what it is, and not like any other, because of this.

Dramatically, a cunning Cleopatra who redeemed herself in Antony's last days, coming to love him absolutely in his defeat and their *liebestod*, would be effective but also banal. Shakespeare was in any case no doubt content to give his audience the traditional figure they expected, the love's martyr of Chaucer and Gower and Garnier's *Marc Antoine*, which Sir Philip Sidney's sister had translated. What he added was his own kind of simplicity, which echoes the simplicity – and the tradition – in the handling of the two great Caesars. The presentment of them all is absolute and on the surface: there is nothing to find behind it. But the sublime simplicity of Cleopatra has its inimitable Shakespearean quality, and as we should expect it is that of the comedy sublime. At the beginning of the Actium campaign we have the perfect example of it. Antony is discussing with his general the reports of Caesar's swift progress:

ANT.   Is it not strange, Canidius,
    That from Tarentum and Brundusium
    He could so quickly cut the Ionian sea
    And take in Toryne? You have heard on't sweet?
CLEO. Celerity is never more admired
    Than by the negligent.

III. vii. 20–5

The intended put-down of that reply, its silliness and its self-possession, is impenetrable. An actress like Joyce Grenfell might do it justice, but she would not be able to play a straight Cleopatra, for Cleopatra never gives the faintest hint of parodying herself. If it were so she might indeed be cunning. The scene, just before Actium, is one of the most brilliant and compact in the whole play, opening with Cleopatra and Enobarbus alone together:

CLEO. I will be even with thee, doubt it not.
ENO. But why, why, why?
CLEO. Thou has forspoke my being in these wars,
    And sayst it is not fit.
ENO.   Well, is it, is it?

Enobarbus' exasperation, with its despairing repetitions, is an open and comic outcry of the powerlessness that Antony feels before both Cleopatra and Caesar. Critics have suggested that Shakespeare is inconsistent through his usual rapidity (or carelessness) and concentration on the scene rather than the play. Here is the politically steely Cleopatra who does not appear elsewhere? But surely Shakespeare has deftly substituted a Cleopatra determined not to leave Antony for a Plutarchan one who couldn't afford to let him out of her sight. The idea that the queen and her maids 'manage this war' is absurd, as everybody knows it to be, including Cleopatra herself: that is the point of her observation about celerity. It shows what a card she is, a 'great fairy' – it is just the sort of remark that Cleopatra *would* make. Her presence, we might note, divests every scene she is in of military and man-like seriousness: contrast with these scenes the ones – no less supple and brilliant – where Antony is alone in Italy with Caesar, Agrippa, Lepidus and the others. There the tone is genuinely businesslike – hard, watchful, courteous, dangerous. Antony there is holding his own in a real man's world.

Such a world of power is not of course any less inherently and humanly absurd than Cleopatra's world of feminine self-satisfaction. That is wonderfully suggested in the messenger's account of Antony's words for her, and when he spoke them:

> 'All the east,
> Say thou, shall call her mistress'. So he nodded,
> And soberly did mount an arm-gaunt steed,
> Which neighed so high that what I would have spoke
> Was beastly dumbed by him.
>
> I. v. 46–50

It has its animation, its triumphs and its poetry as well as the comedy which in Shakespeare is indivisible from these things, but it is basically as odious as the world of violence and intrigue must always be. The scene on board Pompey's galley, and the decency of its commander, does not obscure the fundamental truth of what he is tempted to do, and what his subsequent murder at the hands of the triumvirate shows he should have done.

But this realism does not extend to the later campaign scenes in which Cleopatra is present. There romance takes over, or rather the kind of feminine reality she represents, a reality none the less moving for being here shown as wholly powerless. All her influence can do is

to remove any kind of represented seriousness from the concluding acts
and battles. The skirmish outside Alexandria is portrayed in the play as
a last chance to recoup Antony's fortunes. In fact it was nothing of the
sort, a truth the play tacitly acknowledges in the dressing up for the
encounter and the banquet after it, as well as in Cleopatra's womanly
yearnings over Antony's challenge of Caesar to single combat (a
challenge which – to further compound our issue – he may well have
made in historical fact). She does not manage the wars, but her attentions have indeed effectively demoralised those who do, and it is true
that both in the play and the historical events behind it her mere
existence has made it impossible for Antony to come to terms with
Caesar.

It is her presence which makes it possible for this play to make a
virtue out of the artificiality of having battles take place just off-stage: a
battle in Cleopatra's vicinity automatically becomes a make-believe,
depriving of any conviction the masculine ploys which the play attempts
to represent. The business of battle is put on one side in a somewhat
similar, if less grand and touching, way at the end of *Julius Caesar*,
where the represented events at Philippi are transformed by parting and
the emotions of friendship – the farewells of Brutus and Cassius, and
the Roman friendship that can still be invoked between the conspirators, their victim, and his avengers.

'Here's sport indeed – how heavy weighs my lord?' This is the
reality which dominates and transforms the ending of the play, the
surrender of the whole issue to helplessness and childhood. The price
paid by the play is the impression that the disasters and imminent death
that bring the lovers so close are not quite real anyway, no more real in
terms of the play's imagination than they are in the necessary artifice of
enactment. For Plutarch as for Shakespeare a legend died with Antony,
the god Hercules forsaking him in music by night; and, taking the hint,
Shakespeare gives the play up to something like music, and its 'strong
toil of grace'. The transforming comedy truth of Cleopatra as 'no more
but e'en a woman' takes over, folding in its arms both the hero and the
heroine herself.

The departure of Enobarbus is significant here, for in spite of
Antony's final explosion after his last ships join the enemy it brings the
pair, as lovers, more helplessly together. 'Is Antony or we in fault for
this?' the queen had asked him at their last meeting alone, and the
query is dazed and child-like in the same way as Antony's own query
to his sardonic lieutenant a little later on, when Caesar has refused the

challenge to single combat. ' ''He will not fight with me, Domitius?'' ''No.'' ''Why should he not?'' ' It is the same note as the break in Antony's voice when he addresses her after the outburst of rage over Thidias – 'Cold-hearted toward me?' – to which her reply is the warmest, most enfolding she has yet given him:

> Ah, dear, if it be so,
> From my cold heart let heaven engender hail. . . .

To Antony's rhetorical indignation her reply has been 'Not know me yet?' – a question in which there is nothing wise or fathomless. Antony has never known her because he has been so insistent on his image of her as all-powerful queen of love and serpent of old Nile. But in that sense there is nothing to know. The query is the reverse of the species of telling stroke in tragedy which suddenly reveals a psychological truth. Such are Lady Macbeth's 'had he not resembled/My father as he slept. . . .' Hermione's cry to Oreste in Racine's *Andromaque* – 'Qui te l'a dit?' – when he has slain on her orders the man she loved; Clytemnestra's grief when told the lie that her son, whom she knows will try to kill her, is dead. Such a stroke of truth is the reverse of anything that will happen in *Antony and Cleopatra*. What moves as its tragedy is that only in dying will the pair be close to one another, but then they will be close indeed. Their weakness blurs all distinctions and brings them, at last, into a deep intimacy with the audience. They are no longer social types, living in Plutarch's larger-than-life world of the powerful and great. Her rhetoric of death turns again to a child's game as she gives instructions to Charmian:

> when thou hast done this chare, I'll give thee leave
> To play till doomsday. Bring our crown and all.

And it is with a child's idea of comfort that she remembers Antony in death:

> As sweet as balm, as soft as air, as gentle –
> O Antony – [*To the asp*] Nay, I will take thee too:
> What should I stay –

She is asleep before she can finish the sentence. Charmian completes it for her, and straightens her up like a nurse removing a toy: 'Your crown's awry./I'll mend it, and then play.' Fortune has followed them all, in its own way, throughout; as requested, the Soothsayer at the beginning told 'but a workday fortune'. To be sleepy is the proper end to a working-day.

CHAPTER 6

THE THING I AM
Coriolanus

Love is far from being the theme of *Coriolanus*, either in the moral tale of Plutarch or the tragedy which Shakespeare makes of it. But because it is not the subject of the play it has a considerable importance in it: Coriolanus could be said to be far more successful in the role of husband and lover than he is in that of soldier and statesman. That is not the point. And yet even in such a play as *Coriolanus*, in which consciousness and reflection are barely involved at all, things hidden or below the surface are still very much to the point. Except in one respect Coriolanus is the most public, the least solitary of Shakespeare's heroes, more so even than Antony, but he has one refuge, both from himself and from us. It is Virgilia his wife, his 'gracious silence'.

The scene in which he greets her has the pungent comedy that made Johnson merely remark, with his usual accuracy, that the play 'is one of the most amusing of our author's performances.' Coriolanus is returned to Rome from the exploit that has earned his honourable eponym.

ALL. Welcome to Rome, renowned Coriolanus!
COR. No more of this: it does offend my heart.
    Pray now, no more.
COM.   Look, sir, your mother!
COR.   O,
    You have, I know, petitioned all the gods
    For my prosperity.   [*Kneels*.
VOL.   Nay, my good soldier, up!
    My gentle Marcius, worthy Caius, and

> By deed-achieving honour newly named –
> What is it? – Coriolanus must I call thee?
> But, O, thy wife.
> COR.   My gracious silence, hail!
> Wouldst thou have laughed had I come coffined home
> That weep'st to see me triumph? Ah, my dear,
> Such eyes the widows in Corioli wear
> And mothers that lack sons.
>
> II. i. 158–70

Like everything in the play this reminds us of the gestures and
demeanours of an always well-filled stage. Like all men who back into
the limelight Coriolanus is genuinely embarrassed and miserable when
surrounded by an admiring crowd. He refuses to look at them, and his
senior colleague has to indicate that it is his mother who stands before
him. Volumnia's 'O' of recollection – what is a mere wife compared
with her own possession of her son? – makes her, in the text, as
audible as Lady Bracknell. But Coriolanus enters another world when
he turns to his wife, no longer the hero with downcast eyes or the
dutiful son of a Roman mother. What he says is remarkable for the
difference between the sentiment and the expression. The latter is
almost a speechless and private language, their intimate talk, just as her
loving silence and wet eyes themselves are. But the words he utters are
not exactly calculated to comfort her. She might herself be a widow,
and in the other town there are many of them, made so by this
husband of hers. But it is characteristic of something in this play, its
crowded world and unconsidered assumptions, that no one reflects on
the meaning or implications of what goes on in that world. And least of
all Virgilia. If she did, if she gave any impression of pitying those
widows or even being aware of them, she would not be the certain
refuge for her husband that she is.

For her it is enough that he is there, and it is the same for him. It is
for his mother to construct what she calls 'the buildings of my fancy',
to see her son as consul as well as conquering hero. She numbers his
wounds like achievements, the cups he has won in the battle of life.
Her tone, as she exults in her son's achievements before he enters, is
gloating, visionary, a little mad even. Both her prose statement and the
couplet that succeeds it are like exultant ruminations on the stage of
her own being, to which such action has been denied; the madness is in
our sense of the obsessional repetition, inside her, of fantasies like
these.

MEN. Hark! the trumpets.
VOL. These are the ushers of Marcius: before him he
  carries noise, and behind him he leaves tears.

>   Death, that dark spirit, in's nervy arm doth lie;
>   Which being advanced, declines, and then men die.
>   II. i. 148ff.

'Such eyes the widows in Corioli wear' seems an assertion of the same
kind – like mother like son – but in fact the tone is so different that
Coriolanus' words are more like a benediction, the conferring of a
secret innocence and freedom on himself in his wife's love. In this all
too public play such privacy seems an exculpation from the deeds of
public life. Coriolanus' escape here from the possession of his mother,
who unites personal will with public 'duty', seems unemphatic, taken
for granted almost. Such fleeting seconds of tenderness and privacy
occur also in the pungently 'amusing' scenes of *Troilus and Cressida*.
But in *Coriolanus* the caricature of a society at war – in all senses – and
the patterns of behaviour this gives rise to, has a Roman sobriety, is
both more comprehensive and more subtle.

The personalities of Menenius and the tribunes are as much formed
by such a society and its values as is that of Volumnia. The divided
nature of Coriolanus himself demonstrates its drives and its rigidities.
Both Menenius and Volumnia, in their different ways, depend on the
image of their own rock-solid conditioned prejudices which he seems to
embody. The supple Menenius is no less a confirmed aristocrat and
man of the right (the phrase actually occurs, though in reference to
'the right-hand file', the place of honour, rather than to the seating in
an assembly) because he knows how to shift and compromise, and has a
good conceit of his own compliance. But he has a genuine love for
Coriolanus: it is one of the most attractive things about him.

And indeed Coriolanus is lovable, except to his own mother, whose
egotism is proof against any capacity to be really aware of him as a
person. Even the hatred of Aufidius could be said to love what it
reluctantly admires, and both Cominius and Titus Lartius feel a great
and unenvious affection for their colleague. With characteristic
inaccuracy, and reliance on class-formula terms, the tribunes speak of
his 'pride'. What they mean, of course, is his inability to be other than
he is. Coriolanus would not be popular among his own peers, the
patricians, if he were touchy about his position, or proud of his ancestry
and achievements. He is not; his sense of his own position and his

contempt for the plebs, and for those who are all things to all men with them, is deep and instinctive. To them it looks like pride, just as their earthy good sense, home-loving habits, and reluctance to risk their lives for the city, even as they claim they *are* the city, appear to him as contemptible and disgusting baseness. The idea that there can be any accommodation between himself and these creatures seems to him cant and hypocrisy, fit only for politicians prepared to act a part.

Shakespeare here is portraying a kind of class inflexibility common in various ways in all ages and societies. It is even necessary, even beneficial: the self-respect of both parties may depend on it. But in the case of Coriolanus there is a further element, a personal element, which gives the case its particular individuality. Coriolanus is not touchy but he is deeply sensitive. The thought of acting a part, outside that of the man he is, really appals and terrifies him. His mother herself urges him, and that no doubt both induces him to try, and also deeply disquiets him, as if the foundations of his own self – 'the building of her fancy' – were being undermined by what had constructed them.

> I prithee now, sweet son, as thou hast said
> My praises made thee first a soldier, so,
> To have my praise for this, perform a part
> Thou hast not done before.
>
> III. ii. 107–10

Here is his own mother speaking of performing parts. His voice, which often has the edge of hysteria in it, does indeed seem to rise a couple of octaves as he replies:

> Away, my disposition, and possess me
> Some harlot's spirit! My throat of war be turned,
> Which quir'd with my drum, into a pipe
> Small as an eunuch or the virgin voice
> That babies lulls asleep. The smiles of knaves
> Tent in my cheeks, and schoolboys' tears take up
> The glasses of my sight. . . .
>   I will not do't,
> Lest I surcease to honour mine own truth,
> And my body's action teach my mind
> A most inherent baseness.
>
> III. ii. 111–17, 120–3

The combination of rigidity and insecurity is remarkably suggested in the notion of physical attitude producing its mental equivalent. In his hatred and fear of the natural facilities of the actor Coriolanus makes a not easy job for the man who is acting him, and this is part of the 'amusement' and irony in the play. The actor's capacity to make the part a 'moving' one is alienated by the nature of the part, and makes us realise how greatly, perhaps unconsciously, the tragedian relies in the creation of a part upon the image of the actor who is performing it. Shakespeare must certainly have seen Burbage as Hamlet, Macbeth, Othello. In Antony and Coriolanus, as to a lesser extent in Julius Caesar, the image of the actor, and the consciousness which he is bodying forth and making palpable, disappear: the rhetorician takes over. Coriolanus, and Timon who follows him, are paradoxical creations, heroes whose sense of themselves is so determined as to preclude any of the play of human variety and awareness which a good actor conducts and reveals, and transmits to the audience in the form of emotional depth and uncertainty.

Coriolanus refuses to act any part except the one he conceives to be his own, and he does not know how much that one has been entailed upon him by his mother. He can seek to become a Volscian and remain the same man, himself, his mother's son. That is the irony of his situation and his mother's too. His mother brought him up to be a Roman patrician in every sense of the term, but really she brought him up for herself alone, a 'building of her fancy'. It is logical that the result should be he can go over to the enemy, becoming, as it were, his own name, and remaining in the process more than ever himself. The boomerang effect of his mother's upbringing means that he can detach himself from the very principles that upbringing was supposed to inculcate – hearth, home, patriotism, public spirit, social belonging-ness. Instead of a Roman she has created such a true product of her egocentric will that he can 'stand/As if a man were author of himself/And knew no other kin.'

Because he is so entirely the creation of his mother he is also at an unnatural distance from her, the distance at last between Corioli and Rome.

> This fellow had a Volscian to his mother;
> His wife is in Corioli, and his child
> Like him by chance.

Her whole long rhetorical speech is shot through with comedy, much of which is evidently not apparent to her, but it is forceful and moving too, and as ingenious in argument as Menenius himself – indeed the

affinity between the pair, in terms of class and outlook, is brought out
by the crises that lead first to the banishment of Coriolanus and then to
his march on Rome. Yet there is inflexibility in her candour:

> There's no man in the world
> More bound to's mother, yet here he lets me prate
> Like one i'th'stocks.

Both are in the stocks in terms of their ability to approach each other,
yet it does not seem to strike the old lady that it was precisely because
he was so bound to her that he is now leading the army of Corioli on
Rome. He has not escaped *her*, but he has no trouble in abandoning
Rome and banishing his fellow-citizens, and that he can do so is very
largely her own doing.

The climax of *Coriolanus* is by far the most important one in the
Roman or Plutarchan plays, and perhaps anywhere in Shakespeare. The
killing of Caesar merely divides the play, but the clemency of
Coriolanus to Rome, and the scene that leads up to it, draws all the
bustle of the play together to its still point. As a *coup de théâtre* it can
scarcely fail, and an actor like Olivier can make it one of the most
impressive moments of the canon. That being said, it is still not easy to
see just what are, by Shakespearean standards, the inner pressures and
logic of the event. Artistically Coriolanus is effective from his
simplicity, though it is simplicity of a decidedly tormented kind. What
exactly is that 'happens' to him at the climactic moment? A
formalist explanation would be simply that the scene and staging
require him at this moment to yield to the women and spare the city;
and although that type of criticism seldom produces illumination in the
Shakespearean context, it must be admitted here to have its point.
Certainly there is nothing here of the logic and the inwardness of the
Macbeth situation: Coriolanus has no dramatised consciousness,
neither has he Antony's helpless flow of awareness.

We must judge by externals. Something persuades him; and gives
him for a few moments a stillness which seems the reflection of sudden
self-awareness; this pause stands out against all the frenzy of activity
and obsession in the play. It is the closest he comes to Timon's
yearning for another world than this which has failed him, or Antony's
yielding to the child-like consolations of failure, the gentleness of death.
These three last heroes of Shakespearean tragedy are all seen externally,
but something unexpected is glimpsed in and by all of them, something
incongruous with their sense of themselves and the roles they have

chosen. In all cases it is a kind of weakness, that waits outside Antony both as lover and commander, Timon as magnificent man and misanthrope, Coriolanus as strong self and self-avenger.

Coriolanus' moment of weakness, and understanding of it, is brief and soon reversed. But he has seen in himself what the plebeians know and accept about themselves, that they are not heroes but men who would live – 'singing in their shops and going/About their functions friendly'. He recognises, though, just how 'unnatural' for himself such recognition is. And he recognises that such unnaturalness, such incongruity, makes men absurd and the gods laugh. His frozen, sardonic speech, when it comes, will not admit what he has seen in himself. Instead he devotes his perception to the point where he can still take comfort: that this decision is highly dangerous to himself, as dangerous as the moment when he attacked the town of Corioli singlehanded:

> The gods look down, and this unnatural scene
> They laugh at. O my mother, mother. O
> You have won a happy victory to Rome.
> But for your son – believe it, O believe it,
> Most dangerously you have with him prevailed,
> If not most mortal to him. But let it come.
>
> V. iii. 184–9

For once he seems to be talking with an authority which is really his own, instead of the violence habitual to him, entailed on him by the maternal inheritance. The scene, as he seems to record, is indeed unnatural, and in more than one way. For the mother to kneel to the child is so, and this reversal we have seen in its most moving form in *King Lear*, but it is worse for Coriolanus that he should yield to persuasion; and perhaps worst of all that his wife, his 'gracious silence', should now bring that silence itself to bear upon him. His private refuge with her is violated, his feeling about her forced out into the open. The famous stage direction in the Folio – 'holds her by the hand, silent' – almost certainly indicates a carefully engineered effect on the author's part, and the idea of silence here is touchingly ironical. It is his mother who is silent (at last) and whose hand he holds, but her final resort to stillness ('I am hushed until our city be afire/And then I'll speak a little') implies that it is his wife he is attending to, and in a sense privately pleading with. Vigorous and rational though they are, his mother's pleadings have been too much like his own outbursts of emotion and action – 'before him he carries noise, and behind him he leaves tears.' Her pride in her soldier son does not, of course, extend to his behaving like this to his own country. His dementia is, notwithstanding, a logical consequence of her attitudes, and can make anarchic and terrifying the kind of madness that in her is wholly respectable.

However tough and open and extrovert the play may seem, it is also very Shakespearean in its suggestion of a hidden dimension, to which references are few but of a special significance. At this climax the protective, liberating silence of his wife seems to coincide and come together with the prescriptive tyranny of his mother. It is a conjunction that might unnerve a lesser man than Coriolanus, and its impact shows how 'human' he really is. He speaks with the voice of a lost man, for though he has always rushed into danger it has never been a conscious decision. Now he can see clearly what his decision means.

Despite the force of the climax the internal drama itself remains quite unemphatic – think what Racine would make of the whole emotional situation, and particularly the decision of Coriolanus to return to his adopted town, that of his wife and mother to persuade him to spare the city, even though it means his death at the hands of his new allies. In Shakespeare all is blurred by incongruity: nothing is quite certain. We may imagine the hero in his own way exalted by what he has done, and the knowledge of what will come to pass in consequence. At last he is his own man, as his measured accents declare. He, and he alone, is in command of the situation. In persuading her son the mother has shot her bolt at last:

> COR. Aufidius, though I cannot make true wars,
>   I'll frame convenient peace. Now, good Aufidius,
>   Were you in my stead, would you have heard
>   A mother less? or granted less, Aufidius?
> AUF. I was moved withal.
> COR.   I dare be sworn you were.
>   V. iii. 190–4

But at the same time the bitterness in his words is as total as it is calm. No more the hot fury and intemperate rage at all that crossed him. He can no longer make true war but he can make convenient peace, a compromise peace, a reconcilement so that the Volscians may say 'this mercy we have shown,' and the Romans, 'this we received.' What could be better, and what could be less like him? His revenge on the

Roman people – and Coriolanus is a revenge hero as much as Hamlet is – has ended in joyous notes of relief where 'the shouting Romans/Make the sun dance.'

Hamlet may really surrender the matter to providence – 'The readiness is all. Let be.' Coriolanus says 'Let it come,' but he will not only go to meet it, he will play the game out to the end. For now what he thought of as himself and his honour are totally compromised. To get his revenge on Rome by means of Corioli he has had to shift and palter, to be sedulous in ways that he could not have borne to use in order to become consul in Rome. Aufidius has seen it, and for the good of his country has buttoned up his own pride and let himself be worked on:

> AUF. He watered his new plants with dews of flattery,
>   Seducing so my friends; and to this end
>   He bowed his nature, never known before
>   But to be rough, unswayable and free.
>
> V. vi. 23–6

Now the great soldier hopes 'to purge himself with words'. His speech to the Volscian Senate is too glib to convince: it sounds disingenuous. Aufidius has for a long time been a keen theoretical student of his character, a fact deliberately emphasised in the private exchange with the lieutenant (IV. vii. 35–55). And Aufidius, all the better a psychologist because he knows he can never be so effective and charismatic a general as his rival, knows also that people don't change, that Coriolanus is Coriolanus still and can be undone by the fact when the right moment comes. That moment of freedom was illusory. Aufidius kept his counsel at the gates of Rome, but he learnt just the right word to use at the right moment. 'Name not the god, thou boy of tears,' he advises, when Coriolanus invokes Mars. The ensuing explosion is everything he could have hoped for.

The artifice of tragedy formalises and gives shape and being to incoherent and anguished states of mind. The process is exploited as much in the case of Antony as of Macbeth, though in a different way. But in *Coriolanus* states of mind are communal and familial, men in debate in the street or office, or in the field, women gossiping and sewing together. By comparison the familiarity of Cleopatra and her maids seems stylised, deliberately set against the splendours of imperial power. There is nothing mysterious or exclusive about Virgilia, the gracious silence who suggests a kind of sweetness and privacy in the life of the hero, and whose influence in the climactic scene may be more decisive than that of the mother. For all her shyness and her virtue Virgilia is just a Roman lady among other ladies. In the vivacious scene where the news is received of Coriolanus' imminent and victorious return, and the letters he sent are discussed, she says to Menenius: 'Yes, certain, there's a letter for you. I saw't.' And though the text is uncertain, it seems she is as hot against the tribunes ('He'd make an end of thy posterity') as are her mother-in-law and Menenius. Virgilia is not singled out by the play, any more than anyone else is. Her relation with her husband remains invisible, just as does, in its different way, his relation with his mother.

The play as play ignores these, concerning itself with humans in their social relations, the relations of *amour propre* and dignity, honour and policy, what persons of all classes feel they owe to themselves. Self-importance is a universal characteristic and a comical one: it is ironic that only Coriolanus seems free of its most obvious symptoms. His mother, Menenius and the tribunes have it in abundance, as do plebeians and senators alike. Their own sense of self-importance gives them the knowledge and the capacity to compromise with that of others. 'Your dishonour', says the hero in disgust to his senatorial colleagues,

> Mangles true judgment and bereaves the state
> Of that integrity which should become it,
> Not having the power to do the good it would
> For the ill which doth control't.
>
> III. i. 158–61

These lines, as we shall see, are perhaps the strongest argument in the play for Brecht's view of Coriolanus as a Fascist politician and leader. The obsession with 'integrity' in the state is typical of a dedicated tyrant, that of a Robespierre or a Lenin as much as a Hitler, who scorns the instinctive leaning of the merely self-important towards those 'ills' which give the state not integrity indeed, but flexibility and freedom. The immediate dramatic point is that Coriolanus is wholly absorbed in the business of the state as he sees it, an absorption that makes him unique in Shakespearean tragedy. An integrity passionate and articulate, fellowing the speechless one of his wife, makes him the husband who utters the most moving of his speeches in the play:

Now, by the jealous queen of heaven, that kiss
I carried from thee, dear, and my true lip
Hath virgined it e'er since.

V. iii. 46–8

But it also makes him the most dangerous of leaders. The tribunes
realise this, as in their confused fashion do the plebs. The tribunes'
stratagem conveys no more than the truth when they attribute their
own distrust to the people: 'And this shall seem, as partly 'tis, their
own/Which we have goaded onward.'

It is ironic that his mother, in making her son the building of her
fancy, has produced in him an integrity she does not possess herself.
Her possessive fantasy of him does not contain her own caution and
good sense. As well as integrity it has given him the overwhelming
impatience which, when he advances on the city, alarms so much his
family and friends:

COM.   He said 'twas folly,
    For one poor grain or two, to leave unburnt
    And still to nose th'offence.
MEN.   For one poor grain or two!
    I am one of those; his mother, wife, his child,
    And this brave fellow too, we are the grains.

V. i. 26–30

It is the same kind of undistinguishing haste which caused him in
captured Corioli to remember the man there who had helped him, but
then to forget his name when his officers ask it in order that the man
may be released. This touch, invented by Shakespeare and not in
Plutarch, is typical of the general atmosphere of public life in the play,
as is the wily professionalism of the tribunes, counselling the people to
lay the blame on them for their initial acceptance of Coriolanus as
consul. Such a subterfuge goes hand in hand with an understanding of
the other great rule of public life, as expressed by one of the tribunes:

                    Sir, the people
    Must have their voices; neither will they bate
    One jot of ceremony.

II. ii. 37–9

Shakespeare here goes to the real heart of the power struggle
and shows the role played in its confrontations and resolutions by

self-respect and self-approval. The question 'Whose side is Shake-speare on?', often asked in the past, and given today the standard answer 'Neither side, of course,' is in fact more irrelevant even than that answer implies. For the play shows the complex comedy of public behaviour, in which *both* sides make the same kind of assumptions and depend on the same modes of thinking well of oneself and one's attitudes. Shakespeare's art both profoundly and amusingly imagines for us the ways in which public man is always playing a part, the part that gives him the best conceit of himself. It is founded on his observa-tion of the English society of his time and is equally true of English society today, as we can see in television interviews, in the ritual battles of parties, unions, and vested interests of all kinds, and in the degree of real but hidden intimacy between the combatants, Ultimately they all speak the same language.

But Coriolanus does not. The interesting thing is that he refuses the degree of self-knowledge, and self-indulgence, that goes with public behaviour.

> And so much knowledge of ourselves there lies
> Cored, after all, in our complacencies.

Leigh Hunt is writing of 'ourselves' as fixers, pretenders, adjusters of the art of the possible, keepers of the domestic and public peace. Of course politicians do not take themselves quite seriously. But for Coriolanus not to do so would be impossible: he would disappear in a puff of dust. He cannot bear to look at himself and accept there the absurdity of being ordinarily human. It would mean the end of that dreadful absolute which only exists in vision – his mother's vision – and not in reality. 'Death, that dark spirit, in's nervy arm doth lie.' Death for others and for himself. That is the tragedy of Coriolanus. But even at his climactic moment he is not an awe-inspiring tragic figure or anything like one. However much he hates it he *has* to compound with himself on the public stage and cut the same sort of figure as Menenius and the tribunes. Comedy does not release him, but it shows him as more touching in his own infirmity, more exceptional in every way, than those others. He is seen in the way that Antony and Timon are seen.

Brecht was more than usually perverse in his reading of the play, and in his own adaptation, *Coriolan*. For *Coriolanus* is a domestic play, an intimate play; it is not a drama of ideology and debate, such as the theatre since Schiller has accustomed us to, nor has it the responsibili-

ties and organisational themes of Shakespeare's own history plays and
of the scene which is probably his in *Sir Thomas More*, a scene with
resemblances to Menenius' fable of the belly. Brecht's play is boring
and predictable, but the worst thing about it is that it utterly lacks the
humour which is so essential a part of Shakespeare's. Coriolan is a
Fascist leader, a demogogue who despises the people but makes use of
them to pursue his own fantasy of conquest and the corporate state. In
practice, and in history, the Fascist and Nazi leaders were closely in
touch with the people, who shared many of their own prejudices and
resentments; but, apart from that, Brecht's play, in its doctrinaire
exposition of class conflict, misses an even more fundamental and
universal truth depicted in Shakespeare's – that of class resemblances.

For Coriolanus is an exceptional individual and the tragedy lies in his
individuality, not in his status as a representative of his class. He is
isolated from all the social roles that cut across class boundaries and
require their own particular reassurance in the gambits of independence
that make up self-respect. Whatever the group, he is 'not a man of
their infirmity'. The scenes in which the plebeians, inclined in a baffled
way to fair-mindedness, respond when he is forced to appeal to them for
the consulship, are exquisitely ludicrous:

> So, if he tell us his noble deeds, we must also tell him our
> noble acceptance of them. Ingratitude is monstrous; and for the
> multitude to be ingrateful, were to make a monster of the
> multitude; of the which we being members should bring
> ourselves to be monstrous members.
>
> II. iii. 8ff.

Noble deeds require a noble acceptance: one kind of self-respect makes
its bow to another, and Third Citizen shows in this not only generosity
but a very proper kind of wisdom. The people can share collectively in
these achievements by congratulating themselves on them, as the
general public in England congratulated itself on having won the Battle
of Britain. Third Citizen feels that a *quid pro quo* is in order, and that
honour is satisfied with a display of mutual 'nobility': for the plebeians
stood up to 'them' over the issue of free corn. And he combines
dignity with frankness:

3 CIT. You must think, if we give you anything, we
hope to gain by you.
COR. Well then, I pray, your price o'th' consulship?

1 CIT. The price is, to ask it kindly.

COR. Kindly! Sir, I pray, let me ha't. I have wounds
　to show you, which shall be yours in private.
　Your good voice, sir. What say you?

2 CIT. You shall ha't, worthy sir.

COR. A match, sir. There's in all two worthy voices
　begged. I have your alms. Adieu!

3 CIT. But this is something odd.

2 CIT. And 'twere to give again – but 'tis no matter.

II. iii. 70ff.

The people set store by appearances and are deeply shocked by uncere-
monious behaviour. Though they can easily be taken for a ride by a
scurvy politician nothing makes them more suspicious than a manner
which seems too obviously to be taking them for one, though their
reactions here are not unanimous:

2 CIT. 　　　　　　　　To my poor unworthy notice,
　He mocked us when he begged our voices,

3 CIT. 　　　　　　　　　　　　　　　Certainly
　He flouted us downright.

1 CIT. No, 'tis his kind of speech: he did not mock us.

II. iii. 154–7

This 'kind of speech' is more vigorous, to the point of the frenetic,
than any other in the tragedies, and at the same time wholly abstract,
lacking even the metaphor of tone. More than Antony or Brutus, even
Timon, Coriolanus seems to mean what he says. He is not producing
rhetoric for his side, like Ulysses, but speaks of the tribune with a
staccato and impersonal intensity:

　　　　　　　　　　　　If he have power,
　　　Then vail your ignorance; if none, awake
　　　Your dangerous lenity. If you are learned,
　　　Be not as common fools; if you are not,
　　　Let them have cushions by you. You are plebeians
　　　If they be senators: and they are no less,
　　　When, both your voices blended, the great'st taste
　　　Most palates theirs.

III. i. 97–104

In a mouth aroused to passion Shakespeare's later style is often graphic in its compressed syntax and compacted metaphor; but here the common picture provided by metaphor is absent: one feels his hearers know all too well what he is saying but the way he speaks puts him on a quite different wavelength. The words show how impossible the idea of accommodation is for Coriolanus. Those 'ifs' proclaim absolute alternatives: bow down before them your foolishness that gave them power, if they already have it, and, if they don't have it yet, arouse your suicidal softness to action before they have. The instinct of the tribunes is right: there is nothing to be done with Coriolanus in political terms. His speech is as nervy as his arm, in which death lies. It is illuminating to compare such a speech with that of Claudius in *Hamlet*:

> But, you must know, your father lost a father,
> That father lost, lost his, and the survivor bound
> In filial obligation for some term
> To do obsequious sorrow. . . .
>
> I. ii. 89–92

The syntax is intricate, but the intricacy is subtle and accommodating, the clarity pacific, the tone confident of encountering the same sweet reason that it states.

The comedy *au fond* in *Coriolanus* is in its reassertion of human weakness and the tolerations it needs, a variation on the theme of *Antony and Cleopatra*, and of the Roman plays in general. Coriolanus is human, after all, and in his humanity even resembles those whom he so passionately needs to despise. Even the tribunes resemble him in some ways. They are so intent upon their own fief and its welfare that they do not want to hear about the possibility of foreign invasion, and like politicians of the Left in all ages ignore the idea of defence because it does not suit themselves and their constituents. Even when the news of invasion comes they refuse to believe it:

> BRU.   It cannot be
> The Volsces dare break with us.
> MEN.   Cannot be!
> We have record that very well it can,
> And three examples of the like hath been
> Within my age.
>
> IV. vi. 48–52

When the news is confirmed Brutus exclaims 'Would half my wealth would buy this for a lie!' This is the first we have heard that he, the watchdog for the people, is a rich man, and we may remember that Coriolanus refused his share of the spoils in Corioli. But the most significant intrusion of amusement, and the indulgence to human frailty that goes with it in Shakespeare, is the encounter of Menenius with the two sentries at the Volscian camp, when he goes on his fruitless errand to persuade Coriolanus to relent. Like most such scenes in the play it is Shakespeare's own, not found in Plutarch. Menenius is gratified by the general feeling that he can pull it off if anyone can. It is just a question of finding the right moment:

> He was not taken well; he had not dined.
> The veins unfilled, our blood is cold, and then
> We pout upon the morning, are unapt
> To give or to forgive; but when we have stuffed
> These pipes and these conveyances of our blood
> With wine and feeding, we have suppler souls. . . .
>   V. i. 50–5

Indomitable in comic defeat, Menenius gives the sentries as good as he gets, but we can feel what a blow to him it is that his name and title go for nothing.

1 SENTRY. Now, sir, is your name Menenius?
2 SENTRY. 'Tis a spell, you see, of much power.
    You know the way home again.
1 SENTRY. Do you hear how we are shent for keeping
    your greatness back?
                                        V. ii. 91ff.

Menenius cannot believe that the 'old boy net' will not somehow still function, that Coriolanus will not still acknowledge him on terms, as it were, of class solidarity. But Coriolanus has 'forbad all names'.

> He was a kind of nothing, titleless,
> Till he had forged himself a name i' th' fire
> Of burning Rome.
>   V. i. 12–14

The comic downfall of Menenius is a little like that of Parolles in *All's Well That Ends Well*, and he recovers himself in the same key. The title of the comedy is significant, for the failure of Menenius here is a prelude to the success of the ladies the next day. Reason and compromise, 'jaw jaw' instead of 'war war', are the keynote of both, so that 'honour and policy, like unsevered friends', can 'grow together'. Coriolanus, like Malvolio or Don John, is excluded from the happy ending of the play, and a tragic postscript is added that has no connection with the spirit of that ending, just as the hero himself feels no connection, barely even at the play's climax, with the human world he has had to inhabit. That world will always be an 'unnatural scene' to him, and his capitulation to it a deed that the gods will laugh at, as the denizens of *Twelfth Night* laugh at Malvolio. The figure who must be tragic is defeated in Coriolanus by society's instinct for the processes of comedy. He is the victim of the process and so are the wife and mother who have to undo him. The play cannot let us hear more of them, even in their Roman triumph which is also a personal tragedy. But all the tragedy in *Coriolanus* is personal, intimate, almost invisible: intent only on the social and political dialogue, callous comedy ignores that undervoice and therefore itself becomes unconsciously terrible. An example is the amusement over the son of Coriolanus, and his activities. That is Shakespeare's invention, and it goes with the fact that Coriolanus is destroyed in the background after a climax, however 'unnatural' a one, of comedy rejoicing. Brecht preferred a more natural as well as a more 'tragic' ending: his Coriolan ignores all pleas and sacks Rome.

CHAPTER 7

TRAGEDY AND CONSCIOUSNESS

Hamlet

Three of Shakespeare's tragedies – *Hamlet*, *Othello* and *Macbeth* – share as masterpieces a common impact: they all enter and possess the mind and instantly become a part of it. Indeed, immensely realistic as they are, they seem to take place in an area of thinking, feeling and suffering that has taken over from life, in the same way that the area of the play has taken over, while it is in progress, from the lives of the audience.

This sense of entrance into mental being, rather than into a world of action and suffering, distinguishes these plays from *King Lear*, or the Roman plays, or the history plays. Those plays can be watched and enjoyed in a much more detached spirit. There is no detachment with *King Lear*, but no growth and spreading of awareness either: the silence of Cordelia parallels the way the king is reduced to a foolish fond old man, Lear's shadow.

Macbeth and Hamlet find themselves in a position which leaves them nothing but their own reflections on the nature of life. Life becomes impossible for them but consciousness remains, and tragedy is expressed in its clarity and its poetry. *Othello* is also a tragedy of consciousness, but in a different sense. Consciousness is split between the two main characters, Othello and Iago, and shared only by the audience. The audience is aware of Othello's mind and it is also aware of Iago's, two separate entities, though locked together in the dramatic relation that determines the play. Consciousness in *Othello* does not appear to determine the tragic nature of life, as it does in the other two plays, but it reveals the equivocal world of love, the worlds of love and lust, of high romantic emotion and animal passion.

There is nothing fragile about consciousness in *Hamlet* and *Macbeth*. It can dare do anything, feel anything, think anything. Both Hamlet and Macbeth are wholly at home in the situation which the play has wished upon them; they are as acquainted with it 'as the tanned galley slave is with his oar'; their familiarity with it extends to ourselves; with them we sup full of horrors to the point where a kind of relaxation sets in. Consciousness becomes fully aware of everything that it has made for itself, everything that is in store for it, and in the context of the tragic action our sense of this intimacy, this *ease* almost, in the stretch and depth of awareness, has all the amplitude and leisure unique to Shakespearean dramatic art.

But in *Othello* there is something furtive about consciousness itself. It lurks, as if there were some monster in it too hideous to be known. As indeed there is. In Hamlet and Macbeth awareness does not flinch from where it finds itself and what it has to do. The freedom of the mind, those thoughts that wander through eternity, are not afraid of the mind's restless ecstasy:

> My thought whose murder yet is but fantastical,
> Shakes so my single state of man that function
> Is smothered in surmise, and nothing is
> But what is not.

For Hamlet and Macbeth the events of the world have become what is going on in their minds, and the two merge together. In *Othello* what is present in the mind is unadmitted or unrecognised, or concealed:

> Who has that breast so pure
> But some uncleanly apprehension
> Keeps leets and law-days and in sessions sit
> With meditations lawful?

>   III. iii. 142–5

Iago takes it for granted that nasty things go on in the mind which it prefers not to know about and yet cannot stop happening. This is the atmosphere of the mind in *Othello*, an appropriate one, for in much of the play the mind is a place to be avoided.

No wonder what may happen makes the structure of the play fragile, for the mind – a place here better left alone – is to be filled with hatefulness and suspicion. Neither Hamlet nor Macbeth have their minds poisoned. His father's ghost indicates as much to Hamlet: 'Taint not thy mind, nor let thy soul contrive/Against thy mother aught.' And it is a striking thing that even when Hamlet accuses his mother and uses expressions of disgust about her relations with his uncle, his mind does not seem 'tainted', but rather emancipated into a fuller range of human experience. Macbeth's ambition, the wish to become king, makes us enter into him not as murderer and usurper but as a man beset with an absolute problem, the problem not of what to do, but how to live with the consequences of doing it. We enter the consciousness of Hamlet on the same absolute terms, as if the problem that confronted him had released all of his mind into our keeping and understanding.

With Hamlet and Macbeth the consciousness is generalised, universalised, by the specific problem, but this does not happen in the case of Othello. Othello's consciousness in the beginning is too free, too relaxed, to engage our own with the same paradoxical freedom that we share in that exile from ordinary living of Hamlet and Macbeth. And Othello's increasing agony cripples and constricts his mind, taints it, and ours with it. Or might do, if we didn't avoid the process by putting ourselves outside Othello. But where is 'outside' him? That is the problem, for outside Othello's consciousness is Iago's, which might seem to dominate the rest of the play, in a sense to *be* the play, for the audience is compelled to share its activities and superiorities, of which the decisive one is the ability to transform Othello's own consciousness. Iago, as everyone recognises, takes over Othello, and at the decisive point of the action, the point that corresponds to Macbeth's realisation that he is going to murder Duncan, or to Hamlet's realisation that the task laid upon him has severed his relations with his developing self.

Mind dominates *Othello*, but it is not, as in the other two plays, the hero's own mind. And yet neither is it Iago's. The inner drama of Othello lies in the tension between the two, from which the audience is in one sense excluded. But in one sense only. There is not the single freedom, the single intellectual being, in which Hamlet and Macbeth live out their dramatic lives. But instead there is a contrast between two kinds of mind, incarnated in two types of being. Othello and Iago are both instantly understood, not only in terms of their dramatic relation but as kinds of being which are incompatible with each other, yet complementary. All minds contain an Othello and Iago, and the intellectual being of the play places the two in alliance as well as in conflict.

In these plays two factors combine to give them their peculiar atmosphere and mark them out from the other tragedies. One is the use of concealment: the other the further dimensions of meaning which lie behind the phenomenon of concealment, and are revealed by the dramatic exploitation of it. Consciousness in Macbeth and Hamlet develops as an aspect of conspiracy and concealment. It is important to remember that Hamlet begins the play as an unaffectedly open and candid person, a noble and spirited equivalent of the candid man in a comedy setting who must speak his mind, as Iago does, as Enobarbus does. In *King Lear* Kent is put down by Cornwall as such a fellow

> Who, having been praised for bluntness, doth affect
> A saucy roughness, and constrains the garb
> Quite from his nature.
>
> II. ii. 91–3

It is the dramatic type given most subtlety and scope – though still as a type – by Molière in his portrayal of Alceste in *Le Misanthrope*. In *Hamlet* this openness is high-spirited and instinctive:

> Seems, madam! Nay, it is. I know not 'seems'.
> 'Tis not alone my inky cloak, good mother,
> Nor customary suits of solemn black. . . .
> Together with all forms, moods, shapes of grief,
> That can denote me truly. These indeed seem,
> For they are actions that a man might play. . . .
>
> I. i. 76–8, 82–4

At this point we have a highly intriguing contrast between the idiom of King Claudius – suave, pacific, effortlessly cordial and yet formidably fluent – and the lack of any idiom which characterises the openness of Hamlet. For Hamlet to have to hold his tongue is a real penance, if not enough to break his heart; and the feeling that he must do so, in spite of his own nature, makes for the charged atmosphere of the first court scene. The psychological naturalism is instantly established by the audience's sense of a reversal of roles: Hamlet is naturally 'remiss, most generous and free from all contriving', but these qualities are now occluded in him; while the deviousness of Claudius comes out as an open and engaging authority and common sense.

The open man finds something bothering him which he can't be open about: the close man – Claudius – finds it possible to expand in a seeming sunshine of general accord. It is this paradox that gives its disturbing atmosphere to the Danish court. The popular young prince is paralysed, while the inauspicious king deals effectively with the crisis.

The most convincing thing about Hamlet, as we first meet him, is the directness and naïvety of his responses. The man who hears of, and then encounters, his father's ghost, is the man who greets Marcellus and Barnardo – unknown and junior officers – with instant and total courtesy. This instinctual behaviour is not put on – the audience knows that at once – and one might compare the feel of it with that no less engaging parade of courtesy put on by Cassio in *Othello*. Hamlet has it as to the manner born.

No less immediate is the astonishment of Hamlet at what the ghost tells him, in tone as spontaneous as the amazement with which he first heard of it from Horatio and the others:

> HAM.   I would I had been there.
> HOR. It would have much amazed you.
> HAM. Very like, very like. Stayed it long?
> HOR. While one with moderate haste might tell a hundred.
> MAR., BAR. Longer, longer.
> HOR. Not when I saw't.
> HAM. His beard was grizzled, no?
>
>   I. ii. 234–9

The art of all these exchanges is to suggest the directness and simplicity of consciousness, coming up against two things that are cunningly combined: the reality of lies and concealment, and the story that merely suspends disbelief, the story of the play. Hamlet, as consciousness, is amazed by the story he finds himself in. The plausibility of his uncle is not that of a villain, but of a man whose energy and capability have indeed not 'herein barred/Your better wisdoms which have freely gone/With this affair along.' Hamlet dislikes him, and is repelled by the thought of his mother married to him, and in such haste, but this again is a part of his instinctual forthrightness and simplicity. The amazement, in which Hamlet's consciousness begins, is to find that his genial, though to him repulsive, uncle really is a villain, and that concealment and subterfuge lie all about him.

Even so he cannot quite believe it. Perhaps it is 'a damned ghost' that he has seen? But nothing can be the same. His excellent good friends, Rosencrantz and Guildenstern, have been 'sent for' – they are all part of the concealment conspiracy, and so too is Ophelia, to whom he had been so straightforwardly attached. The attachment now takes such an eccentric form that it is interpreted as love-madness by those who are spying on him and trying to divine his motives. Ophelia too is concealing something – or is she? Her fright and uncertainty are part of the nightmare, for the onlooker a pathetic part, but for Hamlet they are sinister aspects of the deception that is all around him.

In these three plays concealment is the agent of consciousness, or the agency to make it visible. The dramatic idea of it is naturalised, we might say, almost as the dramatic function of death is naturalised at the end of *King Lear*, with the death of Cordelia. Macbeth discovers consciousness through concealment, and the onlooker participates in it with him. Intimacy is the greater because Macbeth has the forces of deception in himself, they are not outside him, and the onlooker is with him and them inside. Like Hamlet, Macbeth feels incredulity at what is happening, amazement at the extension of himself which is suddenly implicit, specifically and urgently implicit in King Duncan's comment.

> There's no art
> To find the mind's construction in the face.
> He was a gentleman on whom I built
> An absolute trust.
>
> I. iv. 11–14

Othello might also have uttered lines like those. Iago was a gentleman on whom he built an absolute trust, and his incredulity is both more explosive and more predictable. But Iago is not really a concealed man, for the onlooker knows all about him. Claudius is not known in this sense: in the tactics of *Hamlet* there is only a formal emphasis on seeming one thing and being quite another. In fact Claudius, like Hamlet himself, is constructed on the principle of diversity and contrast in behaviour and in the impression he makes. He has good and bad impulses, is capable of love as of treachery. Yet conscience for him has a single meaning only, the meaning that stems directly from appearance and pretence:

> POL [*to Ophelia*].　　　Read on this book,
> That show of such an exercise may colour
> Your loneliness. We are oft to blame in this,
> 'Tis too much proved, that with devotion's visage
> And pious action we do sugar o'er
> The devil himself.
> KING [*aside*]. O, 'tis too true.
> How smart a lash that speech doth give my conscience!
>
> III. i. 44–50

This is not the sense in which Hamlet says that 'conscience does make cowards of us all.' Hamlet is there uttering commonplaces suggested by the idea of death and suicide. Consciousness is the great enemy of death because it recognises itself and death, in some paradoxical way, as being closely akin. The consciousness that fills *Hamlet* is a tragic consciousness, a sense of tragedy needing no more than the freedom into which the plot has released it. The sense of mind is also the sense of death. Milton, as I remarked earlier, was almost certainly thinking both of this speech of Hamlet's, and of Claudio's speech on death in *Measure for Measure*, when he makes Belial reflect on this aspect of mind at the debate of the fallen angels in *Paradise Lost*:

> For who would lose
> Though full of pain, this intellectual being,
> These thoughts that wander through eternity,
> To perish rather, swallowed up and lost
> In the wide womb of uncreated night,
> Devoid of sense and motion.

Belial is as 'unworthy' as Hamlet feels himself to be, as Claudio is for his sister Isabella when he voices the fear of death which flesh and mind are heir to; and which in these tragedies of Shakespeare serves above all 'to make us feel existence', in Keats's words. Both Hamlet and Macbeth are in one sense perfectly commonplace characters, whose consciousness is universal, a general manifestation of being, intensified only by the dramatic setting.

Their special predicaments only serve to reveal it, and to reveal their resemblance to each other. Macbeth is an impostor, a pretender with a false face; Hamlet is 'free from all contriving'. But Hamlet's 'antic disposition' and Macbeth's 'false face' both serve in practice to ensure their sincerity with us, their closeness to us. It is worth noting, in this connection, that the antic disposition does not seem intended to be very effective, certainly not by the standards of deception that Iago will maintain. Its dramatic function is to draw attention to Hamlet, to make his conduct disquieting, his alarming candour as evident as a Fool's. Macbeth's deception is equally ineffective as such; both Banquo and Macduff have suspicions at once; but what is more important, Lady Macbeth helps to give at the start an instant intimacy in duplicity with her husband: 'Your face, my thane, is as a book where men/May read strange matters.' To the onlooker too Macbeth is 'my thane', and his mind and heart a book. Moreover the onlooker can soon congratulate himself on knowing her husband better than she does, through sharing the knowledge that love gives her.

But our communion with the hero's consciousness is not a question of understanding but of intuitive sympathy in the sense of what he has to do. He has to do his duty, obedience to which paradoxically reveals the freedom of consciousness. Only Othello's task fails to carry the audience, the audience which accepts that Macbeth's duty is to kill the king and usurp his office, just as Hamlet's is to kill his uncle as an act of filial revenge. But in all three tragedies consciousness accepts without comment the necessity for each task; there would be no point in questioning them. Consciousness takes the moral law for granted: about its operation the tragedy is not original, nor thoughtful, nor clever; no debate is to be held. This is particularly important in *Hamlet*, where revenge could easily become the topic – an absorbing one to all parties – which it is in other revenge plays. Not only does Hamlet never question the duty of revenge, but he also accepts its dramatic conventions.

Shakespeare of course covers this formal acceptance with the most convincing naturalism. The certainty of the king's guilt, as revealed by the play, makes Hamlet furiously angry, and that anger provokes both the decision to kill the king when Hamlet sees him praying, and the realisation that to do so would not satisfy the revenge wish that has boiled up in him as a result of the tension over the 'mousetrap' play. Commentators, including Bradley, have been upset by Hamlet's behaviour at this point – Johnson thought the words damning Claudius to hell 'too horrible to be read or uttered' – but in fact they simply confirm the complete conventionality of the revenge motif in Hamlet. As Nashe's *Unfortunate Traveller* shows, written a matter of ten years earlier, it was normal practice in revenge on a villain to contrive his death so that his soul went to hell. Shakespeare knew what his audience expected. More important, and equally typical of Shakespeare's practice, the state that the hero is in explains his behaviour on ordinary naturalistic grounds, just as it explains his behaviour to his mother and the immediate impulse which leads to the stabbing of Polonius. Hamlet's anger and excitement over what seems the grossest and clearest proof of the king's guilt makes his response quite normal, even predictable.

If Hamlet were exercised about the morality of revenge he would be

quite a different person, the sort of person who might figure in a
thoughtful modern spy story or in the theatre at any time, including
Shakespeare's own – such heroes are implicit in the plays of Massinger
and Heywood, just as they are fully developed and studied in terms of
history and idea in the plays of the Romantic movement and up to our
own age. As it is, the duty of revenge removes from Hamlet's
consciousness any question of dilemma or soul-searching. He does not
have to concentrate; his mind floats freely and takes on the colour of
new occurrences. Rosencrantz and Guildenstern report to the king that
when they told Hamlet of the players' arrival 'there did seem in him a
kind of joy/To hear of it.' Consciousness and its activities are a
distraction and a relief from duty.

There is a sense even in which the paradoxical freedom of consciousness, when confined by an unquestioned duty, extends into the movements in the play, and the onlooker's sense of them. In no other of
Shakespeare's plays is one so haunted by a sense of physical movement,
gesture, process, as if these were visible movements of the mind and
consciousness. It is particularly memorable in report:

> He took me by the wrist and held me hard;
> Then goes he to the length of all his arm,
> And with his other hand thus o'er his brow,
> He falls to such perusal of my face
> As he would draw it. Long stayed he so.
> At last, a little shaking of my arm,
> And thrice his head thus waving up and down,
> He raised a sigh so piteous and profound
> As it did seem to shatter all his bulk
> And end his being. That done, he lets me go
> And with his head over his shoulder turned,
> He seems to find his way without his eyes;
> For out o' doors he went without their helps
> And to the last bended their light on me.
>
> II. i. 87–100

The first two lines of Ophelia's account, as innocently laboured as
Sonya's reading aloud to the older members of the family in *War and
Peace*, sets the scene, as if we were spectators outside Hamlet and able
to look objectively into his mind through this account of the motions of
his body. (That the lines are a gift for an actor, particularly an Elizabethan actor skilled in formalised gesture, goes without saying.) Much

of Hamlet's own immediacy of nature, a vital part of the plot atmosphere, is fixed in Ophelia's literal account: more important the lines
mysteriously go with the queen's beautiful words about her:

> And for your part, Ophelia, I do wish
> That your good beauties be the happy cause
> Of Hamlet's wildness. So shall I hope your virtues
> Will bring him to his wonted way again,
> To both your honours.

III. i. 38–42

'Good beauties' is so just and kind a phrase – but, one feels, no more
kind than just – that Ophelia's helplessness as an externally seen object
appears as clearly in it as Hamlet's consciousness does in her own
artless account. In no other of Shakespeare's women does a woman's
helplessness, her beauty seen, desired, and manipulated, appear as it
does in Ophelia. Conditioned to goodness and docility, she is the exact
foil to Hamlet's wildness, which means his native – though also
indulged and princely – immediacy of behaviour. There is no guile in
Ophelia just as there is no true goodness either, the goodness inherent
in Cordelia and Desdemona. But there is a continuity, so justly
imagined as to be taken for granted, between the girl who endures with
suffering but stoical decorum the tasteless gibes of the man on the edge
and climax of his own private nightmare – the man whom she thought
was paying his attentions to her – and the girl who reveals in her breakdown just how naturally familiar she is with the world of sexual
innuendo and speculation. We apprehend that Cordelia or Desdemona
would also know about it, take it for granted, ignore it. But schooled in
proper behaviour as she is, and without much individuality of her own,
Ophelia can still suffer as much as any girl, and she does suffer horribly
from the cruelty of Hamlet, who understandably if mistakenly
associates her behaviour with cunning and concealment.

The subtlety of the conception shows in the apparent uncertainty of
her relations with Hamlet. Apparent only, because the reality is both
obvious and unclear, like so much else in the play. That kind of
obscurity is the opposite of the 'tricks i' th' world' the mad Ophelia
speaks of, and the suspicion and concealment with which Hamlet himself is surrounded. Salvador de Madariaga felt it important that Ophelia
must have a secret erotic relation with Hamlet, which the songs of her
madness reveal. Surely just the contrary is the case. What is not seen in
the play is quite normal and innocent, the kind of innocence that

extends to Gertrude's marriage to Claudius, and his relations with her. Outside the old king's murder, everything else in the play is good and normal, even the love of the murderer for the queen he got by the act. This is in marked contrast with most revenge plays. Most, like Tourneur's *The Revenger's Tragedy*, make no moral contrast between corruption and its scourge, plot and counter-plot, except in a manner so stylised – as with the chaste Castiza of Tourneur's play – that it confirms the uniformity of impression. But with Hamlet we intuit that he did indeed love Ophelia, as honourably as would be natural to him, and that she returned it in a manner proper to her conditioned being. In the same way we 'know' that Gertrude had no knowledge of what took place in the orchard, and that she too has no guilty infatuation for Claudius, but a sentiment of tried and enduring affection. She will not let out what Hamlet has said to her but she will not betray her husband either. Like a sensible woman she will keep quiet and hope that all will pass.

This is important, because it is essential to the feel of the play that no further guile or concealment should be present than that relating to the deed of Claudius – Hamlet's despatch to death of the two envoys is not guile but an immediate and instinctive action. The Quarto text, which is explicit in the scene between Hamlet and his mother in her closet that son enlists mother in a war against her husband – 'And mother, but assist me in revenge,/And in his death your infamy shall die' – is almost certainly a simplification by actors of the proper version, which leaves intrigue entirely to the king. Because it is so totally at variance with the atmosphere of the play it gives a startling insight, as do the Quarto queen's further lines:

> I will conceal, consent, and do my best,
> What strategem so'er thou shalt devise.

So easily could the players – if the Quarto text is indeed a players' version – throw away a vital aspect of the tragedy. For Hamlet and his mother to be 'in it' together against Claudius would be to put them on a par with Claudius and Laertes in their plotting together. It is essential that mother and son should be 'free from all contriving' against the king whom one hates and the other loves. It is both strange and natural that the queen should silently love and protect the man whom she now knows – but such knowing goes against all her instincts – has murdered her former husband. Hamlet accepts it, and indeed it brings mother and son close together in a way that a mutual confiding and plotting could never have done. The most moving thing about the closet scene is how Hamlet's anguished appeals to his mother not to go to her husband's bed die away in a kind of unspoken mutuality: 'And when you are desirous to be blest/I'll blessing beg of you.'

In spite of all Hamlet's words, and her own confusion, the queen's maternal status is not overturned. It is kept intact, most unexpectedly, by her love for the usurper, and her own peculiar kind of dignity in reassuring her son:

> Be thou assured, if words be made of breath
> And breath of life, I have no life to breathe
> What thou hast said to me.
>
> III. iv. 197-9

Further than that she will not, by implication, go. And something here ironically converts Hamlet, despite all appearances, into what Claudius calls Laertes, when he utters histrionic protests of love for his father and revenge:

> Why now you speak
> Like a good child and a true gentleman.
>
> IV. v. 144-5

For all his torments Hamlet is, in essence, a good child and a true gentleman, but that does not mitigate the burdens he is under: it only reveals the complications, both natural and obscure, in which he is involved. His mother's situation torments him, and for that there is no relief, certainly not in revenge. Questions here cannot be answered, or predicaments resolved. Laertes is more than just the foil to, and parody of, Hamlet's function as avenger; he shows in his family feelings and dealings just how false some kinds of seemingly robust simplicity can be. On the face of it – but 'the face of it' is never clear in *Hamlet* – Laertes, 'a very noble youth', is righteously enraged by the killing of his father and the breakdown of his beloved sister. But we do not believe a word of what he says, not only because he speaks fustian – 'I'll rant as well as thou,' is Hamlet's scornful answer to it – but because his attitude to his father and sister is insufferably proprietary: he regards their fates as a personal injury, above all an injury to his pride.

And this is typical of the avenger, whether he rushes to it like Laertes and will use any means to obtain it, or whether like other Elizabethan revengers he self-consciously debates the question with himself, as do, for instance, Tourneur's Charlemont in *The Atheist's Tragedy*, and Clermont in Chapman's *The Revenge of Busy D'Ambois*. They share with Laertes the same egoism, the same assumption that the world exists in order that they should get what they want. Their single-minded concentration is fatally close to that of the artist himself – indeed one of the troubles about revenge tragedy is that the hero obtaining his desires, and in the most aesthetic way possible, whether fairly or foully or by renunciatory patience, resembles and can almost be identified with the writer of the tragedy arranging the way that it should go.

Such a hero must always be dull. Oddly enough the most conventional revenge hero in Shakespeare is Othello, of whom Bradley said that he would have had no trouble in Hamlet's place, nor Hamlet in his. Othello's obsession with revenge on Desdemona, making it a sacrifice and not a murder, has a quality not so dissimilar from that of the artists and exponents of the genre outside Shakespeare. But the true revenger has no other mind than that he devotes to revenge. Othello's consciousness is elsewhere, a manifestation of his love, which remains outside. And his false conviction about Desdemona is too agonising an obsession to be called egoistical. But both he and Laertes do show by contrast how different Hamlet is, and how effectively the play has deprived Hamlet of the very quality the revenge hero should normally display. The duty that he never questions spreads his mind over everything he comes in contact with, giving him not the positive capacities of an avenger but the negative capability that Keats associated with Shakespeare's art.

The avenger simplifies, feeling that one act will cure all. For Hamlet his duty serves to reveal the infinite irreconcilable complications of living. Instead of reducing life to a single purpose, and an apparent single success, Hamlet's task involves him in all the never resolved complexities and contradictions of living, all the whips and scorns of time. The paradox for the avenger is to find that life is too involved with his own instincts and affections for him to be avenged on a part of it. His words to his mother show how well Hamlet feels his mother's connubial happiness with his uncle, despite the bitterness it brings him; nor does it preclude, though he tries to pretend it does, her equal happiness of the same kind with his own father. The avenger wants to feel that all is black and white – 'look here upon this picture and on this' – and this impulse in Hamlet fights against his discovery that the flesh is sullied and the world rotten by nature, that the acceptance of this is at the centre of regeneration. Ophelia may be a silly limited girl, but her 'good beauties' could indeed have helped to reconcile him to the necessities of the world. The queen's sense of this is part of her salvation, and her lamentation for the dead Polonius – 'the unseen good old man' – is not only an unwittingly comical contradiction of adjectives – 'virtue' was concealed like a spy and conspirator – but a proper tribute to a loyal servant and rational man; one who, despite his accommodations, understood the ways in which human beings have to make allowance for and get on with each other.

> I'll wipe away all trivial fond records,
> All saws of books, all forms, all pressures past
> That youth and observation copied there. . . .
>
> I. v. 99–101

But Hamlet finds they are not easily got rid of. The impulse and need to change his whole mode of being, to place himself wholly at his father's disposal – virtually to identify with him – is no more effective in banishing *consciousness*, which no avenger or fanatic can possess, than are Hamlet's attempts at conspiracy to secure a conspirator's ends. Having been offered by Polonius a perfect alibi and disguise for his activities in the idea of unrequited love, he flings it away instantly when he suspects that Polonius has set his daughter before him like the kid before the tiger. Any conspirator worth his salt would have seized the chance of proving to the king and his minister that love was indeed the trouble, and thus setting their suspicions at rest.

But not Hamlet. Shakespeare has of course constructed him out of contradictions, as he does with so many of his characters, but in the case of a revenge play contradiction can take a particularly effective and dramatic form. In determining to be a complete avenger Hamlet finds out just how inapt consciousness is for it, just as Macbeth finds it unsuited to a career of murder and usurpation. Those 'trivial fond records' will not away so easily: they leap into his mind with a kind of joy when he hears of the coming of the players. Hamlet's reaction is far from being unmixed with that blessed 'baser matter' of life. Only later does the idea come to him of trapping the king through their means.

Or does it? Shakespearean fish swim the sea far away from land, and it is part of the mystery of the play that we can never be quite sure. Certainly Hamlet can be cool and swift and adroit – the conspirator's talents – but it is only really at moments, such as on board the ship, when these qualities are not aimed directly at the object of revenge.

Just as a Hamlet who *pretended* to be in love in order to deceive would place himself in the category of successful conspirators, so one wholly unable to exert their qualities would be far too obviously a non-conspirator, and the play would be seen to be an ingenious variation on the revenge pattern – as a modern play might be. What can be said is that Hamlet is not purposeful, as the 'hellish' Pyrrhus 'with eyes like carbuncles' is as he seeks Priam, or, less parodically, as the young Laertes is, as he conspires with the king to kill Hamlet.

Hamlet is not purposeful because he cannot in fact shake off 'all trivial fond records', the very stuff of consciousness. Shakespeare has it both ways. In his dramatic impact the prince has all the elegance, the initiative, the charisma of a hero and a revenge hero, as it is that sort of play. But he is also wholly compromised with human weakness and decency, the instinct to accept others and himself in whatever imperfect circumstances. His father's ghost is the uncompromising voice of duty, but the instincts of one the book and volume of whose brain is mercifully mixed 'with baser matter', as is the case with most sane men, really inclines towards his uncle. Claudius is neither a fanatic nor a psychopath, and this fact in itself enrages the Hamlet who has to become something like both in order to do the deed his father enjoins. In Claudius's speeches we recognise the saving human weakness that has to live, as Hamlet cannot do, in an impossible position, and thus acquires its own kind of dignity and strength. Everything Claudius says is disingenuous, but his words reveal none the less a man who would be good if he could, a man whose instinct, like Macbeth's, is not 'to take the nearest way'.

> But so much was our love
> We would not understand what was most fit,
> But, like the owner of a foul disease,
> To keep it from divulging, let it feed
> Even on the pith of life.
>
> IV. i. 19–23

Love is indeed prepared to have the pith and pride of life sapped by secrecy, by pretence, by forbearance, if there is no other way. It does not take the revenger's way out. Claudius's understanding of these matters is revealed, ironically enough, when he is working on Laertes:

> Not that I think you did not love your father,
> But that I know love is begun by time,

> And that I see, in passages of proof,
> Time qualifies the spark and fire of it.
> There lives within the very flame of love
> A kind of wick or snuff that will abate it;
> For nothing is at a like goodness still,
> For goodness, growing to a pleurisy,
> Dies in his own too much. That we would do
> We should do when we would: for this 'would' changes
> And hath abatements and delays as many
> As there are tongues, are hands, are accidents,
> And then this 'should' is like a spendthrift sigh
> That hurts by easing.

> IV. vii. 110–23

Claudius describes a very proper human process, as proper as that which he outlines to Hamlet at the beginning of the play:

> But, you must know, your father lost a father,
> That father lost, lost his, and the survivor bound
> In filial obligation for some term
> To do obsequious sorrow. But to persever
> In obstinate condolement is a course
> Of impious stubbornness: 'tis unmanly grief.

> I. ii. 89–94

The tone is important, for it shows among other things why Gertrude feels for her husband as she does. He is a man who understands how life must be lived, without excess, and how much ordinary human morality depends on the very weaknesses that enfeeble it. Hypocrisy finds it easier to bemoan its own inactivity than to proceed to decisive action. The action is harmed ('That hurts by easing') but this implies that the doer is all the better – it eases him – for knowing what should be done and comfortably doing nothing. Hamlet's condition is the opposite. But everyday life, always 'a little soiled i' the working', as Polonius puts it, rightly understands that to let things be usually causes less trouble all round than to take action.

Hamlet, too, can talk like his uncle and show the same kind of understanding, as with the advice he gives his mother:

> Assume a virtue, if you have it not,
> That monster, custom, who all sense doth eat
> Of habits evil, is angel yet in this,

> That to the use of actions fair and good
> He likewise gives a frock or livery
> That aptly is put on.
>
> III. iv. 160–5

But Hamlet is a divided man, divided not by instinct but by injunction
and duty. As with so many of Shakespeare's tragic characters – Timon,
Macbeth, even Titus Andronicus – his protestations against his own
nature fail to convince. He knows that piteous action will convert his
'stern effects', and give 'tears perchance for blood'. The phenomenon
is more developed and more subtle in him than in any other, which
makes his consciousness so compelling a spectacle. Claudius is not a
divided man; he is one whom circumstances have led to be more
wicked than most, but also shown to be capable of inspiring deep
affection. In *Measure for Measure* Mariana pleads for her husband
Angelo in the sort of terms that Gertrude might for Claudius. Like her,
she 'craves no other and no better man':

> They say, best men are moulded out of faults,
> And, for the most, become much more the better
> For being a little bad.
>
> V. i. 437–9

A little bad! After Angelo has not only cruelly jilted her – never mind
that – but blackmailed a postulant nun into going to bed with him (as
he thinks) and then treacherously ordered the execution of the brother
for whose life she had seemingly given up her virginity. Beside that,
even Claudius's record looks no worse. But *Measure for Measure* is a
comedy and Angelo's 'intents' were not realised in action. None the
less Mariana's love, and Gertrude's, is not mocked. The point is not
that love may be blind but that its object, in Shakespeare, can not be
held in the tragic frame, submitted to the full rigour of tragedy's
intentions. There is something absurd, and touching, in Claudius's
twice-repeated command to his wife – 'Let him go, Gertrude' – when
the incensed and armed Laertes is in her grip and struggling to get at
his kingly person. To be loved is to be potentially comic, though to the
eye of love tragedy and comedy do not exist as separate entities; and
comedy sets up a counter-impression to the acts which drama lays upon
its villains. The acts of Angelo were only 'in the mind' because they
were committed in the context of comedy: but similarly the deeds of
Claudius and Macbeth are only done in fact because they are done in

tragedy. And Shakespeare's art requires the duality to be perceived. 'Truly sir, I am a poor fellow that would live,' says Pompey in *Measure for Measure*. 'Simply the thing I am shall make me live,' says Parolles in *All's Well That Ends Well*. 'O yet defend me, friends. I am but hurt,' are the last words of Claudius; he might have said 'I am but bad.' A tragedy cannot end well for villain or for hero, but in these appeals the tone is the same.

There are implications both for the prince and the play. The point about Hamlet is not whether he is noble or neurotic, good or bad etc., but that he is unsuited to playing in revenge tragedy. From this, all else follows. Claudius, the villain and victim, is in the same position. Set obliquely to them is the effective revenge character, Laertes, who wishes only – as such a person in the play should – to cut Hamlet's throat in the church, and who invents and speaks in part:

> I bought an unction of a mountebank,
> So mortal that, but dip a knife in it,
> Where it draws blood no cataplasm so rare,
> Collected from all simples that have virtue
> Under the moon, can save the thing from death
> That is but scratched withal.
>
> IV. vii. 141–6

In terms of the play Laertes is a genuine character, who not only helps to give it its proper atmosphere but acquires from it, as a work of art in the convention of revenge tragedy, other aspects and traits which harmonise and go along with it. The relations in *Hamlet* of what is not the play with what is mean that Polonius and his family have more the status of characters in a play than do Hamlet and his uncle. But even here, with them, the revenge drama of *Hamlet* does not find persons exactly suited to its requirements. The 'character' of Laertes, in which egotism and conceit are constant factors among the more or less unstable and forgivable follies common in youth, is completely taken in and comprehended by the onlooker, and it is comprehended in terms of the revenge play. There is nothing surprising in the fact that a belated generosity – 'Exchange forgiveness with me, noble Hamlet' – should be a part of that nature. All fits in well with the kind of play which Laertes has in a sense taken over, his crafty-comic old father and sweet, weak, dependent sister being two more of the same sort. They are what is known as a close family.

That closeness emphasises Hamlet's isolation. His unsuitability for his role of revenger merges insensibly but very effectively into his unsuitability to be in a tragedy, and thus indeed in any kind of play. The paradox of the players' arrival, so joyfully greeted by Hamlet, is that it shows how little he is an actor, however great his interest in the business. It fills him with happy almost childlike absorption, the opposite of playing any role. The news of the actors is paralleled in the last act by the news brought by Osric, to which Hamlet responds in the same vein of immediacy. On both occasions his seizure of the activity of the moment corresponds to the play's air of giving us a succession of things that are really happening – conversations, games, speculations between two persons about a third, like the spousal interchange about Hamlet between Claudius and Gertrude – in order both to cover up for the inventions of a revenge tragedy and also to give them an inner meaning. The relation between the two is as peculiar and as fascinating as all such relations suggested by tragedy's declining to act its own plot with total conviction. Hamlet and Horatio have nothing else to do, as the climax approaches, than to discuss the probabilities of form for the fencing-match:

HOR. You will lose this wager, my lord.
HAM. I do not think so. Since he went to France I
   have been in continual practice. I shall win at the
   odds.

V. ii. 200ff.

He has been, evidently, engaged elsewhere, and for the duration of the action, in the real business of life. The small debate is between two sportsmen, who seem to have entirely forgotten what the play is about, and yet the play's own disturbing presence intrudes as a kind of gain-giving, something all ill about the heart. The relation is haunting, for it is that between the awareness of ill, as consciousness is aware of it, and the presentation of tragedy as a consolation of art.

After Hamlet is dead he is seen by a soldier as a soldier:

> Let four captains
> Bear Hamlet, like a soldier, to the stage;
> For he was likely, had he been put on
> To have proved most royal: and, for his passage,
> The soldiers' music and the rite of war
> Speak loudly for him.

V. ii. 387–92

Again there is a touching contrast between the lack of identity of Hamlet with any role that the play offers, and the martial personality that is conferred on him after death, the same personality that his father wore in his own eyes and that of all others. The occasions that inform against Hamlet are the roles that are thrust upon him, as the necessities of tragedy are thrust upon the events of the play.

Their resistance is of all kinds, creating innumerable tremors in the mind, tremors of pleasure and meaning. The antic disposition is Hamlet's own way of attempting to put on the role of avenger: at least his distraction marks him out from others and gives him the air of one embarked on a strange destiny, thus drawing all attention on himself. The device of madness, which Shakespeare inherited from the previous stories, has ceased to be the instrument and method of the revenger and has become a substitute for it. It is put aside as soon as something interesting happens – the arrival of the players, or of the wager suggestion from the king – and both Hamlet himself and the others take it for granted this should be so. The task of revenge should join the revenger morally and socially to the world in which it is to be enacted. However much he may seem to be, like Orestes and Hieronimo, a lonely and solitary figure, he is really at one with the medium in which he works. The triumph of *Hamlet* is to separate the hero so subtly and so conclusively from the world around him. It is a profound moral achievement, but like all such achievements in great art it makes absolutely no parade of its own moral nature.

Moreover it happens as a part of the deep imaginative working of the play, it is certainly not part of its programme. If it had been, Rosencrantz and Guildenstern would not have been killed. It is in reference to them that Hamlet uses the word conscience, the only scene in which he does so in the play, in the same sense in which the king and Laertes use it. The repetition a few lines later in relation to the king ('is't not perfect conscience/To quit him with this arm?') shows the same feeling and the same resolution – 'The interim is mine;/And a man's life no more than to say "One"' – which is yet wholly unmethodical, and instinctively 'disclaiming from a purposed evil'. Hamlet protests too much, and that he should do so is part of his attempt to play his own role, but the more he does so the more it appears that it is a role, and that the play is a play, like the vengeance of Pyrrhus and the murder of Gonzaga inside it. The tragic blow serves here to release consciousness, and Hamlet's eloquence often movingly reveals the paradox involved and the inspired movement of the play towards the defeat of its own story.

The ghost who had waved Hamlet to a more removed ground, in keeping with the homely atmosphere of coming and going in the play, none the less speaks as a ghost should, and Hamlet's violent agitation leads him naturally into the same idiom, but it gives him away none the less:

> Haste me to know't, that I, with wings as swift
> As meditation or the thoughts of love
> May sweep to my revenge.
>
> I. v. 29–31

Even Hamlet never utters lines that reveal more than that about 'intellectual being'. (Puzzled editors used at one time to insist that 'volitation', or even 'levitation', must be the right word.) The lines bring together the revenger's task and its impossibility here, when it is involuntarily identified with all the free intimacies of consciousness. Hamlet's candour, his instant and vivid response, is wholly compatible with the fact that he never behaves in the way that tragedy requires of him. Instead of making him purposeful and methodical, secret and single-minded, the revelation of the ghost opens him up to every fresh sensation and awareness. He behaves with childlike and irresponsible glee, the unnerving child who, as in Günter Grass's *The Tin Drum*, makes his oblique comment on the nature of adult society. Like other of Shakespeare's generous heroes – Timon for instance – his vehemence often reveals itself by contradiction: meditation and the thoughts of love – all trivial fond records – will not be banished by the task laid on him, but enhanced and transformed. Instead of diminishing with the concentration required by the story, roles become as free as words; Hamlet does not cease to be lover, son, friend and prince, but is more confirmed in each. As the play, by invoking tragedy, turns away from it into multifarious life, speculation, consciousness, so Hamlet himself both follows the process and determines it.

Macbeth

In *Macbeth* the evasion of tragedy occurs quite differently. Here too mind and consciousness take over from tragic action, creating their intimacies with us alongside it and in defiance of it. But whereas in *Hamlet* the process is both startling and intangible, vividly present as an effect but complicated to sort out and define in detail, in *Macbeth* it happens in a simple, elemental way. For tragedy's sake Macbeth is murderer and usurper, a destroyer of the metaphysical order of things. He has cancelled and torn in pieces the great bond of the commonweal, the soul and the service, the order and coherence of state and person. In this respect, and in the discharge of a simplified tragic action, he is related to Clytemnestra and Aegistheus, who destroy the ordered house of Agamemnon. He is more closely akin to the bad kings in Holinshed, whose evil or selfish and irresponsible actions divide the country and bring chaos and war.

And yet of course he is quite different from any of these. If he were really at all like them the play of Macbeth would not be the unique thing it is. It would not have that peculiar intimacy, giving the irrational feeling that we are closer to Macbeth than to any other character in Shakespeare. Much closer than to Hamlet, because Hamlet is all over the place, in accordance with the aesthetic personality of the play he is in. Macbeth is close to us all the time, and that closeness is a function of his own concentration on his state of mind.

Even so, that does not explain the impression. Macbeth never makes overtures, as it were, to the audience, in the ways that Hamlet does, or Richard II, or Troilus. His own intimacy, and he is a man eminently possessed of the capacity for it, goes all to his wife. It is this that gives us the clue to the way it is done, to our relation with him. For it is the fate of Macbeth to lose the most precious thing that he has and taken for granted, that profound reliance on, and relation with his wife. It causes the tragedy, but it is his 'eternal jewel'.

> and my eternal jewel
> Given to the common enemy of man. . . .

Macbeth refers to his soul, pledged to the devil and the powers of darkness, but it is his sense of 'his dearest partner of greatness' that is destroyed by the project she nursed on his behalf and nerved him to perform. And what he and she lose is the audience's gain. Macbeth's intimacy has nowhere else to go but into the invisible air through which the onlooker is perceiving him.

'What he hath lost noble Macbeth hath won.' Macbeth involuntarily gives the audience that inwardness with his wife in which the seeds of the tragedy were incubated. Before they became the deed's creatures she loved him for the qualities she professed to despise in him. They increased her sense of ownership, of him being her man, understood by her. The sense of their communings makes her reading of his letter one of peculiar intimacy, telling of pauses, thinkings aloud, the pair in converse together of the kind that takes the other's understanding for granted. The speech that follows shows her confidence that her superior strength of purpose also means superior knowledge:

> Glamis thou art, and Cawdor, and shalt be
> What thou art promised. Yet do I fear thy nature:
> It is too full o' th' milk of human kindness
> To catch the nearest way. Thou wouldst be great;
> Art not without ambition, but without
> The illness should attend it. What thou wouldst highly,
> That wouldst thou holily, wouldst not play false,
> And yet wouldst wrongly win. Thou'ldst have, great Glamis,
> That which cries 'Thus thou must do', if thou have it;
> And that which rather thou dost fear to do
> Than wishest should be undone. Hie thee hither,
> That I may pour my spirits in thine ear,
> And chastise with the valour of my tongue
> All that impedes thee from the golden round
> Which fate and metaphysical aid doth seem
> To have thee crowned withal.

I. v. 12–27

Like so many speeches in fated and fatal contexts, the great speech that follows ('Come, you spirits/That tend on mortal thoughts, unsex me here') echoes a classic context in tragedy which Shakespeare's powers must instantly have absorbed in his younger days: in this case it is Seneca's *Medea*, probably from an English translation printed in 1581. It is a remarkable and unnoticed example of the simultaneous use and evasion of the tragic *topos*. Lady Macbeth is like Medea in so far as she is about to take part in a tragedy, but in so far as she contributes to our sense of consciousness in the play, to our feeling of intimacy with its dimension and its dilemma, she is being something very different.

The remarkable thing about her speech, whose tone is as typical of her, and the certain sort of literalness which reveals her mental process, as his homely suavity is of Claudius, is that her picture of Macbeth has a curious irrelevance: she is not talking about the real consciousness with which we are becoming intimate. To her he is a man who is afraid to try getting what he very much wants. That is a diagram drawn by a moral idiot, but, more important, it indicates the gap between them, a gap which their deep and backward-reaching intimacy, so much stressed in the text ('My dearest partner – my dearest love') does nothing to bridge. She is sure she understands him, masterfully accepting and taking command of his limitations – 'you shall put/This night's great business into my dispatch. . . .', 'leave all the rest to me.' 'The milk of human kindness' and the 'illness' that should attend ambition are cruder concepts, in Lady Macbeth's mouth, than they now seem to be. She is not saying her husband is too kind a man for this business, and with too healthy a spirit; 'kindness' means human nature, and Macbeth's is not mature or manly, has not learnt the necessary hardness of the world. Her husband is in a sense her child, fed with the milk which is natural to her, and when the word recurs in the Senecan speech which follows, she calls on the spirits that tend on mortal thoughts, schemes of murder, to turn her milk to gall. She will feed him on that to produce an appropriate response, as the armed men in the tale sprang from the sowing of dragon's teeth.

But this tragic pattern, the logic of dire event in mythology, seems quite irrelevant to what is happening to Macbeth. Or rather not irrelevant, for it serves to indicate the difference between the Macbeth seen by the tragedy, and historical morality, and even by his wife, and the Macbeth the onlooker is experiencing and becoming intimate with. The reason why the two seem so different is again the function – here both simplified and highly dramatic – of our sense of Macbeth in terms of his own consciousness. In his position, as in Hamlet's, there is no question about the diagram and interpretation of *character*. Because they bring us close to them, and indeed inside them, we do not say 'Hamlet is indecisive' any more than we say 'Macbeth wants to be king but cannot bring himself to take appropriate action.' His mother and her husband talk about Hamlet in much the same way in which his wife communes with herself about Macbeth. In both cases the hero seems a great way from the conclusions they reach, and only we, the audience, are aware of it. In both cases this increases our sense of intimacy, but with Macbeth there is a simple contrast between our sense of him, and what his wife feels, and later on what his subjects feel, his victims and enemies. The extraordinary vividness and horror of the drama, which Dr Johnson and many others since felt so acutely, comes from the spectacle of someone as much 'like ourselves' as Macbeth is, doing the deed that he does.

Or does he? Consciousness so predominates in Macbeth that Duncan's murder remains an affair of nightmare. Macbeth has con-

sidered the idea for a long time – there is no doubt of that, but he has
considered it in exactly the way in which everyone does consider such
things, a speculation, a wonderful thought that he might some time
become king.

> If chance will have me King, why, chance may crown me
> Without my stir.

Iago knows all about this sort of traffic of the mind, and how 'uncleanly
apprehensions' may at times carry on there 'with meditations lawful'.
Intents are 'but merely thoughts', as the scrupulously fair-minded
Isabella admits in *Measure for Measure*, when Angelo's intended, but
not consummated, crime has been discovered. This too is theologically
sound, as we learn in *Paradise Lost*: 'Evil into the mind of God and
man may come and go.' The inwardness with us of Macbeth is one of a
concentration and agitation of mind, in which the idea is truer than the
reality, the thought than the action:

> My thought, whose murther yet is but fantastical
> Shakes so my single state of man that function
> Is smothered in surmise, and nothing is
> But what is not.
>
> > I. iv. 138–41

When he announces to his wife 'I have done the deed' the feeling is
one of peculiarly dreadful anti-climax. 'Present fears are less than
horrible imaginings,' and the thing itself, though it is so irrecoverable,
also seems trivial. It alters the nature of our intimacy with Macbeth,
though it does not abolish it. Before he does it, Macbeth is like ourselves, like everybody else, like Banquo, who, in the tense hour before
the murder, expresses in more forceful form the idea of evil speculation
and possibility as ranging in the mind:

> Merciful powers,
> Restrain in me the cursed thoughts that nature
> Gives way to in repose.
>
> > II. i. 7–9

At such a moment the activities of the mind become almost palpable
and express themselves in bodily form, as they do in the other two
mind tragedies. In the speech in which he imagines the thoughts that
may come to him when he goes to rest, Banquo hands his sword to his

son Fleance, and then – with a dream-like precision – hands over his
belt with its dagger too:

> Hold, take my sword. There's husbandry in heaven;
> Their candles are all out. Take thee that too.

In the total darkness of the castle courtyard two figures approach with
another torch, and Banquo instantly commands: 'Give me my sword.'
It is Macbeth – 'a friend' – who in a few moments will be drawing his
own dagger as he sees the mental picture of one before him. 'I see thee
yet, in form as palpable/As this which now I draw.'

But this murder, more intensely conveyed than any other in literature, is never seen, only done. Only a whispered dialogue between the
Macbeths conveys that meticulous sense of precise physical movement
which (as in Banquo's undoing of his sword and belt, Othello's groping
for 'another weapon' in the closet of his chamber, or Hamlet's
reported behaviour to Ophelia) suggests so exactly, not action in the
raw physical sense of stabbing and murder, but the tentative yet definite
movements within itself of the mind:

LADY M.   My husband!
  MAC. I have done the deed. Didst thou not hear a noise
LADY M. I heard the owl scream and the crickets cry.
        Did you not speak?
  MAC.   When?
LADY M.   Now.
  MAC.   As I descended?
LADY M. Ay.
  MAC. Hark!
        Who lies i'th' second chamber?
LADY M.   Donalbain.
                                    II. ii. 12–19

Words themselves have become inconsequential even when most
fraught, a mouse-like scurry in the consciousness under strain. There is
irony in her words –'Consider it not so deeply' – because the time of
that deep anguish of consideration has gone. Far from considering it so,
Macbeth's mind now grasps at incongruities, which link up unexpectedly with pieties conditioned in childhood and revealed in the sleep
murmurs of the two brothers, the king's sons, who lie in the adjacent
chamber:

> There's one did laugh in's sleep, and one cried 'Murther!'
> That they did wake each other. I stood and heard them.
> But they did say their prayers, and addressed them
> Again to sleep.
>
>   II. ii. 22–5

'I stood and heard them.' Macbeth registers the stupefied moment after he has done the deed, and its dream-like contiguity with sleep and childhood:

> One cried 'God bless us!' and 'Amen' the other,
> As they had seen me with these hangman's hands.
> List'ning their fear, I could not say 'Amen'
> When they did say 'God bless us'!
>
>   II. ii. 26–9

Lady Macbeth's plea – 'Consider it not so deeply' – is as beside the point, as unintentionally equivocal, as her words when she feared someone had waked and the plan miscarried: 'The attempt and not the deed/Confounds us.' She means their guilt would be advertised by a botched attempt, but she succeeds also in speaking for us all in a different sense: it is indeed not the murder that confounds us, but the by now so intensely imagined idea of it. When she says 'Consider it not so deeply' she refers with equal inadvertence to Macbeth's great speech of fearful meditation, 'If it were *done* when 'tis done' (the sense requires the emphasis), and the 'judgment' that he still had then to ponder, the knowledge that the deed would recoil on him, that Duncan was 'here in double trust', that as king he had been 'so clear in his great office'.

Nothing of that moral agony remains now for Macbeth: he can think of nothing but his inability to respond with a child's conditioned reflex to those hallowed phrases uttered in the broken sleep of the two brothers.

> But wherefore could not I pronounce 'Amen'?
> I had most need of blessing, and 'Amen'
> Stuck in my throat.

The tone is as querulous as a child's asking for comfort. His wife has none to give. Her time of loving reassurance was in the intimacy of planning the deed – 'Leave all the rest to me.' Now she can only urge him not to think about it or it will drive them round the bend. Three times she has repeated the invocation to child and motherhood, the time of milk, and also the time when the child learns by instinct, by rote and repetition, the sanctities of phrase that have nothing to do with reasoning and judgment. Those takings-for-granted instilled in childhood are assumed by Lady Macbeth to have no application to a man's world. Macbeth now finds, in the moment of damnation, that they have every relevance, that they apply overwhelmingly, and 'Wherefore could not I pronounce ''Amen''?' is his recognition of the fact, more despairing and more spontaneous in tone than anything else in the play.

It brings him even closer to us, but not to his wife: 'Be not lost/So poorly in your thoughts.' Macbeth is beyond thinking, but the exclamations he has heard in sleep suggest not only the innocency of childhood but that of sleep itself. And the final touch in this extraordinary scene, the most concentrated in all Shakespeare, is Macbeth's realisation that he has now become a different person: 'To know my deed, 'twere best not know myself.' The freedom of thoughts, even of 'cursed thoughts', has now been replaced by the absolute fact of murder, which banishes both the world of consciousness and the world of sleep.

It is essential to the hypnotic tension of the play that Macbeth should not seem in any ordinary way 'responsible' for his actions. Not only the witches but every other agency is like a portent or apparition – pity striding the blast, heaven's cherubim, the lamentations heard in the air, the voice that cried 'Sleep no more' – do not so much personify the haunted imagination of Macbeth as act as separate and rival powers, distracting us from the difference between the usurper and murderer and the mind which has drawn us in. I suspect that an Elizabethan audience would have heard the knocking at the end of the scene with a feeling of awe and terror analogous to that felt at the end of *Dr Faustus* when the devils come to claim his soul. Certainly De Quincey is misleading when he suggests in his famous essay that the terror in that knocking is caused by a feeling of the natural world without forcing its way in on the murderous cell where nature and life have been suspended. The terror is more primitive than that. It is the feeling shared by both Macbeth and the audience, that something has 'come for' him, that the secure world of thought and possibility, of the individual self with its desires and secrets, has gone beyond recall.

Hence the scene effects it that the division in Macbeth between the imagining and suffering 'intellectual', and the murdering usurper, becomes absolutely logical. I have dwelt on the scene in such detail because it shows how the play both removes itself from its own tragic necessities and conforms to them. Nowhere else in the tragedies is the process more elegantly and economically achieved. Macbeth is both the consciousness of the onlooker, by definition a non-tragic person, and the protagonist of an action who finds he has done something no onlooker could ever do. In terms of structure and psychology the wonderful thing about *Macbeth* as a play is that it exploits to the hilt the advantage and liability of *being* a play. Real murder cannot be done within a work of art, and therefore it is highly effective if a work of art suggests that its hero cannot do a murder, however much he may contemplate it – contemplation being the mode in which any such work of art must present itself. The fact of murder, and the idea of it, are thus brought as close together as possible, without ever coinciding.

The *ideas* of death and of murder are not only more terrible than the real thing – something only a great work of art could establish, and one perfectly suited to what it can establish – but they become one with ideas of every other kind. The fact of killing is terrible but it is also stiflingly banal – Macbeth comes to know that too. The Macbeth we see before us is the man of mind, his deeds are kept out of sight: Macbeth is never where the staged actuality of death is. When Banquo is killed on the stage he is absent; his murder of the sleeping king and his subsequent slaughter of the two grooms, are events heard of; the gross cunning of the latter in particular is hard to connect with Macbeth, nor is the onlooker expected to do so. Such things are as necessary as they are also irrelevant to the mental dimension of the tragedy, aspects of Macbeth seen not by the onlooker of the play but by the participants in it.

This relation of the hero to his own deeds, and to his own rise, fall and death, is clear enough, but just how unusual it is has scarcely been recognised. In every other Elizabethan play with the same kind of subject, including Shakespeare's, the killing of enemies in the rise to power is not only a part of the action, but is shown and enacted as such. In *Macbeth* it serves only to reveal the consciousness of the hero. He becomes aware of how different it is from that of others, especially his wife's: 'You make me strange/Even to the disposition that I owe.' Even after Banquo's murder it is oddly surprising, even slightly incredible, to find that Macbeth has been behaving like any gloomy and suspicious tyrant – 'There's not a one of them but in his house/I keep a servant fee'd' – and giving a banquet with all the false *bonhomie* of

Stalin entertaining his cronies at the Kremlin. It is natural enough that his enemies should refer to him after his fall as 'the dead butcher', but no onlooker inwardly feels any appositeness in Angus's words –

> Now does he feel his title
> Hang loose about him, like a giant's robe
> Upon a dwarfish thief

– an image which Caroline Spurgeon incomprehensibly took as the key one in the play. It would fit Richard III, who is thoroughly identified with his own deeds, but the attempt of play and players to identify Macbeth with them fails to come off. Menteith comes closer to the point than Angus when he replies that 'all that is within him does condemn/Itself for being there.' What is within Macbeth does indeed disown the image he presents to the outside world; and the ill-fitting garment is not the title of kingship, but, ironically, the world of plot and murder which he entered to obtain it.

Shakespeare's instinct for the unexpected in tragic drama seems here to have carried a proverbial image to a logically simple conclusion. 'There is no art to find the mind's construction in the face,' and Macbeth, as a matter of Virgilian commonplace, must 'look like the innocent flower, but be the serpent under't.' The point is formalised at length by the dialogue in Act IV between Malcolm and Macduff at the English court. But with the dramatic imagination at work here it is a short step from being different from what you seem to be to being – more simply – *different*. With the three heroes it is variously the case; as the Queen says to Hamlet: 'Why seems it so particular with thee?' Macbeth is particular as Hamlet and Othello are, as every one of us is inside his own consciousness. Hamlet at court stands out as Macbeth does among his nobles, as Othello does at the senate: the significant fact is that all three are quite unlike the men they are among. Like them Macbeth is singled out by his apparent capacity – an involuntary one – to see and feel more vividly than others.

There is something masterful in him, as in the other two, a natural distinction which in poetic drama manifests itself in the tricks and qualities of speech, and, through the unique vehicle of Shakespeare, in the transparency with which speech reveals emotion, yearning, longing, bitter regret. This comes out in the unnerving comedy of the banquet scene, where Macbeth's attempts to be like his colleagues and subjects sound horribly off-key, and the social efforts of himself and his wife to be gracious are of the kind that can only cause discomfort:

> Ourself will mingle with society
> And play the humble host.
> Our hostess keeps her state, but in best time
> We will require her welcome.
>
> III. iv. 3–6

Movement and intention are as meticulous as always in the play: Lady Macbeth will condescend at a later stage of the festivity. The most compelling thing about the scene is our sense that Macbeth is indeed acting a part, but of a more oddly and pitiably intimate kind than any of the pretences his criminal schemes have laid upon him. His attempts at being the genial host are no more convincing than his attempt at ogrish insouciance when the murderer comes to the door:

MACB. There's blood upon thy face.
MUR.   'Tis Banquo's then.
MACB. 'Tis better thee without than he within.
>
> III. iv. 13–14

For these contradictory reasons Macbeth seems the only *sincere* man present when he bursts out at the ghost's appearance. And it is typical that his exasperated wife should think his behaviour affected.

> O, these flaws and starts,
> Impostors to true fear, would well become
> A woman's story at a winter's fire,
> Authorised by her grandam.
>
> III. iv. 63–6

In all three tragedies the instant reaction is contrasted with the contrived one. It is specially pathetic in this banqueting scene, which in its raw stage presentation has none the less the subtle scope and feel of a Henry James novel, that Lady Macbeth's honest rage at her husband's behaviour is quashed by his own storm of agitation, and eclipsed by the falsity of the social efforts she must make.

> Think of this, good peers,
> But as a thing of custom. 'Tis no other:
> Only it spoils the pleasure of the time.
>
> III. iv. 96–8

Nothing shows Macbeth's isolation more than the uncomprehending-
ness of the loving wife who had reassured him and seemed to enter into
all his hopes and fears.

The vision and idea of it swallows up the play, and has been taken by
some modern critics in a highly metaphysical sense. The Russian philo-
sopher Shestov took the Danish critic Brandes to task for calling
Macbeth a wonderful study in the power of conscience – 'Macbeth is a
criminal who feels all the pangs of conscience on earth.' Rubbish, said
Shestov, Macbeth on the contrary is a vision of mind thrown back on
itself, a man who cannot find confidence and self-justification in his
own being and the actions necessary to it. The poet Robert Bridges was
approaching the same point from a different angle when he protested
that such a man as Macbeth could not possibly have murdered
Duncan. In her study of the theme of damnation in Renaissance literature, Helen Gardner places Macbeth with Dr Faustus and Milton's
Satan as types of the noble soul damned by the evil of the will and
aspiration. But the trouble with all these interpretations is that they
draw the wrong conclusions from the compelling portrayal of consciousness in Macbeth. As with Hamlet it is 'intellectual being' as a
thing in itself, that cannot be resolved into meaning and idea: to turn it
into *idea* is to misconceive the true moral dimension of Macbeth.
Shakespeare himself is as explicit as need be about the idea and
meaning of his tragedy, as a borrowed and conventional form, related
both to history and to the classics. No playgoer could have missed that
point, touched on throughout, and especially in the short scene at the
end of Act II, between Ross and the Old Man. Significantly, Ross
makes the point in a metaphor of the theatre itself:

> Thou seest, the heavens, as troubled with man's act,
> Threatens his bloody stage.
>
> II. iv. 5–6

And the Old Man, of course, falls exactly into the role of tragical and
historical chorus:

> 'Tis unnatural,
> Even like the deed that's done. On Tuesday last
> A falcon towering in her pride of place
> Was by a mousing owl hawked at and killed.
>
> II. iv. 10–13

This is 'meaning' in the sense in which T. S. Eliot said that the 'meaning' of a poem was often like the piece of meat which a burglar threw to a dog to keep it quiet, 'while the poem does its work upon us.'

And yet, of course, the traditional pieties of the natural order and the art form are not separate from the total individuality of the play, the 'Macbethness' of *Macbeth*. The word the Old Man speaks – 'unnatural' – takes us into the midst of it. As in *Hamlet*, mind is so visible and so compelling in *Macbeth* because its concentration, in the context of the drama, is fellowed by a sense of its natural activities and ends outside it. Macbeth, like Hamlet, like Othello, is the most normal, the most comprehensible of men: all are instantly sympathetic, their thoughts directed in ways to which, as Dr Johnson would say, every bosom returns an echo. And it is Shakespeare's art to give this commonplaceness an absolute distinction, making each of them like no one else. Macbeth would not be so deeply moving or so congenial a figure if he were in any sense a Faustus or a Satan type. He has no appetite for mastery or for evil; he lacks the symbolic force of the will which makes them archetypes of an age, of a special historical and spiritual tendency.

And yet he is 'unnatural', just because he has so clear an idea of, and desire for, what is due to nature. The most moving manifestation of mind in Macbeth is his dream of time, 'the nurse and breeder of all good'. Like most people he has an idea of himself in relation to a per-spective of life, leading peacefully and domestically to the grave, governed by order, attended by love and 'troops of friends'. He is the family man of Shakespearean tragedy, a trait he may inherit from Shakespeare's invention of the villain and ecstatic father, Aaron the Moor in *Titus Andronicus*. A family man without a family, which makes the status all the more marked in him, as it is in that other tragic and solitary family man, the young Evgeny of Pushkin's Peters-burg tragedy, *The Bronze Horseman*,

> Get married? Me? Well and why not?. . . . After a year or two
> I can find myself a snug job somehow, and Parasha will be able
> by then to manage the house and bring up the kids . . . and so
> we'll live, and so we'll go down hand in hand to the grave,
> and our grandchildren will bury us.

It is of course the thought of family life – and as host to the king he is in the very context of it at its most symbolic – that makes Macbeth

utter the last protest against his murderous destiny. He has left the
feast to utter his soliloquy 'If it were *done* when 'tis done . . .' and
breaks off, as his wife hastens in to him, with 'How now, what news?'

LADY M. He has almost supped. Why have you left the chamber?
    MACB. Hath he asked for me?
LADY M.   Know you not he has?
    MACB. We will proceed no further in this business.
             He hath honoured me of late; and I have bought
             Golden opinions of all sorts of people,
             Which would be worn now in their newest gloss,
             Not cast aside so soon.

                                                    I. vii. 29–35

Remarking on the difference in tone between soliloquy and this speech,
Caroline Spurgeon says that these arguments he now puts forward are
the kind that he hopes will appeal to her – practical, domestic arguments. But surely not. They are the arguments that come to him in
her presence, which is a very different thing. The sudden show of
resolution is that of the master of the house, and it is easily out-
manoeuvred. The family man has a sense of the fitness of time which
his wife lacks. She sees nothing but the promised goal and 'the future
in the instant', not reflecting on the propriety of period and interval,
but transported by their scheme only 'beyond the ignorant present'. To
Macbeth, time is involved with 'mortal custom' in a great bond that
cannot be cancelled:

             Rebellious dead, rise never, till the wood
             Of Birnam rise, and our high-placed Macbeth
             Shall live the lease of nature, pay his breath
             To time and mortal custom.

                                                    IV. i. 97–100

This makes for irony in the excuses made for him by his wife at the
disastrous banquet:

                         Think of this, good peers,
             But as a thing of custom. 'Tis no other:
             Only it spoils the pleasure of the time.

Macbeth's distraught behaviour at the ghost is presented in her ghastly
parody of wifely knowledge ('My lord is often thus, and hath been from

his youth') as an old weakness, like a tendency to migraine or the sulks, to be taken no notice of by those near to him. But the greater irony is Macbeth's vision of the proper sort of death that his own wife should have had, paying her breath to time and mortal custom:

> She should have died hereafter:
> There would have been a time for such a word.

The Elizabethan future conditional is not so uncompromising as the modern sense of 'ought to have'. A close parallel would be the way we say: 'he should be going to London one day next week.' If all had gone 'well' a time for death would have come in the nature of things, in the right sequence and season.

There is a singular directness about the family situation in *Macbeth*; the speculations that rightly attend Shakespearean possibility and suggestion are not relevant here, and 'how many children had Lady Macbeth?' is indeed one question that need not be asked. An Elizabethan audience would have understood and taken for granted that the Macbeths were childless because their children had died, something too common to call for remark. Macduff's brood of children indicates an opposite good fortune, and the preoccupations, ambitions, revenges – Macduff's 'He has no children,' Macbeth's references to the barren sceptre in his grip – all reinforce the point. In some sense Macbeth will become a father by becoming king, for, as he says to Duncan, 'Our duties/Are to your throne and state children and servants.' This is all part of the pervasively *natural* world of the play, its 'kindness' in the Elizabethan sense, always Shakespeare's theme but never more so than here, where tenderness, babes, children, milk, mother and fatherhood, are as potent against the world of blood and darkness as the sense of mind is against the fact of murder.

The conventions of tragedy require the hero to have an excess, a weakness, a failing which contributes to his downfall. As we should expect, this idea is present in Macbeth and contributes to the view of him held by the other characters, including his wife. She, in a way, is like both the spectator of tragedy and a proper tragic character herself. She expects Macbeth to be one with her. When she loses control of him she loses her own roles, as she does the 'undaunted mettle' that fitted her for the part. He tries to play her role, and she cannot recognise it in him. To that extent the pair remain intimate, sealed against the outside world, as in the weary aftermath of that deplorable banquet, when her love is moving in its very apathy.

But the other characters recognise and appropriately revile the tragical role as Macbeth displays it. And it is singular that their proper attitude both makes them lose character and colour – there are more cipher figures in Macbeth than in any other major play – and also appears to confirm Macbeth's moral superiority. This may be an odd way of putting it, but it is surely an impression founded on the intensity with which Macbeth has been imagined. Partly of course it is the simple literary fact that the interesting villain takes the interest, but there is more to it than that. The rest are public figures: he alone can remain an intensely private one. But more than that, too, it is Macbeth who seems to arrogate to himself all the simplest and most profound responses in the play, even those that should by rights belong to others. When Ross brings to England news of the slaughter of Macduff's wife and children, Macduff's reception of the news is as moving as it ought to be, but it is also quite evidently contrived to be so, like Lady Macduff's conversation with her son, and like similar things in the history plays. But the most haunting phrases of Macduff are the ones that most clearly evoke the state of mind of his terrible opponent.

MAL. Dispute it like a man.
MACD.   I shall do so;
But I must also feel it as a man.
I cannot but remember such things were
That were most precious to me.
                              IV. iii. 220–3

The lines remind us of 'I dare do all that may become a man'; and throughout the play we feel and know how much Macbeth 'cannot but remember such things were/That were most precious to me.' He monopolises such things. His superiority consists in a passionate sense for ordinary life, its seasons and priorities, a sense which his fellows in the play ignore in themselves or take for granted. Through the deed which tragedy requires of him he comes to know not only himself, but what life is all about.

Shakespeare's art countenances straightforwardness, and never more so than in Macbeth, but not that kind of facility. We cannot use any such formula as self-discovery or education by anguish. Macbeth would not be Macbeth if he did not, in an important sense, know what he knows all along. 'Yet let that be/Which the eye fears, when it is done, to see.' At the opening he has the same sense of things as when he has

ped into blood and done deeds 'which must be acted ere they may
scanned.' (Letourneur, the French translator in whom Pushkin first
...d Shakespeare, rendered 'scan' as *pénétrer*, which approaches
Shakespeare's sense by a different image and equally well suggests the
difference between knowing what it is to do, and experiencing the full
significance of what has been done. A double sense in knowing is half
visible to Macbeth, and one of the many equivocations that beset him.)

'To know my deed, 'twere best not know myself.' And, conversely,
to know yourself is not really to know what the deed will be like. We
are intimate with a compulsion that is all too compatible with clear-
sightedness, and with a moral sensitivity that is compatible with the
grossest superstition. Shakespeare's powers are fully equal to creating
Macbeth as the credulous villain and victim of tragedy, and as the
involuntary connoisseur of mind and life: he shows us that in the
human heart the two can be one and the same.

Othello

'Yet I have known those which have walked in their sleep which have
died holily in their beds.' The Doctor's words in Macbeth remind us,
like so much else in the play, of what Goneril calls 'the difference
between man and man'. Some could have done Macbeth's deeds and
not lost a wink of sleep for it. The tragedies of mind bring out the
difference graphically and inevitably, and distinguish those who live in
the mind. Othello is the most unexpected hero to do so.

When she describes how she fell in love with him, Desdemona says:
'I saw Othello's visage in his mind.' Loving goes on there; thinking is
its ally, determining good and bad. The onlooker should see Othello's
visage in his mind too. But the mind takes the opposite course here
from its journey in Hamlet and Macbeth. Their predicament liberates
consciousness, even from the prison of Denmark, the haunting terrors
of Scotland. Their state – 'cabined, cribbed, confined' as it is – is
mysteriously one of freedom for the intellectual being. Like Macbeth,
Othello reveals too the extremes in the human heart: that the tender
lover can also be the inflexible killer. But Othello is not freed by this
sense of his own situation: he has been caught in it as if in a snare. And
instead of being freed by the hero's consciousness of things, and
sharing it with him, we are forced to stand outside Othello's delusion.
The play grips us in its own artifice of incomprehension. And for most

onlookers, nowadays, the sensation seems to be more exasperating than it is either thrilling or painful.

And it may produce a strong desire to get out. Othello is in one trap, and our knowledge of it puts us in another one. This separation is very different from the freedom of mind we experience through Hamlet's need to kill his uncle and Macbeth's need to kill the king. Othello's need to kill Cassio and Desdemona belongs only to him; not only because we know it to be deluded, but because the nature and extent of the delusion is such that we cannot imagine ourselves becoming involved in it. We cannot justify and verify its necessity by our involvement. We know it is necessary for Hamlet to revenge his father, and for Macbeth to become king by killing the king, and our knowledge is, like theirs, a duty: it makes us a party to both transactions. We are freely involved in them, and in the states of mind associated with them. But mind in Othello has walked into a trap, and the play both invites us in and keeps us out. We are close to Othello and yet alienated from him.

Othello brings us face to face with the problem not elsewhere encountered in the tragedies, or indeed in Shakespeare's works in general: the distinction between tragic and comic. Normally the question doesn't arise. But it does here, because, to paraphrase Horace Walpole's *mot*, the play is tragic if we can feel a part of it, comic if we look at it from the outside. And the distinction, like all such distinctions where *Othello* is concerned, is very absolute and abrupt. Nothing could be more surprising, in a way, than to find a tension between comic and tragic treatment suddenly making itself felt.

And it was sensed early on. Writing at the end of the same century in which *Othello* was first produced Thomas Rymer called the play 'a bloody farce'. Noun and adjective bring the ideas of comedy and tragedy together in their most depreciatory sense, and no more accurately unsympathetic judgment on the play has ever been made. In our own time more genteel, but also more intellectualised versions of Rymer's disfavour have been voiced by T. S. Eliot and F. R. Leavis, who both consider and reject the personality that Othello presents to the outside world, pointing out that he is not so much deceived as a self-deceiver, a man presented by Shakespeare as constitutionally incapable of seeing the truth about himself. So the detached, ironic view of the creator contrasts with the tragical and romantic view taken of himself by the created being. No one but Othello himself believes that he is 'one that loved not wisely but too well.'

We note that Eliot and Leavis, like Rymer himself, prefer to see Othello from the outside. However close the play brings them to him they prefer to keep a moralist's fastidious distance. Dr Johnson, a moralist but not a fastidious one, took in his notes on the play a more charitable view: 'Though it will perhaps not be said of him as he says of himself, that he is a man *not easily jealous*, yet we cannot but pity him when we find him *perplexed in the extreme*.' We may feel pity, implies Johnson, but not terror: not that sense of secret communion in a life and destiny which we have with the protagonist in other tragedies. Johnson shows his usual kindness and common sense in reminding us that we feel pity, but pity is as much the response of an outsider as is the hard derision of Rymer and the rather disdainful, intellectual interest of the modern poet and critic. It may occur to us that no one feels sorry either for Hamlet or for Macbeth.

Leavis's essay is called 'The Sentimentalist's Othello'. And indeed there is or has been another widespread reaction to the play which might be called the sentimental one, suggesting not a saccharine self-indulgence but a feeling and sympathy which does not attempt to be discriminating. Very likely the women in the theatre in Rymer's time, as in Shakespeare's, were touched by Othello, felt romantic about his personality and utterance, were secretly rather in love with him. One such would no doubt have been the housewife in Beaumont's play *The Knight of the Burning Pestle*, who loves moving and eloquent speeches. Very likely the men in the theatre were aware of this in some sense, and, in a half-conscious defensive reaction, were the more inclined to see the Moor as a great booby. Leslie Fiedler makes a good general point about this aspect of the play when he observes that jealousy simultaneously creates a comic situation for men and a tragic one for women. Historically speaking, half an audience might well have been disposed to see the play in terms of tragedy and love, the other half in terms of comedy and sex.

A sentimental response to the play is in some sense in league with love, the love to which Desdemona consecrates her soul and fortunes. No doubt in loving Othello with her we are also loving ourselves; but that may be no bad thing, indeed a necessary one, for a kind of self-love – among other things what his reputation means to Cassio – is at the basis of all honour and decency. As with most things in the play, a paradox is involved; unconscious self-love and self-esteem lends itself to ridicule, which may grow to a kind of hatred. This is certainly at the root of Iago's feelings about Othello, whom he sees as 'loving his own pride and purposes.' On the other hand the opposite reaction can take place: Cassio hero-worships Othello for the same reason that Iago hates him. So in a way have some of the critics, like Swinburne, who asserts that 'we love Othello,' and that our feelings about him are different from those we entertain for Shakespeare's other heroes. Perhaps it is natural that the Victorians should have felt about him as Cassio did, rather than Iago. A. C. Bradley describes him as 'coming to us, dark and grand, with a light on him from the sun where he was born.'

Clearly to love Othello, in whatever sense, is to feel with him and to feel his nobility, to see him in his mind. Love, which in the depths of the play displaces drama and tragedy, is in the nature of things subject to conflicting reactions, scepticism and incredulity as well as enthusiasm. 'What can she see in him?' The mixed reactions among onlookers record the same process taking place among the characters of the play. Perhaps it is better, for this reason, even to hate Othello rather than to treat him with detached curiosity. His imperfections, unlike those of Hamlet and Macbeth, are closely connected with the emotions of love. And to disown those imperfections, usually by defining them, is to treat him as an alien, a comedy figure to be exorcised by pity, or found psychologically or sociologically 'interesting'.

It may be that both the welcoming and the defensive reactions to Othello have something in common underground, a tremor of recognition uniting them in spite of difference. Cynicism and sentiment are two sides of the coin of love. Most people are in their minds on terms with both: the sentiment of love revealing amongst other things our own love for ourselves, while the cynicism about it declares our awareness of how we must look to others, and of how their behaviour so often looks to us. To see Othello in his mind is to see where the sentiment of love predominates, love of another and of self combined in the same happy harmony:

> She loved me for the dangers I had passed
> And I loved her that she did pity them.

Desdemona has taught Othello to love himself, and herself in him – the tenderest of offices and also the most commonplace. The gull Roderigo shares one symptom of his love with Othello himself. He says that Desdemona is 'of most blest condition', to which Iago contemptuously retorts 'Blest fig's end! – the wine she drinks is made of grapes.' So it is, but for Iago that is the end of the matter, and he contrives that it shall come to seem for Othello the end of the matter too.

Love and sex are the opposite poles of the play, not coming together, disturbingly unassimilated to one another. The purpose and function of Iago is to replace the sense of one by the sense of the other. Worked on by Iago, Othello comes to express the same view of the matter as he does:

> O curse of marriage,
> That we can call these delicate creatures ours
> And not their appetites. I had rather be a toad,
> And live upon the vapour of a dungeon,
> Than keep a corner in the thing I love
> For others' uses.
>
> III. iii. 272–7

What is remarkable and disquieting is the intensity and directness of the expression, and the depressing banality of what is expressed. The voice and language of love are talking sex. These are the commonplaces of the saloon bar, which vulgarise by public expression of them both secret fears and secret hopes – coveting one's neighbour's wife while fearing for the virtue of one's own. This is Iago country, where lust is both predatory and watchful. Naturally Iago himself desires Desdemona, on the same grounds that he suspects her husband may have cuckolded him.

> Now I do love her too,
> Not out of absolute lust, though peradventure
> I stand accountant for as great a sin,
> But partly led to diet my revenge,
> For that I do suspect the lusty Moor
> Hath leaped into my seat: the thought whereof
> Doth like a poisonous mineral gnaw my inwards;
> And nothing can or shall content my soul
> Till I am evened with him, wife for wife. . . .
>
> II. i. 285–43

Coleridge's famous phrase about these speeches of Iago's – 'the motive-hunting of motiveless malignity' – is in fact very misleading. From prudish motives (Coleridge also detested the sexual underworld of *Measure for Measure*, though it is of a very different kind) it seeks to distract us and turn us away from the sexual underworld of *Othello*. It would be a mistake to suppose that Iago is merely making things up, creating groundless fantasies on which to base his deep hatred for the general and his lieutenant whom he serves. No audience at the time would have been surprised by his suspicions, or thought them to be wholly improbable. And, despite his tone, Iago does not take this kind of thing at all lightly. We could say that it was *because* he hates Othello that he thinks of him as a sexual rival and enemy, but this does not alter the fact that such resentment would be very practical and real. Emilia evidently found it so. She knows, as all her friends would do, how highly motivated are all the mischiefs and malignities that swarm in the sexual underworld. An immediate parallel occurs to her when she wonders who could have turned Othello against Desdemona:

> Some such squire he was
> That turned your wit the seamy side without
> And made you to suspect me with the Moor.
> IV. ii. 146–8

She refers to the place where such speculations are made, the place to which Iago casually introduces Othello, as if confident that both men came there often:

> Utter my thoughts? Why say they are vile and false;
> As where's that palace whereinto foul things
> Sometimes intrude not?
> III. iii. 140–2

The underworld has its own kind of seriousness, its own species of gleeful preoccupation: it is a place of comedy, but black and heartless.

How to reconcile love and sex, how to protect the noble and fragile structure of love against the cheerless black comedy of sexual intrigue? Perhaps there is no way, and perhaps indeed the 'tragedy' in *Othello* – unexpected and yet pervasive, as all such things are in these tragedies – is that there is no way. Such a catastrophe and conclusion would not be exalted ones, merely in a sense a kind of flop. That was the view of Rymer, who saw no way of reconciling the two sides of the play, assuming that one had so obviously cancelled out the other. His tone is that of the comic side, witty, but not witty enough to keep the tone sweet: 'Had it been Desdemona's garter the sagacious Moor might have smelled a rat; but the handkerchief is so remote a trifle no booby this side of Mauritania could make any consequence from it.'

In a modern production of *Othello* little attempt is made to elevate and respect the structure of love. Why should we not prefer the humour and the bracing realism of Iago as we watch the increasingly grotesque agony of *Othello*? Iago's acting vitalises every scene. Dr Johnson saw that his wit and vigour might 'steal upon esteem, though it misses of approbation.' He is the more fascinating to an audience if they are not much involved in the drama of Othello's mind and the love which is cast out from it. A modern audience is probably suggestible to having reason and good sense put on the side of wit and comedy, and to feeling at home with Iago and his view of things.

We could say that what prevents the natural expansion and freedom of mind in *Othello* is the absolute difference between Iago's and Othello's minds. When Othello shows that he is capable of thinking like Iago, and uttering his sort of thoughts, the difference – and from a dramatic point of view quite rightly – does not disappear but takes on an oppressive and nightmarish form. Then what of the peculiar status of mind in these three tragedies? The structure of *Othello* has to be loaded, compensated, the balance kept, by making Othello's own mind a place of apparent and natural romance and innocence, lofty but, as it were, specialised. Can we live there as well as in the mental world of Iago? Can we, as onlookers, live naturally in both? Or do we, as in the critical tradition from Rymer to Leavis, implicitly reject both, and thus make our appreciation of the play an essentially negative thing?

In answering that question it helps to consider again Macbeth's soliloquy when he is nerving himself for the murder of Duncan:

> . . . his virtues
> Shall plead like angels, trumpet-tongued, against
> The deep damnation of his taking-off;
> And pity, like a naked new-born babe,
> Striding the blast, or heaven's cherubim horsed
> Upon the sightless couriers of the air,
> Shall blow the horrid deed in every eye
> That tears shall drown the wind. . . .
>
> I. vii. 18–25

Macbeth's preoccupations lead his mind involuntarily into a spacious and terrifying metaphysical area, the area that Rilke called 'the open'. Yet in this area there is a total blending in poetry of the comic and the tragical. Any such distinction in it would not normally occur to us, but if it does we see that the two do meet, in poetry, without the faintest sign of distinction or embarrassment, just as they do, in a different context of poetry, in *Romeo and Juliet* when Romeo wonders if 'unsub-

stantial death is amorous.' Into Macbeth's mind great portents like
angels appear and enter, yet they are quite at home with every incongruity of the distracted consciousness. We take for granted what is in a
sense the comic and touching upshot of their visitation, that Macbeth
should reveal his wish, not to seek his salvation by renouncing murder,
but to bask in his present reputation and the pleasures it will bring:

> We will proceed no further in this business.
> He hath honoured me of late; and I have bought
> Golden opinions from all sorts of people,
> Which would be worn now in their newest gloss,
> Not cast aside so soon.
>
> I. vii. 31–5

The image in his wife's reply is brutally deflating. So, he has woken up
from his dream of ambition like a drunkard with a hangover?

> Was the hope drunk
> Wherein you dressed yourself, Hath it slept since?
> And wakes it now to look so green and pale
> At what it did so freely?
>
> I. vii. 35–8

Othello's and Iago's speeches not only lack this freedom in
incongruity but hold the onlooker in the grip of their own separate
obsessions. This had been needful, from far back, to the essential structure of the play, which is a dramatic version of the cautionary tale by
the Italian intellectual and moralist Cinthio. In the tale there is no love
and sex polarity, for the ensign Iago is himself in love with Desdemona,
and acts out of jealousy and venomously disappointed passion when she
refuses his suit. This brings Othello and Iago together, makes them in
fact much the same kind of person. It also defines Iago clearly, just as
he is defined, though in a different way, in Verdi's opera. The most
frightening thing about Shakespeare's Iago is how inexact he is in his
own estimation: his pleased definition of himself is merely that he is not
what he seems to be.

The strain imposed on the structure of *Othello* comes from the fact
that love in it must be kept apart from sex, Othello's love and Desdemona's apart from the world of sexual commonplace, whether good or
evil natured. And this goes against the norm of Shakespearean incongruity. We take it for granted in *Hamlet* and *Macbeth*. But in *Othello*
it is like the monster in the thought too hideous to be shown and –

more important – too potentially risible. The structure requires something that normal Shakespearean psychology cannot permit, for 'foul things' of a sort must indeed intrude into every mind, into the 'palace' of Othello's as well, and not just because they have been put there by Iago. Yet if Othello's consciousness were in any sense able to anticipate Iago's insinuations they would not have the force that the drama requires.

However, the resulting charged and polarised atmosphere is not only superbly dramatic, but also true to life, to life as Othello and Cassio see it. Iago's hatred for them is completely realistic in terms of the commonest human experience, because it approximates to the gut resentment that is felt against others for belonging to a different class, or for being Indian, Jewish, black, cultivated, refined, etc., etc. This blind hatred of distinction is used by the play to underlie the polarity of its own structure. Publicity hates privacy, prose hates poetry, envy hates generosity, sex hates love. Lines and glimpses in the play are constantly directed and pointed towards discrepancy, setting in every sense the high style against the low. This makes the play a more searching study of daily hatreds and dignities than any other of Shakespeare's: and the structure makes it so. But at a cost. We must forgo that sense of absolute freedom in the mental world which we enjoy with Macbeth and Hamlet, and never more so than when their torments and preoccupations seem half-conscious and half-hidden.

Envy can always show up decorum. That is one source of trouble, almost a technical one. But by the same token decorum is always liable to show up itself, and this is only desirable if the work of art wished it to happen or is indifferent to whether it happens or not. What is disconcerting, in the early stages of the temptation, is not Othello's liability to jealousy but the way in which hateful incongruities are thrust into the privacy of his consciousness. The play is bound to bring them together, and the result is an absurdity which it cannot quite let out, which must be left lurking below the surface of emotion. Othello is forced to contemplate the fact that his love is not a wholly private affair, something that is solely a part of his own self and his romantic history. And when he has been made to feel that Desdemona has been and is being made love to by another, his exclamation of woe has a startling and plaintive absurdity:

> I had been happy if the general camp,
> Pioneers and all, had tasted her sweet body,
> So I had nothing known.
>
> III. iii. 349–51

The idea is ineluctably comic. Charmingly so in a way, reflecting as it does an incongruous world of sergeant-majors, populating Othello's military past but grotesquely unsuited to the high romantic image of adventure and hazard. Iago's poison forces him to bring such barrack-room ideas together with those of his love. Yet that word 'tasted' is in a touching way his own, here brought painfully into contact with a licentious jest from army life. We may be reminded of it again before the killing of Desdemona:

> When I have plucked thy rose
> I cannot give it vital growth again,
> It needs must wither: I'll smell it on the tree.
>
> V. ii. 13–15

For Othello the barrack-room and his love are wholly incompatible. For Desdemona, as we shall see, this is not so. She is prepared to go to the wars in all senses.

Shakespeare generally does not in the least distinguish between love and sex: *Romeo and Juliet* shows that. Both in comedy and tragedy the two go naturally and properly together, for men and women alike. Claudius and Gertrude, as much as Portia and Bassanio, have their sexual tenderness as well as love for each other taken for granted; even when, as in the latter case, marriage is a combination of fairy story and business arrangement. But in reconstructing and re-imagining the Othello story for his play Shakespeare had to divorce love from sex as a logical result of separating the romantic nobility of Othello from the underworld intrigue of Iago. The only characters for whom love and sex are taken for granted as parts of the same whole are the three women, Bianca, Emilia, and Desdemona herself.

The consequences of this are bound to be striking, and indeed they are at the root of our divided apprehension of the Othello world and the Iago world. The explicit presence of sex as a kind of basic sport, intrigue and power struggle, whereas love is a lofty affair of adventure and romance, gives the play an atmosphere as much Victorian as Elizabethan, and this goes with its popularity in the nineteenth century after Kean's revival. Historically, men do tend to separate love and sex and to regard both as their due, but in different contexts. Where Shakespeare himself is concerned, a sense of the division, and the need to compensate for it with some bridging material, are shown by his emphasis on the pungent common sense of Emilia, and the no less cheerful and sensible temper of Desdemona, which she displays in conversation with the two officers before Othello's arrival in Cyprus.

Impossible of course to say how the division declared itself to the artist: it might seem his imaginative reaction to the idea of two men who are locked in this dramatic relationship. In Cinthio's tale the relation is in every way more ordinary, and has a kind of low-key plausibility. The commander waits in anxious suspense for days for the proofs of his wife's infidelity which his subordinate has promised to obtain. When convinced, he enters with him into an ingenious conspiracy to make the murder look like an accident, caused by a fall of plaster from the ceiling. Between the pair there is none of the gap between the lover and the connoisseur of sex, no sharp division in outlook. Both indeed in their way have had ample opportunity to feel love for the murdered wife, the ensign because of his infatuation with her, and the general because he has been for a long time a tender and happy husband. 'Their affection was . . . mutual.' 'No word passed between them that was not affectionate and kind.' This makes the crime more dreadful but also in its way more probable. The confusion and duplicity, hatred and sorrow, take place not only in the world of a newspaper story but are narrated in order to point a moral, or rather several, about the evils of credulity and gossip, and of marrying outside one's race and community.

Shakespeare's drastic simplification of the bond between commander and subordinate has the effect of squeezing out the onlooker, who can take part, as it were, neither in terms of love as Othello sees it or in terms of sex as Iago does. The pair drag into their area of high tension the habitual concordances of sex and love, and split them violently asunder. Othello's response to Iago's first tentative hints have led the critics, who see him as a study in the vulnerability of egotism, to claim that he meets Iago half-way and makes his work easy and its plausibility absolute. There is truth in this in so far as Iago's suggestions are all about sex, for the mention of sex in connection with the woman he loves is an explosive subject to Othello. The inability to conceive of one in terms of another, where she is concerned, and himself in terms of both, is at the root of the disaster. None the less love and sex, and the barrier between them, not only squeeze out the onlooker from the play: they also squeeze out tragedy. But the variety of ways in which that happens is always an asset to the Shakespearean work of art.

To the onlooker the fact that Othello, in his effortless and terribly formidable way, does not fetch Iago at the outset a blow that would knock him from one end of the stage to another, is one of the great dis-

appointments of the play. Such an act would be a sort of parodic fulfilment of the onlooker's desire to take part. It is denied him, and the
hero can never really recover in his estimation. The first two acts, by
engrossing the spectator so effectively in Othello's life and being, have
prepared him for some such response. The onlooker is similarly expec-
tant of Hamlet going on being Hamlet, and Macbeth Macbeth, and he
was not disappointed. Nothing they do lets down expectation in this
way.

It seems in the proper nature of things that Othello's pride should
respond with instant finality to his subordinate's insolence. And it is
important to note that if the form of the play barely recovers here from
the change in the feel of its hero, that change is brought about by the
introduction of Othello to the subject of sex. It is a subject that Iago is,
as it were, in charge of; and has been since he holloed out to Brabantio,
in the tumultuous opening scene, that an old black ram was tupping his
white ewe. Just as Othello can never recover from his first capitulation
to Iago, so sex in the play never recovers from the fact that Iago is in
charge of it, and corrupts Othello by his own kind of insistence on it.

Both in the foreground and background worlds of this play love
never quite manages to include sex, even when love speaks with the
voice of Desdemona. It is right that sex should be so disturbing an
element in the play, but no bounds can be set to the kind of disturbance
it causes, the more especially when it is referred to with the gross
casualness of Iago: 'To be naked with her friend in bed, an hour or
more. . . .' The purpose of that casualness is to madden Othello, but it
also lends its own kind of frivolous, uncontrolled element to the play's
love/sex polarity. It is curiously shocking – or would be if we were
paying attention to the point at that moment – to hear what Desdemona tells Emilia after the melancholy supper at the end of Act IV,
when Lodovico has arrived from Venice, and Othello has struck her in
public:

> He says he will return incontinent.
> He hath commanded me to go to bed,
> And bade me to dismiss you.
>
> IV. iii. 11–13

In its adjectival form 'incontinent' is only used in Shakespeare in the
sense of 'with sexual desire', though adverbially it can mean 'at once',
'without further reflection', and is so used by Roderigo. The case here
seems ambiguous, but suggests Desdemona's hope that the abrupt

command means Othello intends to come back and resolve his dark mood in making love to her.

Even so the word is disconcerting, the idea to an onlooker not altogether an attractive one. It seems almost to align itself with Iago's casual patronage of the sex instinct, and to hint, in its rapid note of appeal to what is hidden, of sex as an element not resolvable in human loves. But clearly, and gratefully, it is not so to Desdemona. In her plea before the senate she was as explicit as is consonant with feminine dignity that she 'loved the Moor to live with him'.

> If I be left behind
> A moth of peace, and he go to the war,
> The rites for which I love him are bereft me,
> And I a heavy interim shall support
> By his dear absence.
>
> I. iii. 255-9

This is the voice of love and reason, and no less so is Othello's equally dignified and tender statement that he wants her with him, not for sexual satisfaction, 'but to be free and bounteous to her mind' – the mind in which he had seen and loved himself and her.

None the less it is true to say that no other lover in Shakespeare would make such a statement. In his explicit separation here of the motives of sex and love there is not only something indicative of Othello's own nature but an indication of the dualism that haunts the play. It appears in another form when the lovers are united in Cyprus, and seem to sing their passionately loving aria to one another. '*If it were now to die, 'twere now to be most happy....*' '*The heavens forbid but that our loves and comforts should increase....*' For Desdemona, the whole business is natural and growing: for Othello there is a delight in love that cannot contemplate any ordinary consummation.

For Othello love is a private freedom but sex a public knowledge. The pioneers of the army, whom he imagines making free with Desdemona, are an aspect of that public world which becomes such a nightmare to him. After picking up the handkerchief Emilia tells her husband, 'I have a thing for you.' He replies, 'It is a common thing.' The innuendo is spotted by Emilia who exclaims indignantly at it, and Iago instantly ripostes with 'to have a foolish wife'. That sexual badinage will become grim when Othello calls Desdemona 'Thou public commoner', and behaves to her as if he were in a brothel. Iago is sure that the desire for sex unites us all – 'And knowing what I am

know what she shall be.' For him a lust for 'these required conveniences' is a matter for the will to give way to or reject; for the will
controls 'unbitted lusts, whereof I take this that you call love to be a
sect or scion.'

The tone of such platitudes is familiar, and it is more a comment on
their nature and use in life rather than a weakness of the play that it
has no way for males to talk about sex other than Iago's way. But there
are exceptions. The most significant is Cassio, the unknowing cause of
all the trouble, whom Iago admits to have 'a daily beauty in his life'.
His conduct to Bianca, though not edifying, has at least a kind of
tender geniality that distinguishes it from mere sex; and it is Cassio
who, at the summit of the play's happiness, can publicly unite by his
chivalrous eloquence explicit sex and love together in an epithalamium
for the wedded pair:

> Great Jove, Othello guard,
> And swell his sail with thine own powerful breath,
> That he may bless this bay with his tall ship,
> Make love's quick pants in Desdemona's arms,
> Give renewed fire to our extincted spirits,
> And bring all Cyprus comfort.
>
> II. i. 77–82

It is the only moment of the play when love and desire are united as
bringers of public joy and celebration, even though it is in the absence
of the lovers.

In *Othello* even Shakespearean double entendre acquires a note of
incongruity, and this speech of Cassio's is the only one which knits up
all heroic and amorous effect by means of it. The suggestiveness of *bay*,
tall ship, and so forth, mark a mutuality in the style of eroticism. But
this is in contrast with the style of Othello himself. He seems not to
grasp the implications of what he says, any more than those of what is
taking place. He seems ignorant of that commonest of Elizabethan
sexual puns which he has uttered in 'If it were now to die,' and such
incomprehension, however tender and dignified, adds incongruously to
the speech as an omen of disquiet. The touchingly farcical image of 'I
had been happy if the general camp . . .' begins a speech that ends
'Othello's occupation's gone.' The two senses of that word were
notorious – both Shakespeare and Ben Jonson in their plays affect to
deprecate its cant meaning – and the audience must have been aware of
it; but Othello seems not to be. The effect is to cut off his knowledge of

sex from the range of his emotional feeling; and this produces a discrepancy not only exploited by Iago and derided in his wit, but on offer, as it were, to the audience. In such a context it can seem as if the play, and its author himself, were siding against Othello.

Of course the general specification of the play as tragedy corrects this. The point is made clear through Iago:

> The Moor, howbeit that I endure him not,
> Is of a constant, loving, noble nature;
> And I dare think he'll prove to Desdemona
> A most dear husband.
>
> II. i. 282–5

That we know from our own eyes, but they also see how Othello has been isolated by his absurd situation. How is a cuckold to be turned into a tragic hero? How, for that matter, was a Jewish money-lender to be turned into a passionate Shylock? In comedy the thing seemed to happen by itself and naturally, but in tragedy it has to be arranged. And the way it is done is partly, and precariously, a question of timing.

In Cinthio's tale, where the pair have been happily married for some time, the motive for murderous jealousy and grief has to be turned back on Othello's Moorishness, a condition so outlandish in terms of a mixed marriage that no amount of cohabitation would cure it. Time, in the story, breaks things up, and produces the catastrophe. The timing of the play has been endlessly discussed, and long before A. C. Bradley, and the intelligent student who suggested a double time-scheme to him, it had been suggested that when the action reaches Cyprus it can be seen as winding itself up either in a matter of hours, or in a matter of weeks or months. More important, perhaps, is the impression the play gives of the events that *preceded* it, and the way it vividly recalls Othello's courtship. Cassio went wooing with Othello and acted as go-between. Perhaps the hint that Desdemona gave about her feelings for Othello could in fact have been suggested by him? For she, as Othello then said with proud simplicity,

> bade me, if I had a friend that loved her,
> I should but teach him how to tell my story
> And that would woo her. Upon this hint I spake.
>
> I. iii. 164–6

What was spoken in happy tranquillity is recalled by Othello in violent agitation. That friend is now the enemy, his manoeuvres with Desdemona timeless and dateless. Time and emotion melt together, and the first incision that Iago cuts is designed to make them one in memory.

> IAGO. Did Michael Cassio, when you woo'd my lady,
> Know of your love?
> OTH. He did, from first to last. Why dost thou ask?
>
> III. iii. 95–7

The query suggests a whole new range of possibilities. Was it indeed the *friend* whom Desdemona loved, and was thinking of when she uttered the hint. The compression of time brings back the moment and perhaps something else: for Cassio seemed not to know what had taken place in that pregnant little scene when he met Othello and Iago in the flurry of the nocturnal opening crisis. Suppose Othello had not told him – had not wished to tell him – of the imminence of his elopement with Desdemona. The contradiction between Cassio's apparent ignorance in that tiny exchange, and what we later hear of his service in Othello's wooing, is like the tricks that time itself plays. It becomes a device to make the atmosphere more uncertain for the protagonist, more bewildering.

More bewildering for Othello, but not more confusing for us. There is no confusion involved in the play, and nothing in the matter of time or relation that looks like mere carelessness. Time is like Othello's blackness, a factor constantly present but never decisive, never leant on by the playwright to underpin his case. The play eludes with ease any attempt to pin it down to a solution: why it happened, what caused it, what weakness in Othello was involved? Even jealousy as such is not the reason. Jealousy is a long-term affair, with its own rules and customs, its own subterranean animosities and grudges. In *The Winter's Tale* they lie beneath the surface, like reefs laid down in the past. Jealousy is a very intimate topic. What we have in *Othello* is something much more open and elemental: the substitution of the simple public concept of sexual appetite for the complex private reality of daily love. That is what Iago contrives to force on Othello.

And it is this nightmare that Othello strangely refers to as 'the cause', in the exhausted, almost drowsy incantation he utters before he kills Desdemona. It is a love incantation, intended to displace the wickedness of sex. A paradox, which Shakespeare might well have been quite conscious of manipulating, is that the black man should be invested not with witchcraft and devilry but with the true power of love, as Shylock had been endowed with the voice of humanity. Iago, the trusted officer and true Venetian, becomes on the other hand the spokesman of sex in its crudest, least regenerate form. But of course this is not something the play makes a point of showing, as a play would today. It emerges naturally from the relationship.

> It is the cause, it is the cause, my soul:
> Let me not name it to you, you chaste stars,
> It is the cause.
>
> V. ii. 1-3

It is wholly in keeping with *Othello* that the 'cause' should not be named or defined: it does not have to be for it is all around us in the play. It is sex itself, the absurdity and horror that stands between Othello and the tragic fate he is determined to have. He cannot live in the dungeon, the toad-ridden cistern of sex as presented by Iago. Tragedy can only be consummated by the removal of this monstrous and farcical image of sex, the sating of bodies, the beast with two backs. It is this image which lurks in the background of Othello's speech and makes its tragic sublimity disquietingly parodic, even as Iago parodied, in deadpan style, his master's vehement invocation of the Pontic sea, and its 'icy current and compulsive course'.

Macbeth, going to commit murder, had spoken in the same vein.

> Witchcraft celebrates
> Pale Hecate's offerings; and withered Murther,
> Alarumed by his sentinel, the wolf,
> Whose howl's his watch, thus with his stealthy pace,
> With Tarquin's ravishing strides, towards his design
> Moves like a ghost.
>
> II. i, 51-6

But in *Macbeth* such a speech seems wholly native to its situation. In *Othello* the incongruity between tragedy and comedy has been growing with every new reference of Iago's. It is time for Othello to use tragical violence on that detestably comic vision of sex which Iago has summoned up. And to kill it requires the killing of Desdemona. As the action has progressed sex has usurped love, a frightful comedy has usurped the tragic expectation. Those inanely casual images dropped by Iago ('Or to be naked with her friend in bed/An hour or more, not meaning any harm') have become so vivid to Othello that tragedy must be restored, since love cannot be.

The play's construction, unique in Shakespeare, keeps sex and love, like tragedy and comedy, together yet apart, sensationally revealing each others' natures and characteristics. The same is true of tragedy and comedy themselves, here sharply revealed in image and setting instead of mixing naturally together. The process is unfair to both: tragedy is bound to look a little bit absurd, comedy and sex malicious and mechanical. Polarising the two viewpoints are Othello and Iago, both isolated: though for much of the time Iago is in fact not so isolated, for he can appeal to the audience and find it on the side, not of his intrigue, but of his outlook and style. The great risk the play runs is the isolation of Othello, 'a fixed figure' to be pointed at by the audience, and perhaps with a secret derision by the finger of the dramatic mechanism itself.

Certainly there is every indication that once the relationship of Othello and Iago had begun to be imagined by Shakespeare it developed too swiftly to be kept under control. The comic/tragic polarity is itself taken apart in the process, though the verse and style require it as a visible mechanism. *Macbeth* is probably the tragedy that followed, and we can see there too, on a bigger scale even, the character who is at once created for the tragic and yet imagined and perceived in terms of the domestic. Iago's hatred makes him comparable in a limited way. He is the person known at some time in every community – school, regiment, office, household – who hates quietly and deeply, hates others for being what they are. His hatred is often expressed as a derisive geniality that no one takes seriously.

> She was a wight, if ever such wight were,
> To suckle fools and chronicle small beer.

Everyone receives such cynicism with 'ohs' and laughs at it, as at any other readily identifiable social ploy. But Iago is kidding on the level, like the snob who makes a point and a style of pretending to be snobbish. He really does loathe innocence and goodness and their humdrum happy preoccupations. Quite a lot of people are like Iago, and conceal it with 'old fond paradoxes to make fools laugh i' th' alehouse'. We are not exactly intimate with this domestic side of Iago, as we are with that of Macbeth, but most people would recognise it, and would recognise its connection with the really terrifying hatred that seethes out of Iago when he finds the perfect way of making that hatred cause havoc, without breaking his cover.

Hell and night
Must bring this monstrous birth to the world's light.

It is in an area of complete psychological truth, therefore, that Iago the social type joins up with Iago the villain of tragedy. Empiric observation marries easily with the 'Spartan dog', the black and bloody villain: null and empty in nature as it is, Iago's hatred in action fits naturally into a correspondingly negative rhetoric, just as his lordship of sex and comedy is wholly compatible with his role as villain. Macbeth is a different matter. The difference between our sense of his mind, and his role as a bloody tyrant, is itself the dramatic surprise and success, as emphatic as the difference between his sense of the open promise of time, and his deception by 'the fiend that lies like truth.' Mind in *Macbeth* is both in league and at variance with tragic action, the incongruity involved being a part of its compelling intimacy.

But in *Othello* such an incongruity threatens the whole stability of the structural relation, making tragedy and comedy look equally at a disadvantage. It separates the heroic Othello from the gull who is made 'egregiously an ass' by Iago; and cuts off any intimacy with Othello, his 'visage in his mind', from the pity or distaste felt for him in his rage and pathos. (It is a striking fact that when he says: 'I'll chop her into messes! Cuckold me!' – the sentiment is much more repulsive than any of Macbeth's murderous utterances, which seem assumed and put on.) Mind in *Othello* is divorced from emotion, as sex is from love.

But whatever the stresses and strains produced by these divisions the rewards in art are none the less enormous. Even the risk of alienating the onlooker from the tragic action produces a corresponding gain: that action and behaviour remain in the play perennially controversial, and the focus of sexual and social awareness sharp and clear. In a production today, the implications of this are usually more interesting than the actual intrigue can be, and a lot of weight is usually put on Emilia's role as a figure of common sense and common humanity, correcting the romantic excesses of the lovers. But no figure in these three tragedies has such a symbolically positional status. Besides, Emilia, for all her virtues, has a stupidity and lack of imagination comparable in its own way to that of her husband; while her views on the sex war, from the feminine angle, are as pungent as his. Certainly the role of the women is important, but it is Desdemona alone who, because of her love, can remain unconscious of the tragedy/comedy element, as she does of the polarity between sex and love.

For her Othello is no more 'the noble Moor whom our full senate/Call all in all sufficient,' than he is the hollow man of bombast and self-love seen by Iago. Love needs neither to praise nor to deflate. Could Desdemona have heard her husband's last speech before he kills himself she would have understood it, as she understood and loved when he came to visit and told her of his 'travel's history'. She would have understood in it both the soldier and the man who loved her, the man whom Leavis characteristically finds nothing but a spectacle of self-pity ('Contemplating the spectacle of himself, Othello is overcome with the pathos of it'). Loving as she does, she is not herself subject either to that kind of critical definition and diagnosis, the kind that Iago, and even her own father, seek to make about her. Why did she love? To her father it was witchcraft; to Iago, lust. Is she physically attracted to Othello? Naturally she is and equally naturally she isn't: the question is irrelevant because she loves him. In his wife's eye and mind ('But here's my husband') Othello is none of the things spectators have found him, neither heroic nor credulous, no monster and not a god either, but a man capable alike of good and bad. Her unchanging and undiscriminating love restores the balance between the comic and the tragic and sustains the whole precarious structure.

> Unkindness may do much
> And his unkindness may defeat my life,
> But never taint my love.

That emotion irradiates the play. The few glimpses we have of it do not belong to the world of the tragic or comic vision, the world of Iago and Emilia or of 'the plumed troop and the big wars/That make ambition virtue,' or even of those 'antres vast and deserts idle/Rough quarries, rocks, and hills whose heads touch heaven.' The glimpses we have are of a private world – too private for a play – and one called into being by a recognition, a marriage of true minds.

> This to hear
> Would Desdemona seriously incline:
> But still the house affairs would draw her thence;
> Which ever as she could with haste dispatch,
> She'd come again, and with a greedy ear
> Devour up my discourse: which I observing,
> Took once a pliant hour, and found good means
> To draw from her a prayer of earnest heart

That I would all my pilgrimage dilate,
Whereof by parcels she had something heard,
But not intentively.

I. iii. 145–55

A sign of love: the impulse to catch up on and complete all the instalments; to possess, and systematically, everything in that past. It is the same possession that will bid Othello wear his gloves and feed on nourishing dishes and keep him warm; and attempt to further his interests in the same way, and with the same single-mindedness, by pleading for Cassio. 'Our general's general' Cassio calls Desdemona. She has committed herself to love as to the wars, and she will be killed by it: but that fate is no more tragic than it is comic that she should fuss the great commander about his gloves. For Desdemona love and sex are undistinguished aspects of the private life, the life that the play and its characters cannot touch, that even Othello's madness cannot touch. *Othello* is a tragedy of privacy, a phrase that itself expresses incongruity, for as with most Shakespearean tragedy, success is achieved by a treatment unsuited to the form. And it is that lack of suiting which makes the theme perennial; the tearing down of a privacy is a subject which fits our age, as it might fit any age. It lets in chaos, and lets out love.

ANNOTATED BIBLIOGRAPHY

(This includes books referred to in the text, and books and articles not referred to which I have found useful for general reading, or for the study of a particular play.)

General

Aristotle, *The Poetics*, annotated and translated by S. H. Butcher, London, 1895.

Battenhouse, R. W., *Shakespearean Tragedy: Its Christian Premises*, Bloomington, Ind., 1969.

Bethell, S. L., *Shakespeare and the Popular Dramatic Tradition*, London, 1944.

Bowers, F., *Elizabethan Revenge Tragedy*, London, 1952.

Bradbrook, M. C., *Themes and Contentions of Elizabethan Tragedy*, Cambridge, 1979.

Bradley, A. C., *Oxford Lectures on Poetry*, London, 1909.

Bradley, A. C., *Shakespearean Tragedy*, London, 1915.

Bullough, G., *Narrative and Dramatic Sources of Shakespeare*, London, 1973.

Bush, D., *English Literature in the Earlier 17th Century*, Oxford, 1945.

Charlton, H. B., *Shakespearean Tragedy*, Cambridge, 1948.

Clemen, W. H., *The English Drama before Shakespeare*, London, 1980.

Coleridge, S. T., *Coleridge's Shakespeare Criticism*, ed. T. M. Raysor, London, 1930.

Creizenach, W., *The English Drama in the Age of Shakespeare*, London, 1916.

Croce, B., *Ariosto, Shakespeare and Corneille*, trans. D. Ainslie, London, 1920.

Eliot, T. S., *Elizabethan Essays*, London, 1953.

Ellis-Fermor, U., *The Jacobean Drama*, London, 1947.

Ellis-Fermor, U., *The Frontiers of Drama*, London, 1948.

Evans, B., *Shakespeare's Tragic Practice*, Oxford, 1980.

Fiedler, L. A., *The Stranger in Shakespeare*, London, 1973.

Greg, W. W., *The Shakespeare First Folio*, Oxford, 1955.

Gregory-Smith, G., *Elizabethan Critical Essays*, Oxford, 1904.

Gundolf, F., *Shakespeare und der deutsche Geist*, Berlin, 1911.

Halliday, F. E., *Shakespeare and his Critics*, London, 1949.

Halliwell, R., *On the Character of Sir John Falstaff*, London, 1841.
Worth comparing with the essay by Maurice Morgann.

Hazlitt, W., *Lectures on the Literature of the Age of Elizabeth*, and *Characters of Shakespeare's Plays*, London, 1870.

Holinshed, *Shakespeare's Holinshed*, ed. W. G. Boswell-Stone, London, 1907.

Holloway, J., *The Story of the Night*, London, 1961.

Huxley, A., 'Tragedy and the Whole Truth' in collected essays, *On Art and Artists*, London, 1960.

James, H., Preface to *The Tempest*, in *Selected Literary Criticism*, ed. M. Shapiro, London, 1958.

Jameson, Mrs A., *Shakespeare's Heroines*, London, 1897.

Jones, E. W., *Scenic Form in Shakespeare*, Oxford, 1971.

Jones, E. W., *The Origins of Shakespeare*, Oxford, 1977.

Joseph, B. L., *Elizabethan Acting*, Oxford, 1951.

Jusserand, J. J., *The English Novel in the Time of Shakespeare*, trans. E. Lee, London, 1901.

Kitto, H. D. F., *Greek Tragedy*, London, 1950.

Kitto, H. D. F., *Form and Meaning in Drama*, London, 1956.

Kitto, H. D. F., *Poiesis: Structure and Thought*, Cambridge, 1966.

Knights, L. C., *Drama and Society in the Age of Johnson*, London, 1937.

Kott, J., *Shakespeare Our Contemporary*, London, 1965.

Krook, D., *Elements of Tragedy*, New Haven, Conn., 1969.

Lawlor, J., *The Tragic Sense of Shakespeare*, London, 1960.

Leech, C., *Shakespeare's Tragedies*, London, 1950.

Mehl, D., *The Elizabethan Dumb Show: The History of a Dramatic Convention*, London, 1965.

Montaigne, *Essays*, trans. J. Florio, London, 1603.

Morozov, M. M., *Shakespeare on the Soviet Stage*, trans. D. Margarshack, London, 1947.

Murry, J. M., *Keats and Shakespeare*, Oxford, 1942.

Nichol Smith, D., *Eighteenth Century Essays on Shakespeare*, Oxford, 1935.
Includes Maurice Morgann's 'Essay on the Dramatic Character of Sir John Falstaff'.

Nicoll, W. D., *World Drama: From Aeschylus to Anouilh*, London, 1949.

Nietzsche, F. W., *The Birth of Tragedy*, ed. O. Levy, London, 1909.

Ornstein, R., *The Moral Vision of Jacobean Tragedy*, Madison, Wis., 1960.

Rather modish and earnest, but with a consistent viewpoint that can be argued against.

Palmer, J., *Political Characters of Shakespeare*, London, 1945.

Partridge, E., *Shakespeare's Bawdy*, London, 1947.

Plutarch, *The Lives of the Noble Grecians and Romaines,* trans. Sir T. North, London, 1603.

Pollard, A. W., (ed.), *Shakespeare's Hand in the Play of Sir Thomas More*, Cambridge, 1923.

Pushkin, A. S., *The 'Little Tragedies', with other Verse and Prose*, ed. A. Yarmolinsky, London, 1939.

Pushkin, A. S., *Letters*, ed. J. T. Shaw, Oxford, 1963.

Reed, H., *Lectures on English History and Tragic Poetry*, London, 1856.

Richardson, W., *Essays on Shakespeare*, London, 1789.
Contains essays on Falstaff that may be compared with Morgann's, and on Shakespeare's female characters.

Righter, A., *Shakespeare and the Idea of the Play*, London, 1961.

Schücking, L. L., *Character Problems in Shakespeare's Plays*, London, 1922.

Silk, M. S. and Stern, J. P., *Nietzsche on Tragedy*, Cambridge, 1980.

Sisson, C. J., 'The Mythical Sorrows of Shakespeare', British Academy Lecture, London, 1932.

Spurgeon, C. F. E., *Shakespeare's Imagery*, Cambridge, 1935.

Stauffer, D. A., *Shakespeare's World of Images: The Development of His Moral Ideas*, New York, 1949.

Steiner, G., *The Death of Tragedy*, London, 1961.

Sternfeld, F. W., *Music in Shakespearean Tragedy*, London, 1963.

Stewart, J. I. M., *Character and Motive in Shakespeare*, London, 1949.

Stoll, E. E., *Art and Artifice in Shakespeare*, Cambridge, 1933.

Swinburne, A. C., *A Study of Shakespeare*, London, 1918.

Thorndike, A. H., *Tragedy*, London, 1908.

Tolstoy, L., *What is Art? and Other Essays*, trans. A. Maude, Oxford, 1928.

Van Doren, M., *Shakespeare*, London, 1941.

Wilson Knight, G., *The Shakespearean Tempest*, Oxford, 1932.

Wilson Knight, G., *The Wheel of Fire*, enlarged edn, London, 1949.
Contains the essays discussed in my sections on *King Lear* and on *Timon of Athens*.

Early tragedies

Baker, H., *Induction to Tragedy: A Study in a Development of Form in 'Gorboduc', 'The Spanish Tragedy' and 'Titus Andronicus'*, Louisiana, 1939.

Brooke, H., *Shakespeare's Early Tragedies*, London, 1968.

Cunliffe, J. W., *The Influence of Seneca on Elizabethan Tragedy*, London, 1893.

Mason, H. A., *Shakespeare's Tragedies of Love*, London, 1970.

Sommers, A., '"Wilderness of Tigers": Structure and Symbolism in Titus Andronicus', *Essays in Criticism*, no. 10, 1960.

Wilson, H. S., *On the Design of Shakespearian Tragedy*, Toronto, 1957.

Hamlet

Charney, M., *Style in Hamlet*, Princeton, 1969.

Cruttwell, P., 'The Morality of Hamlet – "Sweet Prince" or "Arrant Knave"?', *Stratford-upon-Avon Studies*, no. 5, London, 1963.

Eliot, T. S. *Elizabethan Essays* (on *Hamlet*), London, 1953.

Gardner, H., *The Business of Criticism*, Oxford, 1959.
Contains a valuable section on Hamlet criticism.

Jump, J. D. (ed.), *Hamlet: A Casebook*, London, 1968.
Contains ten useful essays.

Lewis, C. S., 'Hamlet: The Prince or the Poem?', British Academy Lecture, London, 1942.
A good corrective to psychological studies.

Madariaga, S., *On Hamlet*, London, 1948.

Traversi, D. A., *An Approach to Shakespeare*, revised edn, London, 1969.
The *Hamlet* is one of the best in a study which takes a strongly ethical approach to Shakespeare, and is not very illuminating on the other tragedies.

Waldock, A. J. A., *Hamlet: A Study in Critical Method*, Cambridge, 1931.

Wilson, J. D., *What Happens in Hamlet*, Cambridge, 1935.
Good on details of plotting and staging.

Troilus and Cressida

Campbell, O. J., *Shakespeare's Satire*, New York, 1943.

Edwards, P., *Shakespeare and the Confines of Art*, London, 1968.
A valuable study in the peculiarities of the play.

Morris, B., 'The Tragic Structure of Troilus and Cressida', *Shakespeare Quarterly*, no. 10, 1959.

Nowottny, W., '"Opinion" and "Value" in *Troilus and Cressida*', *Essays in Criticism*, no. 4, 1954.

King Lear

Danby, J. F., *Shakespeare's Doctrine of Nature*, London, 1949.
A companion piece to the important essays by Wilson Knight. A Christian interpretation.

Everett, B., 'The New *King Lear*', *Critical Quarterly*, no. 2, 1960.
Calls in question the validity of any religious view of the play.

Gardner, H., 'King Lear', John Coffin Memorial Lecture, London, 1967.
A judicious essay denying that Lear learns from experience.

Greg, W., 'The Date of *King Lear* and Shakespeare's Use of Earlier Versions of the Story', the *Library*, no. 20, 1940.

James, D. G., 'Keats and *King Lear*', *Shakespeare Survey*, no. 13, 1960.

Levin, Y., 'Tolstoy, Shakespeare and Russian Writers of the 1860s', *Oxford Slavonic Papers*, no. 12, Oxford 1968.

Mack, M., *King Lear in Our Time*, Berkeley, California, 1965.

Orwell, G., 'Lear, Tolstoy and the Fool', in *Selected Essays*, London, 1957.

Schlegal, A. W., *Lectures on Dramatic Art and Literature*, trans. London, 1846.
Historically very interesting. Representative of the Romantic view and the influence of Shakespeare in Germany.

Sisson, C. J., *Shakespeare's Tragic Justice*, Toronto, 1962.

Stroup, T. B., 'Cordelia and the Fool', *Shakespeare Quarterly*, no. 12, 1961.

Walton, J. K., 'Lear's Last Speech', *Shakespeare Survey*, no. 13, 1960.

Welsford, E., *The Fool*, London, 1935.
The standard scholarly work. Good on the relation of kingship with motley and the fool.

West, R. H., 'Sex and Pessimism in *King Lear*', *Shakespeare Quarterly*, no. 11, 1960.

Othello

Allen, N. B., 'The Two Parts of Othello', *Shakespeare Survey*, no. 21, 1968.
A penetrating discussion of the time scheme, which argues that the last three acts were written first, and the first two intended to contrast with them in tempo and mood.

Gardner, H., 'The Noble Moor', British Academy Lecture, London, 1956.

Honigmann, E. A. J., *The Stability of Shakespeare's Text*, London, 1965.
A section advances the theory, based on Greg's findings, that the Quarto is a first version, and that the Folio text clearly represents additions and second thoughts.

Hopgood, R., 'Shakespeare and the Included Spectator', in *Reinterpretations of Elizabethan Drama*, ed. M. Rabben, New York, 1969.

Jones, E., *Othello's Countrymen*, London, 1965.
A survey of the tradition of the character of Moor or black man.

Leavis, F. R., 'Diabolic Intellect and the Noble Hero: The Sentimentalist's *Othello*', in *The Common Pursuit*, London, 1952.
An essay that takes up the point made by T. S. Eliot in 'Shakespeare and

the Stoicism of Seneca' (*Elizabethan Essays*) that Othello is a character study in delusion and self-pity.

Shaffer, E. S., 'Iago's Malignity Motivated: Coleridge's Unpublished *Opus Magnum*, *Shakespeare Quarterly*, no. 19, 1968.

Stoll, E. E., *Othello: An Historical and Comparative Study*, Minneapolis, 1915.

Macbeth

Bradbrook, M. C., 'The Sources of Macbeth', *Shakespeare Survey*, no. 4, 1951.

Brooks, C., 'The Naked Babe and the Cloak of Manliness', in *The Well-Wrought Urn*, New York, 1947.
Far-fetched but interesting. Pursuers of imagery are fond of *Macbeth*, and this piece should be compared with Caroline Spurgeon and with the more sober explorations of W. H. Clemen in *The Development of Shakespeare's Imagery*, London, 1951.

De Quincey, T., 'On the Knocking at the Gate in *Macbeth*', *London Magazine*, 1823. Reprinted in *Shakespeare Criticism: A Selection*, ed. D. Nichol Smith, Oxford, 1916.

Ewbank, I., 'The Fiend-like Queen: A Note on *Macbeth* and Seneca's *Medea*', *Shakespeare Survey*, no. 19, 1966.

Foakes, R. A., '*Macbeth*', *Stratford Papers on Shakespeare*, Toronto, 1963.
A balanced summing-up.

Knights, L. C., 'How many Children had Lady Macbeth?' in *Explorations*, London, 1946.

Julius Caesar and *Antony and Cleopatra*

Cecil, Lord, D., *Antony and Cleopatra*, in *Poets and Storytellers*, London, 1949.

Charney, M., *Discussions of Shakespeare's Roman Plays*, Boston, Mass., 1964.

Daiches, D., 'Imagery and Meaning in *Antony and Cleopatra*', *Modern Literary Essays*, Edinburgh, 1968.
A controversial but decidedly interesting essay.

Foakes, R. A., 'An Approach to *Julius Caesar*', *Shakespeare Quarterly*, no. 5, London, 1954.

Fowler, W. W., 'The Tragic Element in Shakespeare's *Julius Caesar*', in *Roman Essays and Interpretations*, London, 1920.

Frye, N., *Fools of Time*, Toronto, 1967.

Knights, L. C., 'Personality and Politics in *Julius Caesar*', in *Further Explorations*, London, 1965.

Leavis, F. R., '*Antony and Cleopatra* and *All For Love*: A Critical Exercise', *Scrutiny*, no. 5, 1936.
Exemplifies Leavis's methods. A highly illuminating essay.

MacCallum, M. W., *Shakespeare's Roman Plays and Their Background* (new edn of T. J. Spencer), London, 1967.
First came out shortly after A. C. Bradley's *Shakespearean Tragedy*, and applies the same sort of method of character study to the Roman plays. Still a very worthwhile book.

Murry, J. M., *The Problem of Style*, London, 1922.
Comments on the style of *Antony and Cleopatra* which are penetrating and not at all dated.

Velz, J. W., *Shakespeare and the Classical Tradition: A Critical Guide to Commentary 1660–1960*, Minneapolis, 1968.
A useful reference book.

Coriolanus

Bradley, A. C., '*Coriolanus*', in *Studies in Shakespeare*, ed. P. Alexander, London, 1964.

Burke, K., '*Coriolanus* and the Delights of Faction', *Hudson Review*, no. 19, 1966.
An odd but interesting essay, formalising the play's action.

Ellis-Fermor, U., '*Coriolanus*', in *Shakespeare the Dramatist*, ed. K. Muir, London, 1961.

Ernright, D. J., '*Coriolanus*: Tragedy or Debate?', in *Discussions*, ed. M. Charney, London, 1957.

Frye, N., 'The Tragedies of Nature and Fortune', *Stratford Papers on Shakespeare*, Toronto, 1961.

Granville-Barker, H., *Prefaces to Shakespeare* (fifth series), London, 1947.
The last of the Prefaces and the only one that really contributes to the subject. The approach – how the liaison des scènes in each play evolves – really pays off here.

Harding, D. W., 'Women's Fantasy of Manhood: A Shakespearean Theme', *Shakespeare Quarterly*, no. 20, 1969.
An interesting psychological approach. The title is self-explanatory.

Muir, K., 'In Defence of the Tribunes', *Essays in Criticism*, no. 4, 1954.

Murry, J. M., 'A Neglected Heroine of Shakespeare', in *Countries of the Mind*, London, 1922.
A valid and not sentimental post-Morgann impression.

Rabkin, M., '*Coriolanus*: The Tragedy of Politics', *Shakespeare Quarterly*, no. 17, 1966.

Timon of Athens

Bradbrook, M. C., 'The Tragic Pageant of *Timon of Athens*', in Shakespeare the Craftsman, London, 1969.

Ellis-Fernor, U., '*Timon of Athens*: An Unfinished Play', *Review of English Studies*, no. 18. Reprinted in *Shakespeare the Dramatist*, ed. K. Muir, London, 1961.

This and the Bradbrook essay make a typical contrast; the first assuming *Timon* to be a complete work of art, the second that it is unfinished.

Gomme, A., '*Timon of Athens*', *Essays in Criticism*, no. 9, Oxford, 1959.

Honigmann, E. A., '*Timon of Athens*', *Shakespeare Quarterly*, no. 12, 1961.

Knights, L. C., '*Timon of Athens*', in *The Morality of Art: Essays Presented to G. Wilson Knight*, ed. D. W. Jefferson, London, 1969.

Maxwell, J. C., '*Timon of Athens*', *Scrutiny*, no. 15, Cambridge, 1948.

A scholarly essay, pointing out the problems and weighing the probabilities.

Muir, K., '*Timon of Athens* and the Cash Nexus', *Modern Quarterly Miscellany*, no. 1, 1947.

A valuable essay though difficult to get hold of. It focuses on the financial and social aspects of the *Timon* situation.

Williams, S. T., 'Some Versions of *Timon of Athens* on the Stage', *Modern Phililogy*, no. 18, 1920.

How productions attempted to solve the difficulties of staging *Timon*.